ZEITGESCHICHTE

Ehrenpräsidentin:
em. Univ.-Prof. Dr. Erika Weinzierl († 2014)

Herausgeber:
Univ.-Prof. DDr. Oliver Rathkolb

Redaktion:
em. Univ.-Prof. Dr. Rudolf Ardelt (Linz), ao. Univ.-Prof.in Mag.a Dr.in Ingrid Bauer (Salzburg/Wien), SSc Mag.a Dr.in Ingrid Böhler (Innsbruck), Dr.in Lucile Dreidemy (Toulouse), Prof. Dr. Michael Gehler (Hildesheim), ao. Univ.-Prof. i. R. Dr. Robert Hoffmann (Salzburg), ao. Univ.-Prof. Dr. Michael John / Koordination (Linz), Assoz. Prof.in Dr.in Birgit Kirchmayr (Linz), Dr. Oliver Kühschelm (Wien), Univ.-Prof. Dr. Ernst Langthaler (Linz), Dr.in Ina Markova (Wien), Univ.-Prof. Mag. Dr. Wolfgang Mueller (Wien), Univ.-Prof. Dr. Bertrand Perz (Wien), Univ.-Prof. Dr. Dieter Pohl (Klagenfurt), Dr.in Lisa Rettl (Wien), Univ.-Prof. Mag. Dr. Dirk Rupnow (Innsbruck), Mag.a Adina Seeger (Wien), Ass.-Prof. Mag. Dr. Valentin Sima (Klagenfurt), Prof.in Dr.in Sybille Steinbacher (Frankfurt am Main), Dr. Christian H. Stifter / Rezensionsteil (Wien), Univ.-Doz.in Mag.a Dr.in Heidemarie Uhl (Wien/Graz), Gastprof. (FH) Priv.-Doz. Mag. Dr. Wolfgang Weber, MA, MAS (Vorarlberg), Mag. Dr. Florian Wenninger (Wien), Assoz.-Prof.in Mag.a Dr.in Heidrun Zettelbauer (Graz).

Peer-Review Committee (2018–2020):
Ass.-Prof.in Mag.a Dr.in Tina Bahovec (Institut für Geschichte, Universität Klagenfurt), Prof. Dr. Arnd Bauerkämper (Fachbereich Geschichts- und Kulturwissenschaften, Freie Universität Berlin), Günter Bischof, Ph.D. (Center Austria, University of New Orleans), Dr.in Regina Fritz (Institut für Zeitgeschichte, Universität Wien/Historisches Institut, Universität Bern), ao. Univ.-Prof.in Mag.a Dr.in Johanna Gehmacher (Institut für Zeitgeschichte, Universität Wien), Univ.-Prof. i. R. Dr. Hanns Haas (Universität Salzburg), Univ.-Prof. i. R. Dr. Ernst Hanisch (Salzburg), Univ.-Prof.in Mag.a Dr.in Gabriella Hauch (Institut für Geschichte, Universität Wien), Univ.-Doz. Dr. Hans Heiss (Institut für Zeitgeschichte, Universität Innsbruck), Robert G. Knight, Ph.D. (Department of Politics, History and International Relations, Loughborough University), Dr.in Jill Lewis (University of Wales, Swansea), Prof. Dr. Oto Luthar (Slowenische Akademie der Wissenschaften, Ljubljana), Hon.-Prof. Dr. Wolfgang Neugebauer (Dokumentationsarchiv des Österreichischen Widerstandes, Wien), Mag. Dr. Peter Pirker (Institut für Staatswissenschaft, Universität Wien), Prof. Dr. Markus Reisenleitner (Department of Humanities, York University, Toronto), Dr.in Elisabeth Röhrlich (Institut für Geschichte, Universität Wien), ao. Univ.-Prof.in Dr.in Karin M. Schmidlechner-Lienhart (Institut für Geschichte/Zeitgeschichte, Universität Graz), Univ.-Prof. i. R. Mag. Dr. Friedrich Stadler (Wien), Assoc.-Prof. Dr. Gerald Steinacher (University of Nebraska), Assoz.-Prof. DDr. Werner Suppanz (Institut für Geschichte/Zeitgeschichte, Universität Graz), Univ.-Prof. Dr. Philipp Ther, MA (Institut für Osteuropäische Geschichte, Universität Wien), Prof. Dr. Stefan Troebst (Leibniz-Institut für Geschichte und Kultur des östlichen Europa, Universität Leipzig), Prof. Dr. Michael Wildt (Institut für Geschichtswissenschaften, Humboldt-Universität zu Berlin).

zeitgeschichte
45. Jg., Heft 4 (2018)

Reflections on Camps –
Space, Agency, Materiality

Edited by
Antje Senarclens de Grancy and Heidrun Zettelbauer

V&R unipress

Vienna University Press

Inhalt

Antje Senarclens de Grancy / Heidrun Zettelbauer
Editorial 451

Artikel

Antje Senarclens de Grancy
Different Housing Spaces – Space, Function, and Use of Barrack-Huts in
World War I Refugee Camps 457

Ulrike Krause
Protection | Victimisation | Agency? Gender-sensitive Perspectives on
Present-day Refugee Camps 483

Robert Jan van Pelt
Labour Service Barrack-Huts in Germany and the United States, 1933–45 507

Heidrun Zettelbauer
Unwanted Desire and Processes of Self-Discipline. Autobiographical
Representations of the *Reichsarbeitsdienst* Camps in the Diary of a Young
Female National Socialist 537

Annika Wienert
Camp Cartography: On the Ambiguity of Mapping Nazi Extermination
Camps 575

Abstracts 599

Rezensionen

Veronika Duma
Henning Fischer, Überlebende als Akteurinnen 605

Oliver Rathkolb
Christian Merlin, Die Wiener Philharmoniker. Band 1: Das Orchester und seine Geschichte von 1842 bis heute, Band 2: Die Musiker und Musikerinnen von 1842 bis heute 607

Olaf Stieglitz
Matthias Marschik/Rolf Sachsse, Rauchende Sportler 609

Autor/innen 613

Antje Senarclens de Grancy / Heidrun Zettelbauer

Editorial

Camps – considered to be (more or less) enclosed and temporary environments and to be flexible tools for the (voluntary or forced) isolation of specific socially, politically or ethnically defined groups – are a global and ubiquitous mass phenomenon of the present. The growing body of scholarly literature on camps and their comprehensive dimensions indicates the significance this issue is assuming in the contemporary world and reflects its importance in current policies and societal debates. In the fields of Philosophy, Political and Cultural Theory, camps are currently understood as prototypical cultural sites of the Modern, referring to Zygmunt Bauman's fundamental suggestion to look at the 20th century as the "century of the camps". Such an approach also relates to Giorgio Agamben's reflection on "the camp" – implicitly identified as the concentration camp – as a site where a fundamental relationship between the law and the absence of law is established, and the state of exception turns into the rule.[1] Such an approach can be correlated with perspectives taken by Contemporary History researchers on camps, which still focus on concentration and extermination camps in the context of the National Socialist regime or the Soviet gulags. As sites of excessive violence, terror and murder, such camps are discussed by historians as radical archetypes of the modern camp history and its 'final point'. Since the 1990s in particular, many studies have opened up a broad range of questions about the Nazi concentration camp system, and recent publications have enabled new and concise overviews to be made in this context.[2]

In public history debates, NS-camps still appear to represent the 'normative model' of the camp, whereas scholars have been continuously shifting towards a more extensive historical, transnational and global understanding of the phenomenon over the past decade. Authors of recent studies have highlighted the

---

[1] Zygmunt Bauman, "A Century of Camps?," in: *The Bauman Reader*, edited by Peter Beilharz (Oxford: Blackwell, 2001), 266–280; Giorgio Agamben, *Means without End: Notes on Politics*, Theory out of Bounds (Minneapolis and London: University of Minnesota Press, 2000), 37–45.
[2] Nikolaus Wachsmann, *KL: A History of the Nazi Concentration Camps* (New York: Macmillan, 2015).

lines of historical continuity, tracing the camp phenomenon back to pre-modern times (e. g. by referring to 'total institutions' such as workhouses for the poor or traditions of military culture).³ They have revealed possible connections between colonial camps formed around 1900⁴ and the subsequent camp systems. For instance, the issue of civilian internment is now integrated in the core of World War I and Empire Studies⁵ and is investigated in the context of World War II. Currently, different attempts are being undertaken to write a concise global history of the concentration camp since the end of the 19th century up to the present.⁶ The principal concept of camps grounded on educational or hygienic discourse or its explicit or implicit technologies indicates that the camp is a crucial tool that can be used for modern biopolitics, crisis management or warfare. Subsequently, the physical, material and architectural dimensions have become the focus of a large variety of theoretical and empiric studies.

In addition to such transnational pre- and post-histories of the concentration camp – including politics of memory – authors of other camp studies have focused on different camp types, ranging from highly institutionalised to loosely informal structures.⁷ The many purposes of camps as a major element of 20th- and 21st-century history can be loosely grouped together, but they are often closely intertwined: They range from being sites that enable individual development and autonomy (e. g. holiday, peace or protest camps) to spaces for control and discipline (e. g. civilian internment, POW or concentration camps) and on to locations that are intended to meet urgent needs (e. g. humanitarian refugee, post-disaster or homeless camps).⁸

Currently, researcher in the fields of Philosophy, Political Theory, Architectural History as well as those who adopt the interdisciplinary perspectives of Urban or Gender Studies discuss camps as specific, modern spaces that represent sites with the highest possible functionality. A deeper understanding of con-

---

3 Christoph Jahr and Jens Thiel (eds.), *Lager vor Auschwitz. Gewalt und Integration im 20. Jahrhundert* (Berlin: Metropol Verlag, 2013); Bettina Greiner and Alan Kramer (eds.), *Welt der Lager. Zur "Erfolgsgeschichte" einer Institution* (Hamburg: Hamburger Edition HIS Verlagsges., 2013).
4 Aidan Forth, *Barbed-Wire Imperialism. Britain's Empire of Camps, 1876–1903* (Oakland: University of California Press, 2017); Jonas Kreienbaum, *"Ein trauriges Fiasko". Koloniale Konzentrationslager im südlichen Afrika 1900–1908* (Hamburg: Hamburger Edition HIS Verlagsges., 2015).
5 Stefan Manz et al. (eds.), *Internment during the First World War: a mass global phenomenon* (London and New York: Routledge, 2018).
6 Dan Stone, *The concentration Camp. A Short History* (Oxford: Oxford University Press, 2017); Andrea Pitzer, *One Long Night. A Global History of Concentration Camp* (New York: Little, Brown and Company, 2017).
7 Irit Katz et al. (eds.), *Camps Revisited. Multifaceted Spatialities of a Modern Political Technology* (London: Rowman & Littlefield, 2018).
8 Charlie Hailey, *Camps: A Guide to 21st-Century Space* (Cambridge, MA: MIT Press, 2009).

temporary camps as social, cultural and urban spaces has been particularly derived by researchers pursuing Migration and Refugee Studies, who approach camps from an interdisciplinary and multi-methodological perspective, as well as those conducting architectural research. Trained architects working with an extended concept of architecture are investigating the spatial aspects of institutional refugee camps, which have often been in continuous existence for many decades.[9] In the past few years, the shapes and functions of informal and makeshift encampments such as the "Calais Jungle" in France are of equal interest to spatial theorists, sociologists and urban designers. The analyses of Calais and comparable examples indicate that a paradigm change is taking place, insofar as such studies illuminate not only the fears and imagined scenarios of menace that exist within present European society, but also serve as research fields for the development of new urban and cohabitation concepts.[10]

Keeping these perspectives in mind, the authors of this special volume explore camps as (cultural) spaces in a broad sense and deal with their complex and paradoxical dimensions as modern sites. As editors, we do not intend to outline a consistent concept in topics, theory or methodology, but instead to open up a wide range of approaches in order to underline the potential of this field of research. Against this backdrop, the contributors define space as a socio-cultural and tangible analytical category, focusing on camps with their specific rules, logistics, and materialisations. They investigate them as physical and social products that have been conceived and created by camp designers and inhabitants, as mental factors for socialisation and self-discipline, as expressions of cultural representation, and/or as constitutive elements of memory.

The authors of this special volume examine the space of the camp in general as a subject, which affects social configuration together with the camp's physical and architectural qualities and symbolic functions. They are interested in the processes that occur when allegedly rational decisions are made or heteronomous acts take place as part of the daily camp routines; they examine how these processes and structures oscillate in their cultural meanings. They study how different subjects can lend new interpretations to seemingly fixed acts of significance by taking possession of space or vice versa how the existing scopes of action shift into spaces of control and discipline. Overall, the contributors intend to comprehend the ambivalent, ambiguous, inconsistent and paradoxical aspects of camp spaces.

The case studies assembled in the volume all reflect an interest in specific

---

9 Manuel Herz (ed.), *From Camp to City. Refugee Camps of the Western Sahara* (Zurich: Lars Müller Publishers, 2013).
10 Fiona Meadows (ed.), *Habiter le campement. Nomades, voyageurs, contestataires, conquérants, infortunés, exilés* (Arles: Actes Sud, 2016).

institutional and highly formal camp structures as well as share aspects of their symbolic representation. In particular, the authors focus on the following specific camp types: refugee camps during World War I and in the present (Antje Senarclens de Grancy and Ulrike Krause), inclusion camps of the National Socialist *Reichsarbeitsdienst* and labour service camps in the U.S. (Robert Jan van Pelt and Heidrun Zettelbauer), and extermination camps (Annika Wienert). The articles are positioned within different disciplinary contexts (Contemporary History, Visual Studies, Architectural History, Refugee and Gender Studies) and present a wide range of understandings, definitions and approaches to space and the complex relations between governance and agency. The authors stress the entanglement of social structures, cultural discourse, institutionalisation, individual perception and appropriation. Key aspects that are presented are the coincidence of proximity and distance, control and intimacy, disciplinary action and self-organisation, internment and scopes of (re)action or protection and surveillance. The mutually linked topics and the common points of reference in the assembled articles show the manner in which the camp issue can serve as cross-sectional matter in the current approaches being taken in the fields of Cultural Theory and Contemporary History.

Artikel

Antje Senarclens de Grancy

Different Housing Spaces – Space, Function, and Use of Barrack-Huts in World War I Refugee Camps

Introduction

In his 1939 lecture "Education of the Architect" in Mexico, Hannes Meyer, Swiss architect and former director of the Bauhaus in Dessau, referred to the social function of architecture. In a terse sentence he pointed to a fundamental discrepancy that seems to lie in the nature of architecture, using the example of a modern building type: "The standardised barrack-huts of the Mexican railway worker as an element of a progressive, democratic state represents a higher form of housing than the barrack-huts in a labor camp in present-day Germany, although they are both exactly the same in construction and appearance!"[1] Meyer is known as one of the most emphatic representatives of the rationalist and functionalist *Neues Bauen*. However, in this quote he states that one and the same object, a simple accommodation without any comfort, can become something *fundamentally different* through different uses – in opposition to the dictum "form follows function."

Guiding Question[2]

In its use as a camp barrack, the standardised and primarily use-neutral barrack-hut – as argued below and shown by the example of refugee camps of World War I – is a different housing space, 'different' in relation to other uses, in the sense of Meyer's statement. This means that the very essence of this building, its ex-

---

1 Hannes Meyer, "Erziehung zum Architekten" [1939], in: Hannes Meyer, *Bauen und Gesellschaft. Schriften, Briefe, Projekte*, ed. Lena Meyer-Bergner (Dresden 1980), 204–213, esp. 206. From 1939 on, Meyer was the director of the newly founded Institute of Planning and Urbanism of the Instituto Politécnico Nacional in Mexico City.
2 This article has been developed as part of an ongoing research project on the relational history between camps and modern architecture using the example of refugee camps in the Habsburg Monarchy in World War I.

istence, changes in each case when used for a particular purpose.³ The camp barrack is not only a simple temporary dormitory for specific inhabitants, but a complex spatial structure. It is not solely generated by factors such as architectural design, space distribution, construction or equipment, as well as material and symbolic functions,⁴ but also – and in particular – by its use. According to Henri Lefebvre, this space is at the same time the precondition and the result of social practice.⁵ Finally, it only becomes apparent through the *use* of the barrack-hut as to whether that, what was intended by the decision-makers and conceived in the administrative offices and on the drawing boards, was actually achieved.

Different types of exclusion or inclusion camps in the "century of camps"⁶ as well as the respective historical contexts have to be precisely differentiated.⁷ However, what they have generally in common is that standardised camp barracks are the result of top-down generated concepts. This means that their planning or selection takes place without involving the future residents. In this regard, they are comparable to the settlements of modern social housing. If, in the following, not only the objective-oriented *planning* but also the *use* of camp barrack-huts is to be discussed, we can benefit from the findings of architectural-historical research, which since the 1990s has increasingly investigated the use and the user perspective of modern architecture.⁸ In this understanding, architecture is constituted not only by the architect's design intention, but also by the use and appropriation of the building as an object. Contrary to this view, the players of modern architecture have drawn their attention since the 1920s to the

---

3 In addition to the fundamental process of changing spaces through use, the refugee camps and their barrack-huts can also be described as heterotopic spaces in the sense of Foucault's "other spaces," "in which the real sites, all the other real sites that can be found within the culture, are simultaneously represented, contested, and inverted. Places of this kind are outside of all places, even though it may be possible to indicate their location in reality." Michel Foucault, "Of Other Spaces" [1967], in: *Diacritics* 16/1 (1986): 22–27.
4 Regarding the semantic field of architectonic functions, see Adrian Forty, *Words and Buildings. A Vocabulary of Modern Architecture* (London: Thames & Hudson, 2000); Ute Poerschke, *Funktionen und Formen. Architekturtheorie der Moderne* (Bielefeld: transcript, 2014).
5 See Henri Lefebvre, The Production of Space (Malden, Oxford et al.: Blackwell, 1991 [1974]).
6 Zygmunt Bauman, "A Century of Camps?", in: *The Bauman Reader*, edited by Peter Beilharz (Oxford, 2001), 266–280.
7 See Bettina Greiner and Alan Kramer (eds.), *Welt der Lager. Zur "Erfolgsgeschichte" einer Institution* (Hamburg: Hamburger Edition, 2013); Christoph Jahr and Jens Thiel (eds.), *Lager vor Auschwitz. Gewalt und Integration im 20. Jahrhundert* (Berlin: Metropol-Verlag, 2013); Irit Katz et al. (eds.), Camps Revisited. Multifaceted Spatialities of a Modern Political Technology (London: Rowman & Littlefield, 2018).
8 See recent examples: Kenny Cupers (ed.), *Use matters: an alternative history of architecture* (New York: Routledge, 2013); Kirsten Wagner, "Hermeneutiken des Architekturgebrauchs. Zur Sichtbarkeit des Lebens", in: *Theorie der Architektur. Zeitgenössische Positionen*, edited by Sebastian Feldhusen and Ute Poerschke (Gütersloh–Berlin: Bauverlag and Basel: Birkhäuser, 2017), 410–435.

users of their buildings, but as a rule imagining them as abstract, universal beings whose needs could be met by normalised planning and construction.[9] From an inscribed authoritarian point of view, individual appropriations or changes were understood as a disruptive factor that should be purified by education and training.[10]

Recent architectural historiography often refers to Philippe Boudon's case study published in 1969 about the workers' housing estate Pessac in Bordeaux from 1924 by Le Corbusier and Pierre Jeanneret, which was produced serially, cost-effectively and according to hygienic standards.[11] In his empirical study Boudon shows in which way the inhabitants continued to develop "architecture as the seemingly finished"[12] and shaped the space through their everyday actions. In the preface to this study, Henri Lefebvre names three distinct levels presented by Boudon: the theoretical level (the architects' conception and planning), the level of architectural practice, where ideological considerations are supplemented by factors like the needs of the future occupants, and finally the level of the reality of the city and the effects of a living mode.[13] According to Lefebvre, in the reality of living in a house as an activity, "the collective and individual social work" proves to be more outstanding and more complex than the "abstract rationality" of the architects.

If the focus is now not on the use of a modern housing estate, but that of camp barrack-huts as architectural-spatial works, central distinguishing features must be added: The line between public and private space is drawn differently in the camp context than in that of housing complexes. In the case of certain camp types, private space (in the sense of a "loophole"[14] denying access to social control) is kept to a minimum or completely non-existent for most occupants.[15] When it comes to the use of accommodation buildings in camps, *use* means not

---

9 See Paul Emmons and Andreea Mihalache, Architectural handbooks and the user experience, in: *Use matters*, edited by Cupers, 35–50; Walter Prigge (ed.), *Ernst Neufert. Normierte Baukultur im 20. Jahrhundert* (Frankfurt/M.–New York: Campus, 1999).
10 See Sabine Kraft, "Eingeübtes Wohnen", in: arch+ 176/177 (2006): 48–50; Theres Sophie Rohde, *Die Bau-Ausstellung zu Beginn des 20. Jahrhunderts oder "Die Schwierigkeit zu wohnen"*, unpublished PhD. Thesis, Bauhaus University Weimar, 2014.
11 Philippe Boudon, *Lived-In Architecture. Le Corbusiers Pessac Revisited* [1969] (Cambridge/Mass.: MIT Press, 1972).
12 Wagner, "Hermeneutiken des Architekturgebrauchs", 413.
13 Henri Lefebvre, "Preface", in: Boudon, *Lived-In Architecture*, no pagination.
14 Michelle Perrot, "Introduction", in: *A History of Private Life*, vol. IV: *From the Fires of Revolution to the Great War*, edited by Philippe Ariès and Georges Duby (Cambridge/Mass. and London: The Belknap Press of Harvard University Press, 1990), 9–12, esp. 9.
15 However, regarding the existing degree of privacy we must also differentiate within the camps, such as in the case of smaller and more comfortable "luxury" or "intelligentsia barracks" for socially higher standing people in refugee camps in World War I or the officers' barracks in prisoner of war camps.

only the occupants' actions, but also those of the camp management, adapting the space according to its objectives and using it as a biopolitical dispositif.

In the following, a specific example will show how standardised accommodation barracks[16] in the camp context are formed into a complex work through a range of design decisions as well as adaptation and appropriation actions on different levels and thus are transformed into *different* living spaces in the sense of Hannes Meyer's constructivist statement. Therefore, we have to ask how the barrack-huts were designed according to the goals and requirements formulated by the decision makers in the planning offices and at the drawing boards, which functional or material adaptations were required by the camp administration in order to achieve the original goals, and how the barracks could be appropriated or transformed as living spaces by the inhabitants. The camp system of the refugee camps of the Habsburg Monarchy during World War I serves as a field of investigation. In particular, I will focus on the huge large-capacity barracks of the first year of the war, built from the autumn of 1914 onwards as temporary emergency structures, each building for hundreds of refugees. Later they were adapted in some cases or supplemented by smaller types of barrack-huts. My analysis is based on three of the essential functions that these housing barracks had to fulfill from the perspective of the government in order to achieve the objective – protection and reassurance for the population in the hinterland: (a) temporary accommodation, (b) distribution in space, and (c) staging.

Camps Instead of Housing Estates

To reach this objective, it is necessary to know the reasons for this specific camp system.[17] As a result of refugee movements and forced evacuations ordered by the

---

16 In the "century of the camps," there are numerous examples in which existing building types and spaces, such as castles, schools or industrial buildings, were transformed into prisoner of war camps, refugee camps, internment and concentration camps. However, it is probably due to the temporary, rudimentary and serial building type of the modern barrack-hut that this building could become a synonym for the camp itself.

17 See e.g. Walter Mentzel, "Die Flüchtlingspolitik der Habsburgermonarchie während des Ersten Weltkrieges", in: *Aufnahmeland Österreich. Über den Umgang mit Massenflucht seit dem 18. Jahrhundert*, edited by Börries Kuzmany and Rita Garstenauer (Vienna: Mandelbaum, 2017), 126–155; Martina Hermann, "'Cities of barracks': Refugees in the Austrian part of the Habsburg Empire during the First World War", in: *Europe on the Move. Refugees in the Era of the Great War*, edited by Peter Gatrell and Liubov Zhvanko (Manchester: Manchester University Press, 2017), 129–155; Julia Thorpe, "Displacing Empire: Refugee Welfare, National Activism and State Legitimacy in Austria-Hungary in the First World War", in: *Refugees and the End of Empire. Imperial Collapse and Forced Migration in the Twentieth Century*, edited by Panikos Panayi and Pippa Virdee (Basingstoke: Palgrave Macmillan,

government of the Habsburg Monarchy and carried out by the military, hundreds of thousands of people from the war zones[18] arrived in the cities of the hinterland (Vienna, Prague, Graz, Brno, etc.) during the summer of 1914. The mass accumulation of people in the urban centers led to a situation perceived in many ways as threatening, to a chaotic supply situation and subsequently to a dramatic increase of the already blatant housing misery. On the part of the Austro-Hungarian government, no forward-looking plans with regard to expected refugee movements had been elaborated before the war. Therefore, under extreme time pressure, quasi as an "impromptu"[19] response and allegedly without any standards or models "in world history,"[20] the state had to find a solution for this problem: On the one hand, it was about protecting the local population against the feared outbreak of epidemics and against conflicts with a supposedly 'penetrating' group of people (meaning mostly destitute refugees[21]), as well as about controlling politically suspicious persons. On the other hand, in the sense of public welfare, it was about creating mass housing and supplies for people who were now homeless.

For this purpose, the government, or more specifically the Ministry of the Interior (*k.k. Ministerium des Innern*), assessed that it would not be sufficient to build barrack housing complexes outside the cities as a provisional version of social housing[22] and to provide the refugees with food and medical care. Rather, it was considered unavoidable to organise these facilities as outwardly closed systems, surround them with barbed-wire fences and guards, and to carry out a series of sanitary restraints (quarantine, disinfection). Thus, the practice of isolation and internment of civilian and military groups in camps was used as a measure of a governmental crisis management, which had already become a global mass phenomenon since the end of the 19th century.[23] In a meeting on 13

2011), 102–126; Walter Mentzel, "Kriegserfahrungen von Flüchtlingen aus dem Nordosten der Monarchie während des Ersten Weltkrieges", in: *Jenseits des Schützengrabens. Der Erste Weltkrieg im Osten: Erfahrung – Wahrnehmung – Kontext*, in: Bernhard Bachinger and Wolfgang Dornik (Innsbruck et al.: Studien Verlag, 2013), 359–390.

18 First from Galicia, Bukovina and the Balkans, then from South Tyrol, Trentino, Gorizia/Gradisca, Friuli, Istria and the coast (Küstenland).
19 "Die Ausstellung in der Bognergasse (Flüchtlingsfürsorge)", in: *Neue Freie Presse*, 21 January 1916, 1–3, 1.
20 "Beteiligung des k.k. Flüchtlingslagers in Wagna an der Kriegsausstellung in Triest", in: *Lagerzeitung für Wagna*, 9 August 1917, 2–4.
21 Those refugees with sufficient financial resources and who were "socially higher standing" were accommodated in communities and not in camps.
22 The *Volkswohnungen* for the socially weak, planned by Leopold Simony and Theodor Bach and financed by the Kaiser Franz Joseph I Jubilee Foundation founded in 1895, formed a preliminary stage of the later social housing of "Red Vienna."
23 See e.g. Aidan Forth, *Barbed-Wire Imperialism. Britain's Empire of Camps, 1876–1903* (Berkeley: University of California Press, 2017); Jonas Kreienbaum, *"Ein trauriges Fiasko"*. Ko-

September 1914, the Ministry of the Interior specified the measures to be taken for the entire Monarchy.²⁴

The enclosed spaces for the temporary concentration of a particular population group were not only built manifestations of an 'othering' process, which involves a marked distancing from others who are classified as 'foreign,' but corresponded to those exclusion camps, which Giorgio Agamben defines as places in a permanent state of exception.²⁵ Although civilian citizens of the Monarchy, the refugees accommodated in the camps were deprived of regulated legal protection.²⁶ Disguising their very purpose, the camps were officially called "collective settlements" (*Sammelniederlassungen*)²⁷ or, in terms of building types, "barrack camps" or "barrack cities." Unofficially, or in the daily press, there was also talk of "concentration camps."²⁸ Around 1900, this term mainly referred to the colonial camps of the Spanish-American War ('reconcentration' policy) and of the "Boer War" in South Africa, meaning a detention situation rather than the later intention to exterminate in World War II.²⁹

A photograph from a 1915 propaganda publication showing rudimentary sleeping places in a housing barrack being disinfected by camp staff wearing protective suits illustrates two of the main purposes of the camps: cost-saving accommodation as well as measures against the spread of diseases. From autumn 1914 on, more than 15 barrack camps for up to 30,000 people³⁰ were built on

---

loniale Konzentrationslager im südlichen Afrika 1900–1908 (Hamburg: Hamburger Edition, 2015); Greiner and Kramer (eds.), *Welt der Lager*; Matthew Stibbe, "Ein globales Phänomen. Zivilinternierung im Ersten Weltkrieg in transnationaler und internationaler Dimension", in: *Lager vor Auschwitz*, edited by Jahr and Thiel, 158–176; Matthew Stibbe, "The Internment of Civilians by Belligerent States during the First World War and the Response of the International Committee of the Red Cross", in: *Journal of Contemporary History* 41/1 (2006): 5–19. See also footnote 84.

24 "Ergebnis der Beratung in Angelegenheit der Fürsorge für galizische Flüchtlinge", ÖStA, AVA, MdI, Präs., Sign.19/3, Zl.12.240; Walter Mentzel, *Kriegsflüchtlinge in Cisleithanien im Ersten Weltkrieg*, unpublished PhD. thesis, University of Vienna, 1997, 219.

25 Giorgio Agamben, *Means without End: Notes on Politics*, vol. 20: Theory out of Bounds (Minneapolis and London: University of Minnesota Press, 2000), 37–45, esp. 39.

26 Only after the Austrian *Reichsrat* reconvened on December 31, 1917 was a law issued "concerning the protection of war refugees."

27 K.k. Ministerium des Innern (ed.), *Staatliche Flüchtlingsfürsorge im Kriege 1914/15* (Vienna: 1915), 11.

28 See e.g. "Braunau a. Inn. Konzentrationslager", in: *Der Bautechniker* 25 (1915): 316; Heinrich Mannheimer, "Säuglings- und Kinderfürsorge im k.k. Barackenlager Wagna bei Leibnitz", in: *Lagerzeitung für Wagna*, 20 September 1916, 3–5.

29 See e.g. Christoph Jahr and Jans Thiel, "Prolegomena zu einer Geschichte der Lager. Eine Einführung", in: *Lager vor Auschwitz*, edited by Jahr and Thiel, 7–19, especially 14–16.

30 The largest ones were established in Lower Austria, Styria, Upper Austria, Bohemia and Moravia and had inhabitants strictly separated according to nationality and confession.

Fig. 1: Refugee camp Wagna (Styria), disinfection of a housing barrack, from a publication of the Styrian Lieutenancy (*Statthalterei*), Graz 1915. (Source: Library of TU Graz)

behalf of the Austro-Hungarian government. Architectural planning and efficiency-oriented administration operated smoothly like cogs in a machine.[31]

Temporary Accommodation for the Homeless

Barrack-Huts used as 'Fillable Containers'

Initially, the purpose of the dormitories in the closed refugee camps was to provide temporary accommodation for a huge number of homeless people as a substitute for housing in the cities. The buildings that the decision-makers in the Ministry had in mind were empty casings. Since the refugee camps were initially intended as ephemeral facilities, the focus was primarily on low cost, rapid manufacturability, easy disassembly and reusability when choosing the building type. To reduce costs, low durability was accepted. All these criteria were met by the construction type of the serially produced, principally use-neutral wooden barrack-hut.[32] As a more durable alternative to the tent, and a proverbial 'roof

---

31 Civil-servant engineers or self-employed academically trained architects were responsible for site planning in refugee camps.
32 See Walther Lange, *Der Baracken-Bau mit besonderer Berücksichtigung der Wohn- und*

over one's head,' their open, empty space could be 'filled' with homeless people. The barrack-huts thus formed the core elements of the entire system of the barrack camps.

Fig. 2: Refugee camp Gmünd (Lower Austria), barrack-huts, 1915. (Source: Stadtarchiv Gmünd)

The decision to use simple barrack-huts to solve the refugee problem did not primarily mean taking a deprecative attitude towards the people to be cared for.[33] In 1914 – at the beginning of the "century of the camps" – the serial building type of the barrack-hut was imagined as a relatively neutral object, and not yet necessarily associated with misery. Above all, barrack-huts were cheap, temporary living spaces in times of housing shortage. Their use-neutral space also made them the ideal instrument for completely different purposes (hospitals, schools, camps, etc.) and allowed to utilise these mobile buildings as governmental techniques.[34] Originally derived from the military context, various standardised

---

Epidemie-Baracken (Leipzig: Baumgärtner's Buchhandlung) 1895; Ernst Seidl (ed.), *Lexikon der Bautypen. Funktionen und Formen der Architektur* (Stuttgart: Reclam, 2006), 55–56.

33 Within the refugee camps, however, the staff and physicians' dwellings as well as the "intelligentsia barracks" for socially higher-ranking refugees were structurally and aesthetically of a much higher-quality, which illustrates the strict hierarchy of the camp society.

34 See Axel Doßmann et al., *Architektur auf Zeit. Baracken, Pavillons, Container* (Berlin: b_books, 2006); Axel Doßmann et al., "Barackenlager. Zur Nutzung einer Architektur der Moderne", in: *Auszug aus dem Lager. Zur Überwindung des modernen Raumparadigmas in der politischen Philosophie*, edited by Ludger Schwarte (Bielefeld: transcript, 2007), 220–245.

barrack systems (Doecker, Brümmer, Adrian[35]) were developed internationally since the last decades of the 19th century. Timber construction companies used to produce serial sheds, gazebos and camp barrack-huts[36] using similar materials and construction principles. Municipalities bought standardised barrack-huts to be prepared for emergencies such as natural disasters and epidemics. In the early 20th century, contrary to today's negative connotations of barrack-huts, this construction type was challenging even for prominent and established architects, seeking in times of need solutions to current questions of prefabrication and minimal or temporary living space.[37] In the 1920s, the German *Baracke* could even have turned into an optimistic metaphor for industrially produced and hygienically clean buildings of the *Neues Bauen* ("Baracken der Zukunft"[38]).

However, the term "barrack-hut" not only referred to the strictly formal architecture of rationally planned, standardised and serially manufactured buildings, which are part of the modern history of prefabrication and architectural standardisation.[39] Around 1900, in German the term *Baracke* was rather ambiguous and opened up a semantic field: Evolving from former meanings, it designated a makeshift and improvised ground-level dwelling, and thus on the one hand a self-organised and random construction, and on the other hand a rundown or dilapidated building. Linked (in German) with adjectives such as primitive, miserable, sad or squalid, a latently deprecative meaning of the concept of barrack-huts could be augmented, for example in descriptions of the makeshift buildings of the settler movement in Vienna after World War I. Today, however, the informal, self-expanding spatial structures of the Bidonvilles or Favelas are becoming increasingly interesting for architects, urban planners and architectural historians.[40]

---

35 *Brümmer'sche zerlegbare, transportable Häuser, Hauptkatalog A der Deutschen Barackenbau-Gesellschaft m.b.H. Köln*, Barmen 1902; "Preisverteilung in der Deutschen Städteausstellung in Dresden", in: *Deutsche Bauzeitung* 38 (1903), 78: 502; André Guillerme et al., "Le front de l'industrialisation de la construction. 1915–1920", in: *Les Cahiers de la recherche architecturale et urbaine* 28 (2013): 37–56.
36 Barrack-huts were used for all kinds of camps: prisoner of war camps, civilian internment camps, detention camps, etc. Cf. generally, Robert Jan van Pelt's article in this issue.
37 See e. g. Antje Senarclens de Grancy, "Spitalsbaracken, 1915, Projekt", in: *Otto Wagner*, edited by Andreas Nierhaus and Eva-Maria Orosz (Salzburg and Vienna: Residenz 2018), 464.
38 Ilja Ehrenburg, *Visum der Zeit* (Leipzig: Paul List Verlag 1929), 91–99, esp. 93. See also Osamu Okuda, "Versinkende Villen – aufsteigende Baracken. Paul Klee und die Bauhaus-Debatten über den Konstruktivismus", in: *Aufstieg und Fall der Moderne*, edited by Rolf Bothe and Thomas Föhl (eds.): (Ostfildern–Ruit: Kunstsammlungen zu Weimar, 1999), 336–343.
39 Etymology: French: *baraque*, Spanish/Italian: *baracca* for a makeshift or emergency building. In English, finally, *barracks* means a building or group of buildings where soldiers live, a circumstance that refers to the military origin of the standardised barrack-huts.
40 See e. g. the special issue: *Bidonvilles & Bretteldörfer. Ein Jahrhundert informeller Stadtentwicklung in Europa*, *dérive* Nr. 71 (2018).

When in 1918 architect Hermann Muthesius wrote in a building manual: "Misery generates barrack-huts,"[41] he meant both the improvised homes of the homeless during and after World War I and the replacement buildings designed by architects, with which they hoped to improve the emergency situation. Due to years of use and lack of maintenance in the war and post-war period, the barrack-huts for the refugees of the Habsburg Monarchy, originally rationally planned as a biopolitical solution to a mass problem, became increasingly desolate. Consequently, the housing conditions in the camps hardly differed from that of the poor in industrialised cities, and the barracks changed from one meaning to another. "Barrack-hut" turned into an architectural image of misery.

Appropriation as a Housing Space

At first, however, the wooden dwellings were built in the enclosed, transitory space of the refugee camps. In doing so, the camp planners did not utilise the then commercial and technically mature barrack models, the widespread Doecker barracks for example.[42] Instead, they developed different models with huge open interiors and a minimal infrastructure for each camp in a very short time. From the outset, the Ministry and the camp administration operated with the term "housing" (*Wohnen*) in relation to the shelters provided for the refugees of the Monarchy, as the term "housing barracks" (*Wohnbaracken*) shows in all plans. Dwelling can be described as a social field of practice, which includes activities such as sleeping, eating and cooking, but also reading and regenerative activities and everyday routines. However, in the barrack-huts, dwelling, especially in the sense of a spatial appropriation and creating a (longer-term) homely environment,[43] was only possible within a very limited framework. When the refugees arrived in the camps in the fall and winter months of 1914, they found little more than fixed wooden boards with raised headboards for sleeping. The rooms were poorly insulated, and their equipment was not suitable for the cold season. In winter, the water froze in the huts.[44]

---

41 "Not treibt zu Baracken." Hermann Muthesius, *Kleinhaus und Kleinsiedlung* (München: Verlag von F. Bruckmann, 1918), 342.
42 The so-called Doecker barrack manufactured by the company Christoph & Unmack was created as a model for an architectural competition for a "building for the treatment of wounded and infectious patients for war and peace purposes" at the World's Fair of Antwerp in 1885. Regarding the history of standardised barrack-huts, see Robert Jan van Pelt's article in this issue.
43 Irene Nierhaus and Nierhaus Andreas (eds.), *Wohnen zeigen. Modelle und Akteure des Wohnens in Architektur und visueller Kultur* (Bielefeld: transcript, 2014).
44 Flüchtlingsfürsorge. Barackenlager Chotzen und Wagna, AVA, MdI, Allg., Sign.19, Zl.22.099,

The rudimentary interior of the empty barrack-huts was only partly a factor in the restrictions and misery in the camps. Contemporary parallels could be found in completely different contexts, if one were to limit the description of life in the camp huts to the characterisation as a collective form of living in a basic dwelling without comfort. As part of the Body, Life and Culture Reform movement around 1900, gazebos or air huts with primitive sleeping places served for overnight accommodation, like those on Monte Verità near Ascona, at holiday camps and sanatoriums, similar to the simple dormitories for alpinists in mountain huts in the context of the exploration of the Alps.[45] Nevertheless, the stay at these rudimentary, comfort-free, collective and temporary living places occurred – in strong contrast to the refugee barrack-huts – through the free decision of individuals for these simplest living conditions. There was always the alternative of a self-determined 'return' into a 'normal' (urban) environment, while the inhabitants of the refugee camps were not allowed to leave their living places in order to find more suitable lodgings on their own initiative. However, what made living in the camp fundamentally different from other simple ways of life, was the permanent monitoring of the intimate sleeping space by the camp management. The housing space in the camp thus had a public character.[46] Privacy, it should be noted, is not an absolute concept but the result of social negotiations. Inscribed in the degree of (conceded and achievable) privacy was a social hierarchy, as can be seen, for example, in the phenomenon of bed-lodgers (*Bettgeher* or *Schlafgänger*) in the modern metropolis, which was still widespread at the time of World War I.

We can understand spatial appropriation as the active and self-determined handling of space and as the development of space through action.[47] This leads to the question as to how one can prove the adaptation of a (public) space in the camp, which offered little more than a 'roof over one's head,' to a living space. In the daily newspapers, there are only a few indications of the occupants' actions, for example when, in default of straw sacks or mattresses, they used clothes and

---

11 May 1915; see e. g. "Eine polnische Kolonie in Chotzen", in: *Arbeiter-Zeitung* (Vienna), 30 October 1914, 7.

45 Nils Aschenbeck, *Reformarchitektur. Die Konstituierung der Ästhetik der Moderne* (Basel: Birkhäuser, 2016); Doris Hallama, "Hüttenbauen im Hochalpinen. Zur Architektur der Schutzhütten", in: *Wege und Hütten in den Alpen*, edited by Deutscher Alpenverein et al. (Köln-Weimar-Wien: Böhlau Verlag, 2016), vol.1, 121–202; Martin Green, *Mountain of Truth. The Counterculture begins – Ascona, 1900–1920* (Hanover and London: University Press of New England, 1986).

46 Regarding the relationship between public and private space in living, see Ulla Terlinden, "Naturalisierung und Ordnung. Theoretische Überlegungen zum Wohnen und zu den Geschlechtern", in: *Wohnen und Gender. Theoretische, politische, soziale und räumliche Aspekte*, edited by Darja Reuschke (Wiesbaden: Verlag für Sozialwissenschaften, 2010), 15–26.

47 See e. g. Ulfert Herlyn, "Stadt- und Regionalsoziologie", in: *Einführung in Praxisfelder der Soziologie*, edited by Hermann Korte and Bernhard Schäfers (Springer, 1997) 243–261.

blankets as a makeshift to pad their sleeping places, consisting of wooden planks.[48] In contrast to homeless shelters in the cities of that time, which were only used for overnight accommodation, the refugees were at least able to leave their belongings in the housing barracks during the day. The "Arbeiter-Zeitung", which more than other Austrian daily newspapers reported on the individual living conditions of the refugees, wrote in 1914 about a minimum of personal furnishing in the camp in Chotzen/Choceň: "On the cupboards above the bedsteads the poor luggage is stored. Sparse furniture, property of the refugees, outworn clothes, here and there a necessary piece of duvet or blanket to cover."[49]

Disciplining, however, was always inscribed in the concept of the camp. The following year, in the same daily newspaper, the positive assessment of the individual use of the housing barrack was associated with the observance of (self-)discipline: "The living spaces [in the camp Mitterndorf] have an unequal appearance, depending on the sense of cleanliness and beauty of the inhabitants. There are rooms kept scrupulously clean, whose walls are decorated with wallpapers and pictures, and whose inhabitants, despite the difficulties of refugee life, are eager to make the accommodation space as comfortable as possible. But in many cases, however, one sees dirt and neglect, which can not be eliminated despite the exertion of influence by the administration."[50] It depended on the decisions, regulations and disciplinary measures of the camp administration, whether or how much belongings the refugees were allowed to take with them into the camps,[51] but also – as the reference to the "exertion of influence by the administration" shows – how the existing space could be handled. These conditions included not only the existence of rules for living in the barracks, but also the separation of functions: As an example, the day-structuring and socially significant activity of cooking, which was important for a bourgeois or peasant living, was outsourced and centralised in kitchen barracks.[52]

---

48 "Eine polnische Kolonie in Chotzen", in: *Arbeiter-Zeitung (Vienna)*, 30 October 1914, 7; "Ein Besuch in den Flüchtlingsbaracken bei Leibnitz", in: *Volksblatt für Stadt und Land*, 24 January 1915, 9–10.
49 "Eine polnische Kolonie in Chotzen", in: *Arbeiter-Zeitung (Vienna)*, 30 October 1914, 7.
50 "Das Flüchtlingslager in Mitterndorf", in: *Arbeiter-Zeitung, Morgenblatt*, 5 September 1916, 6–7.
51 "In the living spaces you can see poor remains of household appliances and furniture, which the refugees did not want to leave behind and carried on while fleeing."
52 Depending on the number of occupants, 8, 12 or more housing barracks were assigned to a kitchen hut, which – in clear analogy to prisoner of war and military camps – made it possible to easily organise administrable camp sections.

Distribution in Space

The Jump in Scale of the Huge Halls

In addition to supplying the refugees with accommodation space, the barrack-huts also served the purpose of making the mass of human beings in the camp controllable and administrable. In that case, according to the modern interpretation context, the bodies had to be 'distributed' and 'organised.'[53] Although in the autumn of 1914 the construction of a large number of accommodations was the top priority, special barrack models were developed, as already mentioned, for each of the camps, which involved a great deal of planning effort. The reason for this decision can only be that, on the one hand, the number of people to be accommodated exceeded the capacity of conventional emergency lodging by far, while on the other, a resource-saving solution had to be found within a given budget.

In the different camps, each barrack-hut housed hundreds of people: around 500 in Wagna, 600 in Chotzen/Chocen,[54] and 250 in Gmünd.[55] In 1914, the huts at the Wagna camp had a floor area of about 680 sqm, which was significantly increased by open galleries to raise the occupancy rate. In the huts in Gmünd, only 1.3 sqm of floor space per person was available (while, for example, the Doecker standard barrack-huts, each with 18 sleeping places, provided around 4 sqm of floor space per person). The dramatic reduction of existing standards, for example concerning the "airspace allocated to each inmate,"[56] was deliberately accepted by the representatives of the Ministry. The amount of people in the huge barrack halls meant a numerical break not only with respect to conventional barrack-hut models,[57] but also to already common 'total institutions' such as poor and homeless asylums or hospital dormitories. How could this remarkable jump in scale be justified?

In the contemporary press, the refugee situation was repeatedly described as a "vast current," "inundation," or "flooding,"[58] also expressing the Ministry of the

---

53 See the chapter "The art of distributions" in: Michel Foucault, *Discipline and Punish. The Birth of the Prison* (London: Vintage Books/Random House, 1995), 141–149.
54 "Eine polnische Kolonie in Chotzen", in: *Arbeiter-Zeitung (Vienna)*, 30 October 1914, 7.
55 Mentzel, "Kriegsflüchtlinge", 296.
56 K.k. Ministerium des Innern (ed.), *Staatliche Flüchtlingsfürsorge im Kriege 1914/15* (Vienna: 1915), 11.
57 For example, the Doecker standard barrack comprised approximately 45 sqm and was generally recommended for a total of 18 people.
58 Friedrich v. Wiser, "Staatliche Kulturarbeit für Flüchtlinge", in: *Österreichische Rundschau* 45 (1915) 5, 203–211; "Das Flüchtlingslager Wagna in Steiermark", in: *Reichspost, Morgenblatt*, 16 February 1916, 6; "Die Ausstellung in der Bognergasse (Flüchtlingsfürsorge)", in: *Neue Freie Presse*, 21 January 1916, 1–3.

Interior's representatives' inability to cope with the situation. In such metaphors, people affected by homelessness, housing misery, and the loss of their livelihood took the form of a 'natural disaster'.[59] Consistently pursuing this image, the refugee camps could be easily "compared to waterworks, locks and dams that curb a free and unrestrained stream pouring according to rules and laws, forcing effervescent floods into profitable work,"[60] as a journalist of the "Neues Wiener Journal", who worked in the war archive during the war, wrote in 1916. This picture not only illustrates the extent of the task to be accomplished, but literally interprets it as social engineering.[61] Rather, the camps and, in particular, the huge barrack-huts are conceivable as catch basins, which can now be 'filled' with people, imagined as "water masses"[62] and abstracted in statistics.

Space Allocation in the "Human Depot"

Following the discursive associations, the "masses of people," which could be 'dammed' in the huge, initially almost empty barrack-huts, now had to be arranged to cope with the 'chaos of bodies' within this 'container.' Using the example of the prison, Michel Foucault describes how, under the banner of the Enlightenment, a process of disciplining, monitoring and controlling the population is set in motion, in which each individual is given his or her place.[63] In this light, the empty space of the barrack-huts was not left to the free access of individuals, but parceled out, that is, subdivided into controllable units. The sleeping place was not freely chooseable but was assigned to the individuals by the camp administration in the sense of a 'tableau' for the division of the manifold, whereby family or village communities were taken into account in order to avoid social conflicts.

Since the Ministry of the Interior conceived the care of the refugees in the sense of the poor relief and welfare as was usual around 1900, it appeared obvious that the typology of large-scale barrack-huts was connected to rooms in homeless shelters – only in temporary construction instead of buildings for permanent use in 'normal times.' The minimalism of the equipment in the camp

---

59 Cf. Stefan Benedik et al., *Die imaginierte "Bettlerflut". Temporäre Migrationen von Roma / Romnija – Konstrukte und Positionen* (Klagenfurt and Vienna: Drava-Verlag, 2013).
60 Egon Dietrichstein, "Oesterreichische Flüchtlingsstädte", in: *Kriegs-Ausgabe 1916*, 32, 463–467, esp. 463.
61 Cf. David Kuchenbuch, *Geordnete Gemeinschaft. Architekten als Sozialingenieure – Deutschland und Schweden im 20. Jahrhundert* (Bielefeld: transcript, 2010).
62 K.k. Ministerium des Innern (ed.), Staatliche Flüchtlingsfürsorge im Kriege 1914/15, Vienna 1915, 11.
63 Foucault, *Discipline*.

barrack-huts – wooden sleeping places with raised parts for the head and simple boards used as shelves – actually corresponded to this in urban homeless shelters. A local example was the asylum and workhouse (*Asyl- und Werkhaus*) of the city of Vienna, built in 1912, with seven dormitories for up to 100 people each.[64] More models and experiences were also available in the chapter "Refuges for the Homeless"[65] in the "Handbuch der Architektur," a standard work for architecture and the construction sector. In this book, international examples of large dormitories were presented, such as the *Städtische Obdach*, built in 1890 in Berlin-Fröbelstraße, a huge inner city complex for a total of 4000 people, with 70 people per dormitory.

An essential element in the design of the camp barracks was, as in the urban asylums, that the dormitories for the refugees provided an almost complete overview and were thus controllable. An – at least visual – separation in sleeping or living cells (after the war a leitmotif of the architects of the *Neues Bauen* movement) was almost completely omitted. For example, in the Wagna and Gmünd camps, the only privacy screen provided by the designers consisted of half-height partitions, which, at regular intervals, formed units for several people.[66] The standard of then-current examples was not achieved – such as the Viennese men's asylums built in 1905 and 1910 like English "Rowton Houses" with single sleeping cabins with doors[67] that guaranteed a minimum of privacy according to normative, bourgeois philanthropic ideas.

In the two-dimensionality of the ground plans for the barrack-huts – later they were presented as prototypes in propaganda exhibitions on refugee aid – the carefully drawn dividing lines between the sleeping places resemble those of shelves in material storages, warehouses or library depots, such as Otto Wagner's 1910 designs for the Vienna University Library.[68] From the perspective of the

---

64 K.k. Reichshaupt- und Residenzstadt Wien, Magistratsabteilung XI (ed.), *Das Asyl- und Werkhaus der Stadt Wien*, Vienna 1913.
65 *Handbuch der Architektur*, vol. 4, half vol. 5, Darmstadt 1891. See also: Architekten- und Ingenieur-Verein zu Berlin (ed.), *Berlin und seine Bauten*, Berlin 1896, vol. II and III, 481–483.
66 Franz Haimel, *Flüchtlingslager Wagna bei Leibnitz. Mit einer Abhandlung über die Alt-Römerstadt Flavia Solva*, 2 vol. (Graz: Steiermärkische Statthalterei, 1915).
67 See Kaiser Franz Joseph I. Jubiläums-Stiftung (ed.), *Männerheim (Wien XX.Bezirk, Meldemannstraße Nr. 27)*, (Vienna: Kaiser Franz Joseph I. Jubiläums-Stiftung, 1905); Kaiser Franz Joseph I. Jubiläums-Stiftung (ed.), *Männerheim. Wien XVII., Wurlitzergasse Nr. 89*, (Vienna: Kaiser Franz Joseph I. Jubiläums-Stiftung, 1910); Jane Hamlett, *At Home in the Institution. Material Life in Asylums: Lodging Houses and Schools in Victorian and Edwardian England*, (Basingstoke: Palgrave Macmillan), 2015, 135–159.
68 Andreas Nierhaus and Eva-Maria Orosz (eds.), *Otto Wagner* (Salzburg and Vienna: Residenz, 2018), 424. Like the overall plans of the camps, the floor plans of the large-scale barrack-huts of the first months, such as those of Wagna or Gmünd, are comparable to the distribution of items on the shelves of a warehouse, following the principles of inventory management. They

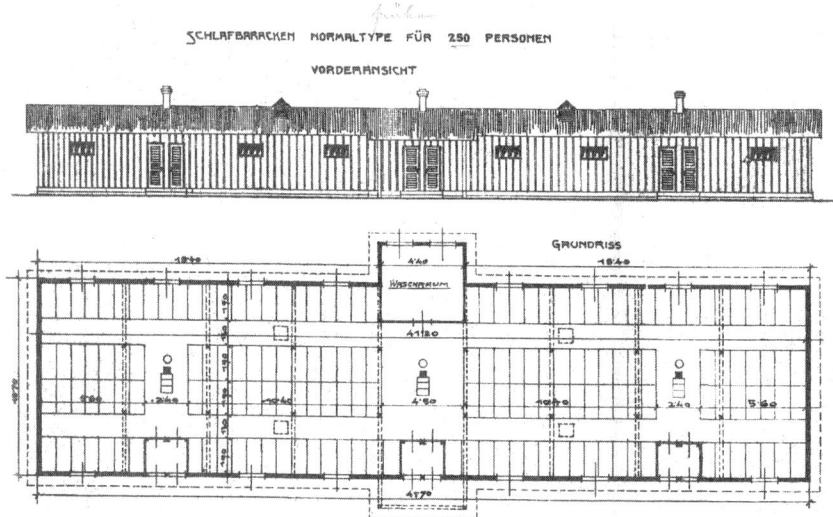

Fig. 3: Refugee camp Gmünd (Lower Austria), view and floor plan of a sleeping hut for 250 persons, 1915. (Source: Stadtarchiv Gmünd)

camp administration, it seemed that the sheer mass of the homeless could be rationally mastered in this way. The barrack-huts were something like the "human depots"[69] (*Menschenmagazin*) of the residential buildings of the Gründerzeit city, which had already been criticised around 1890 by the urbanist and theorist Camillo Sitte.

This principle continues even on the larger scale of the camp plan. Within the strict grid of straight camp roads, the housing barracks constituted the most frequently reproduced basic module. Comparable to contemporary modern metropolitan planning, the grid plan enabled rapid movement, smooth communication and visual control of open spaces, as well as a circulation of air necessary for hygiene. 50, 100 and more of the huts were lined up repetitively and put together rationally to form a modern "cell conglomerate"[70] (Otto Wagner). In this way, the barrack-huts could serve as organisational units for the daily processes in the camp and as a linchpin between administration and inhabitants,

---

find their visual and organisational correspondence in the shelves of the administration offices of the camps. See Monika Dommann, "Wertspeicher: Epistemologien des Warenlagers", in: *Zeitschrift für Medien- und Kulturforschung* 3/2 (2012): 35–50.

69 Camillo Sitte, "Das Wien der Zukunft (1891)," in: *Camillo Sitte Gesamtausgabe*, vol. 2: *Schriften zu Städtebau und* Architektur, edited by Klaus Semsroth et al. (Vienna et al.: Böhlau Verlag, 2010), 295–308, 300.

70 Wagner used this term for the modern appartment houses of the late 19th century. Otto Wagner, *Moderne Architektur. Seinen Schülern ein Führer auf diesem Kunstgebiete*, (Vienna: Anton Schroll Verlag, ³1902), 141.

such as for the food distribution or the delivery of the post.⁷¹ The street grid reproduced the operation principle of a table or an office shelf. In the barrack-hut, people would appear as objects in a folder and thus easily accessible for purposes of camp administration.

Perception, Reactions, and Measures

Now, the question is how this order devised by the camp designers affected the perception of the inhabitants or how it worked on a daily basis. For the individuals, living in the huts probably meant radically new sensory impressions compared to the usual living spaces in their places of origin. They suffered the experience of spending months and even years together with hundreds of other people sleeping in a huge room with high ceilings and almost no visual or acoustic separation. Since in most cases the barrack-huts had only small window openings, the rooms were also dark during the day and artificial lighting did not work well due to their size. In the living areas, therefore, a dim atmosphere prevailed, as repeatedly mentioned in the sources. Lithographs made by the young Viennese artist Max Pollak in 1915 after a visit to the barrack-huts in the Nikolsburg/Mikulov camp recall images of the metropolitan slums such as those in Gustave Doré's graphic cycle "London. A Pilgrimage" (1872) or the social documentary photographs of Hermann Drawe in Vienna (1907), in which sharp criticism of the downside of Modernity is practiced.⁷²

The experience of narrowness and cramped conditions on the ground stood in stark contrast to the oversised open space above. The dimensions of the sleeping places were so tightly calculated – in Wagna, for example, 80 cm width per person – that the unfamiliar or familiar bodies almost touched each other while lying down. In addition, no individual adjustments were possible and the paths through the room were pre-structured since the arrangement of the beds was set and the planks firmly mounted. All everyday activities, even those of an intimate nature, from reading letters and writing, dressing and undressing to sexual activity and sleeping, were visible to all and acoustically perceptible. The sources also report complaints about the noise and odor nuisance and other stress triggers caused by the large number of people in the huts.

Paradoxically, all of these factors were consequences of rational top-down decisions. In social practice, the 'filling' of the refugees in huge halls and the

---

71 The numbering of the barrack was shown in the camp plans and marked visibly on the outer walls of the huts.
72 See Emil Kläger and Hermann Drawe, *Durch die Wiener Quartiere des Elends und Verbrechens* (Vienna: Mitschke, 1908).

allocation to specific sleeping places in the open space did nothing to calm the situation. On the contrary, it caused stress, conflicts and chaotic conditions, which contributed to depression, revolts and escape attempts, as well as high infection rates due to physical closeness and lack of hygiene – all in all, everything that was supposed to be avoided through the establishment of 'orderly' camps. Only through disciplinary measures, which were permanently reconsidered and reformulated by the camp administration and implemented with great effort, could an instable balance of order be maintained in the housing huts.

Fig. 4: Refugee camp Wagna (Styria), inside a family barrack-hut, 1915. (Source: Library of TU Graz)

For example, the daily camp newspaper published in Wagna largely served the announcement of prohibitions and reports of punishments. As in other disciplining institutions, homeless shelters or boarding schools, rules were laid down and strictly controlled (night rest, restrictions on everyday activities such as smoking or cooking because of the fire risk).[73] Above all, the establishment of the function of the barrack commander (*Barackenkommandant*) – called *Wojt* (Polish: community leader[74]) or *Kapo* or *Capo di baracca* (Italian: head of the barrack) – can be understood as a measure to control, calm the situation and maintain hygienic conditions. These were appointed from the ranks of the refu-

---

73 E.g. "Aus dem Barackenlager", in: *Lagerzeitung für Wagna*, 27 January 1917, 3.
74 "Ein Tag im Leibnitzer Flüchtlingslager", in: *Kleine Zeitung*, 25 December 1914, 6.

gees and had to supervise the cleanliness of the barrack-huts, the handing out of food, the disinfection and the discipline in the halls and to daily report to the administration. In this way, they reproduced military authority, but on the other hand they also corresponded to the occupational profile of the janitor in urban housing blocks, in his authority as an agent of the landlord.[75]

Appropriations and Transformations of the Space

Despite the rudimentary equipment, the room of the housing barracks was not in a static condition. If paillasses were provided for sleeping to isolate the wooden floor, they had to be stacked up in the morning to make room for the day.[76] In sparse sources, however, attempts by the refugees can be found to transform the open space according to their own needs with the few means available, contrary to the regulations and in the sense of agency. Several former refugees reported from the Braunau camp, that the residents within the dormitories produced "tent-like" spaces with blankets and cords for a visual delimitation between men and women, children and adults.[77] Thus, they divided the unity of the hall and created privacy. In November 1915, the "Lagerzeitung für Wagna" wrote: "It was perceived that in various barrack-huts the blankets are used as curtains in front of the different barrack compartments instead of as protection against the cold. The refugees are made aware that this mischief will definitely not be tolerated and that the barrack commissioners are instructed to initiate the necessary to abolish this practise immediately."[78]

These appropriations of the public space of the camp barrack – as a transformation into an at least semi-public, if not private space – signified resistance against the panoptic overview conceived by the camp designers for easier control in the sense of surveillance in a 'total institution.'[79] The actions of the barrack commanders, ordered by the camp administration, and the removal of the partitions aimed at restoring the original order. In the preserved sources, resistance in this performative sense is often only comprehensible through pro-

---

75 Peter Payer, "Hausmeister in Wien. Aufstieg und Niedergang einer Respektsperson", in: *Wiener Geschichtsblätter* 51 (1996), supplement 4.
76 Max Winter, "Die Barackenstadt in Neu-Gmünd", in: *Arbeiter-Zeitung* (Morgenblatt), 22 September 1915, 5–7, esp. 6.
77 Mario Eichta, Braunau 1915–1918. I Profughi di Lavarone e del Trentino. Die Alt-Tiroler Flüchtlinge aus Lafraun (Cremona: Persico Europe, 1997), 136.
78 "Verlautbarungen. Unfug bei Verwendung der Bettdecken", in: *Lagerzeitung für Wagna*, 13 November 1915, 5.
79 Erving Goffman, *Asylums: Essays on the Social Situation of Mental Patients and Other Inmates* (New York: Anchor Books, 1961); Foucault, *Discipline*.

hibitions and punishments, as in the case of unauthorised opening of or climbing over the camp fence as transgressing the camp's external borders.

The ephemeral interventions of the refugees into the spatial structure can also be read as – timeless – creative reinterpretations of the unitary space of the huts. In his study on the housing estate Pessac mentioned above, Boudon emphasises, as a surprising success of its architecture, that the residents assign new functions to the standardised rooms through individual transformations, for example by erecting new partitions or removing old ones, to turn a garage into a kitchen or to enlarge a sleeping room.[80] Similarly, the camp inhabitants gave their temporary living place "plurality and creativity"[81] and produced a condition that Michel de Certeau calls an "art of using those [products] imposed on it."[82]

In some cases, the initiative of the camp inhabitants could even have an effect on the camp management as originator of the barrack-hut concept, as the continuation of the above-mentioned statement on the 'mischief' of the textile partitions in the Wagna camp shows: "Should there be a need to provide curtains to some hall compartments, the camp administration is ready to grant the necessary material on request of the respective barrack commissioners."[83] This quote shows that the room of the barrack-huts was not irrevocably finalised by the designers in the building department, as intended by those responsible, but indeed participatorily continued by spatial appropriations and transformations of the residents. It also shows some flexibility on the part of the camp administration, which was the result of a pragmatic weighting of discipline and freedom for the residents, without giving up the hegemonic position of authority.

However, there is another, far-reaching modification of the camp concept, which can be traced, at least indirectly, to the residents' complaints and protests about the catastrophic conditions: Under pressure from members of parliament (*Reichsrat*) and representatives of relief committees, who were aware of the completely inadequate housing in large-scale barrack-huts (and because the government finally realised that the war would last longer), the camp planning changed after the first few months and followed new parameters.[84] The model of the huge open-space barrack was abandoned in favour of smaller units. First, the

---

80 Boudon, *Lived-In Architecture*.
81 Michel de Certeau, *The Practise of Everyday Life* (Berkeley: University of California Press, 1984), 30.
82 Certeau, *The Practise*, 31.
83 "Verlautbarungen. Unfug bei Verwendung der Bettdecken", in: *Lagerzeitung für Wagna*, 13 November 1915, 5.
84 Already at the beginning of December 1914, after a visit to the Nikolsburg/Mikulov camp, several members of parliament submitted a memorandum to the Minister of the Interior, demanding "in particular the installation of compartments in the halls of the barracks." "Das Barackenlager in Nikolsburg", in: *Dr. Bloch's Österreichische Wochenschrift*, 4 December 1914, 14–15.

large halls were subdivided and finally the construction of small single-family huts was preferred. The camps were equipped with a dense, modern infrastructure, including all areas of life, and architecturally transformed, upgraded and conceived for the purpose of permanent residence.[85] At least conceptually, the cohesion of the camp boundary gradually loosened. The subsequent camp planning can thus be interpreted as a precursor or variant of later social housing.

Staging

Hegemonic Representation of State Welfare

Going beyond the primary purpose of emergency accommodation, order, and control, refugee camps were also assigned a communicative function within the framework of general war propaganda. They aimed to show the local population that the 'impending danger' of the other was banned behind the guarded camp boundary by measures of the public authorities, but that at the same time the refugees, being citizens of the Habsburg Monarchy, were looked after. At the same time, this reveals the ambivalence of the state's interest, since concurrently, on pure suspicion of espionage, persons of the same population group were held prisoner in civilian internment camps.[86] The borders between the different camp types blurred, as even the refugee camps acted as internment camps in various cases.

Regarding the refugee camps, the Ministry of the Interior was fully aware of the exceptional situation of "the concentration of a large number of persons in one and the same [...] room" and the concerns "in hygienic, social, and moral respect."[87] Even though the precarious situation was constantly improved, life in the camp barracks created new physical and mental misery. The obligation of public care for the refugees, assumed by the planners and managers of the camps on the one hand, and the actual results achieved on the other hand were far apart. Despite (forced) hygienic measures, sickness and mortality rates were dramatically high. Hunger and cold as well as the rigidly restricted freedom of movement

---

85 This consisted of a sewer and electricity network, hospital, school, church, synagogue, people's hall, cinema, etc. Accordingly, the authorities spoke of "barrack cities," and the propaganda presented the refugee camps as "housing colonies" and (ideal) cities.
86 See Matthew Stibbe, "The Internment of Political Suspects in Austria-Hungary during the First World War: A Violent Legacy?", in: *Gender and Modernity in Central Europe. The Austro-Hungarian Monarchy and Its Legacy*, edited by Agatha Schwartz (Ottawa: University of Ottawa Press, 2010), 203–218; Stefan Manz et al. (eds.), *Internment during the First World War: A Mass Global Phenomenon* (New York: Routledge, 2019).
87 K.k. Ministerium des Innern (ed.), *Staatliche Flüchtlingsfürsorge im Kriege 1914/15* (Vienna, 1915), 11.

Fig. 5: Exhibition "The War Aid" ("Die Kriegshilfe"), organised by the Ministery of the Interior, Vienna, 1915 (Source: Österreichisches Staatsarchiv)

put great strain on the refugees. In order to prove the legitimacy of state decisions and to disguise the failure of the state with regard to public care, strict censorship and broad media strategies were necessary to convey a positive image of the camps to the public. These included staged photographs of the interior of the camp barracks, made by professional photographic studios. They usually show clean, tidy and freshly wallpapered rooms or compartments, where the residents can be seen sitting or standing in modest attitude, the women often with white headscarves.[88] These pictures suggest order, cleanliness, care as well as a successfully controlled situation.

In 1915, after the first year of refugee care, the "War Aid Exhibition"[89] in

---

88 See e. g. Haimel, *Flüchtlingslager Wagna*. Only a tiny number of the numerous preserved official photographs of the refugee camps show the interior of the housing barrack-huts, even though for hundreds of thousands of people, they formed the center of their often longstanding stay. Censorship reports, reports by deputies and private relief committees, refugee logbook entries and interviews conducted with former camp residents from the 1980s provide evidence of the actual living conditions in the camps. See e.g. Paolo Malni (ed.), *Gli spostati. Profughi, Flüchtlinge, Uprchlici 1914–1918*, vol.1: *Fotografarsi. Sriversi* (Rovereto: Laboratorio di Storia di Rovereto, 2015).

89 See Julia Thorpe, "Der rote Faden der Vertreibung: Österreich-Ungarns Flüchtlinge im Ersten Weltkrieg und ihre Darstellung in der Kriegshilfeausstellung von 1915", in: *Stick- und Knüpfmuster ruthenischer Flüchtlinge im Ersten Weltkrieg. Aus der Sammlung des Volks-*

Vienna, organised by the Ministry of the Interior, played a special role for the persuasion of the public. This show presented the model character of the refugee camps in the sense of bourgeois welfare and as a collective task in times of housing shortage and a humanitarian and cultural peak performance of the Austro-Hungarian Monarchy. Countless photographs as well as detailed façade and floor plans of the housing barracks as abstract 'prototypes' for future realisations suggested the interpretation of the camps as 'normal' housing complexes, if not as quasi-Utopian living places.[90] By means of hierarchical display and entertainment strategies of colonial exhibitions and folkloristic or ethnological presentations at world fairs, the camp inhabitants were showcased as bearers of an exotic culture.[91] At the same time the camp was presented as a cultivating instrument and didactic program.[92] These disguising strategies actually worked, at least in the first years of the war. A large, colored model of one of the camps led to visitors' associations with a "giant toy under glass."[93] Cynically neglecting the true living conditions, others characterised the camps as idyllic housing colonies and "peaceful barrack homes."[94]

The Camp as a Living Exhibition

The housing barracks of the refugees were, as already stated, no private places. Their living space belonged to the public sphere. When passing through one of the large barrack-huts, one could take a look at the open bunks with the sleeping places of the refugees – principally comparable to the effect of the large windows in modern residential buildings: Not only would they let in a maximum of light, but also visually display the living area to the outside.[95] Again, this effect depends

kundemuseums Wien, edited by Kathrin Pallestrang (Vienna, 2014), 31–45; Julia Thorpe, "Nostalgic histories of War. Refugees in Austria-Hungary, 1914–2014", in: *Beyond Memory. Silence and the Aesthetics of Remembrance*, edited by Alexandre Dessingé and Jay M. Winter (New York: 2016), 65–77.

90 See Antje Senarclens de Grancy, "The Evidence of Architecture", in: *Exhibiting Matters. GAM – Graz Architecture Magazine* 14 (2018): 182–197.
91 See Werner Michael Schwarz, *Anthropologische Spektakel. Zur Schaustellung "exotischer" Menschen, Wien 1870 – 1910* (Vienna: Turia + Kant, 2001); Anne Dreesbach, *Gezähmte Wilde. Die Zurschaustellung "exotischer" Menschen in Deutschland 1870–1940* (Frankfurt/M. et al. 2005).
92 Maureen Healy, "Exhibiting a War in Progress: Entertainment and Propaganda in Vienna, 1914–1918", in: *Austrian History Yearbook* 31 (2000): 57–85.
93 Tea Lapenna, "Kriegshilfe", in: *Reichspost, Morgenblatt*, 16 December 1915, 1–2.
94 "Die Ausstellung in der Bognergasse (Flüchtlingsfürsorge)", in: *Neue Freie Presse*, 21 January 1916, 1–3, esp. 3.
95 See e.g. Beatriz Colomina, *Privacy and Publicity. Modern Architecture as Mass Media* (Cambridge/Mass.: MIT Press 1994).

on the freedom of choice for or against such an exposure and on the question of who can dispose of the space, as shown in the example of the textile partitions.

The fact that during official visits to the camps, the camp management manipulated the image of the barrack-huts and the actual living conditions of the refugees, shows that the state was trying to present their alleged control of the situation. This can be illustrated by the following example. On 11 January 1916 Archduchess Maria Josepha visited the camp in Mitterndorf as a representative of the imperial family and as a patron of a relief committee. In the diary entry of the teacher Filomena Boccher, a refugee from Trentino, one can find the exact counterpart to the reports about the official visit published in the press. While the press was talking about the Archduchess' satisfaction with the size and features of the housing block she was visiting (a new type of a family hut with smaller units),[96] Boccher noted that the Archduchess had entered a room, which "seemed prepared for her visit, as it was clean, not crammed with beds like the others, and on the beds lay beautiful white sheets. The Archduchess certainly did not suspect that there were rooms like the one where I live, where 17 people lie on miserable paillasses, [...] back to back, without a blanket, with the door and broken windows through which cold air streams fiercely, causing the poor old people to freeze [...]."[97]

Among the camp visitors, the refugees' wooden dwellings repeatedly evoked associations with similarly constructed exhibition pavilions.[98] This effect was – more or less consciously – reinforced by the camp planners in the sense of the "Exhibitionary Complex"[99] of the great exhibitions of 19th century. As the war progressed, the camp gates were more and more elaborated, strikingly reminiscent of the entrances to large exhibition areas, such as Hans Poelzig's main entrance to the *Jahrhundertausstellung* in Breslau in 1913 or the entrance to the exhibition of the artist colony at Mathildenhöhe in Darmstadt in 1901.[100] There, the facilities housed within the exhibition gate (box office, exchange office, police inspection, fire station) corresponded to the camp guard and a registration office at the Gmünd camp. In both cases, the gate and the fence marked a separate, controlled area with its own objectives and rules. In this sense, the refugees' living in the barrack-huts can be compared to colonial shows or other exhibition

---

96 "Besuche", in: *Wiener Zeitung*, 13 January 1916, 10. (Camp visited on 11 January.)
97 Filomena Boccher, *Diario di una maestra in esilio nel "Lager" di Mitterndorf* (Roncegno, 1983), 42.
98 See "Das Flüchtlingslager in Gmünd", in: *Badener Zeitung*, 3 April 1915, 6; Ernst Decseys, "Steiermarks italienische Stadt. Ein Besuch in Wagna", in: *Neue Freie Presse, Morgenblatt*, 30 March 1916, 1–3.
99 Tony Bennett, "The Exhibitionary Complex", in: *Thinking about Exhibitions*, edited by Reesa Greenberg et al. (London and New York, 1996), 81–112.
100 See Annette Ciré, *Temporäre Ausstellungsbauten für Kunst, Gewerbe und Industrie in Deutschland 1896–1915* (Frankfurt/M. et al.: Peter Lang, 1993).

types and can be interpreted as a living ethnological exhibition.[101] In this function, the inhabitants were assigned the role of passive objects or exhibits – an aspect that can be associated with the aforementioned interpretation of the camp as a "human depot" like that of a museum collection.

Conclusion – Different Housing Spaces

The large housing barrack-huts in the refugee camps of the Habsburg Monarchy in World War I served as a case study for investigating the relationships between space, function, and use of a given building type. Considering the very specific framework conditions of different camp contexts, a general nature of camp barracks cannot be derived from the results of this case study, or at least only to a limited extent. However, basic aspects illustrating the social functions of built space can be summarised.

It was shown that the housing barrack-huts of the refugee camps in their spatial-material existence were not completed by the architectural design of the planners on the drawing board, but that only through processes and actions in and with them they became the "collective and individual social work" (Lefebvre) of a camp barrack. The barrack-huts were constituted through the assignment of different functions and actions in and with the space: the biopolitical aims and the conceptions of the Ministry; the design decisions of the planners in the construction offices who translated these ideas into a material form and organised the space according to the modern paradigms of rationality and efficiency; the regulations of everyday life by the camp management; acts and appropriations of the refugees to whom these rooms had been allocated as living spaces; and finally, through the external visitors' reception of the camps. As a special feature of the camp context, the user perspective, a key issue in current architectural history research, was not restricted to the inhabitants to whom the sleeping places had been assigned. Rather, the camp administrations, who used the barrack-huts to achieve the overriding goals on behalf of the Ministry, were included as users as well.

As was shown, the reason for the fact that the camp barracks became a "lower form of housing," as Hannes Meyer puts it, did not lie primarily in the material condition and equipment of the building type of the barrack-hut, but rather depended on the way camp planners and camp management dealt with the room

---

101 See Rebecca Houze, "Home as a Living Museum: Ethnographic Display and the 1896 Millenial Exhibition in Budapest", in: *Centropa: Journal of Central European Architecture and Related Arts* 12/2 (2012): 131–151; Saloni Mathur, "Living Ethnological Exhibits: The Case of 1886", in: *Cultural Anthropology* 15/4 (2000): 492–524.

or used it as a dispositif. Hence, it was not, or not only, the rudimentary facility and the lack of comfort that caused the misery of the refugees, but other factors, too: the suppression of self-initiative regarding an adaptation of the bare room, the total availability and panoptic controllability of the space, the disciplining actions as well as the general conditions of the camp as an enclosed space with massively restricted freedom of movement, risk of infection, hunger and cold. The absolute size of the barrack halls was less problematic than the disproportionate occupancy of the space, that is, the huge number of individuals and the resulting stress factors such as noise, smell and permanent observation. The rudimentary space of the barrack-huts caused the plight of its inhabitants (only) combined with the disciplinary restrictions and the extreme health risks of the specific camp conditions.

Ulrike Krause

Protection | Victimisation | Agency? Gender-sensitive Perspectives on Present-day Refugee Camps

Introduction[1]

Refugee camps generally serve as humanitarian spaces for the immediate protection and assistance of refugees, especially after extensive movements to host countries have taken place. Governments of host countries decide whether or not refugees have to stay in camps while in their territory, and if so, governmental and humanitarian actors play crucial roles in establishing and maintaining camps with their aid structures. Among the humanitarian actors, the United Nations Office of the High Commissioner for Refugees (UNHCR) is central due to its mandate for refugee protection.[2]

However, in this article, I argue that camps are not only about refugees' shelter, care, and safety. On the contrary, they constitute spaces of order and control as well as spheres of limitation and isolation for refugees.[3] A gender-sensitive reading shows how humanitarian aid in camps influences social relations and thus also gender relations among the refugees; labels of vulnerability are applied to the people which women appear to embody par excellence due to their ascribed helplessness, whereas young men are often portrayed as 'troublemakers'.[4]

---

1 This article is partly based on findings that were presented in a recent chapter in German, cf. Ulrike Krause, "Flüchtlingslager: Im Spannungsverhältnis zwischen Schutz, Macht und Agency," in: *Über Grenzen. Migration und Flucht in globaler Perspektive seit 1945*, edited by Agnes Bresselau von Bressensdorf (Göttingen: Vandenhoeck & Ruprecht, 2019).
2 See UNGA, "Statute of the Office of the United Nations High Commissioner for Refugees", (A/RES/428(V) (New York: 1950).
3 See e.g. Michel Agier, *Managing the Undesirables. Refugee Camps and Humanitarian Government* (Cambridge: Polity Press, 2011); Bram Jansen, *The Accidental City: Violence, Economy and Humanitarianism in Kakuma Refugee Camp Kenya* (University of Wageningen, 2011); Ulrike Krause, "Zwischen Schutz und Scham? Flüchtlingslager, Gewalt und Geschlechterverhältnisse," in: *Peripherie: Zeitschrift für Politik und Ökonomie in der Dritten Welt* 35 (2015) 138/139: 235–259.
4 Simon Turner, *Politics of Innocence: Hutu Identity, Conflict and Camp Life* (New York–Oxford: Berghahn Books, 2010), 20; Elisabeth Olivius, "Refugee Men as Perpetrators, Allies or Trou-

Of course, these humanitarian structures and ascriptions as well as the often drastic experiences during their periods of flight and encampment affect the refugees – the people, the very individuals. Yet they not only rely on and are restricted by humanitarian affairs, as well as face various uncertainties and dangers. They also strive to cope with the conditions, challenge power structures, engage in livelihoods, and seek more stability.

Such critical reflections of refugee camp phenomena are placed in the centre of this article. By drawing on the growing body of multidisciplinary literature and, in part, on original research conducted with refugees in Uganda[5], I aim to explore how refugee camps are set up and function, how they affect refugees, and how the people cope with camp structures and limitations. It is, therefore, not the intention to present findings of a single-case study, but to bring together insights from various empirical studies to shed light on comprehensive camp features, questions of (humanitarian) power, and refugees' own practices from a gender-sensitive perspective. As a result of the analysis, I reveal that refugee camps are shaped by various forms of ambivalence: humanitarian power and refugees as beneficiaries, protection and violence, provisional setups and protracted situations, inclusion and exclusion, invisibility and visibility, female victims and male perpetrators, etc. In this vein, I show that refugee camps are neither 'neutral' spaces of humanitarianism nor 'safe harbours' for refugees but purposefully established enterprises in which women, men, girls, boys, and other people determined as refugees (try to) create meaningful lives, despite the adversities they face.

To this end, the first and main part of this article is focussed on the roles of humanitarian actors in terms of their measures and hierarchical structures in camps along with consequences of isolation, victimisation, and objectification of refugees. Then, the perspective is switched to refugees and insights of how the people cope with conditions in camps are presented. The final summary concludes the article with an urban interpretation of refugee camps.

---

blemakers? Emerging Discourses on Men and Masculinities in Humanitarian Aid," in: *Women's Studies International Forum* 56 (2016): 56–65.

5 For additional publications, see Ulrike Krause, "Zwischen Schutz und Scham"; Ulrike Krause, "Wie bewältigen Flüchtlinge die Lebensbedingungen in Flüchtlingslagern? Ergebnisse aus einer empirischen Analyse zu kongolesischen Flüchtlingen in Uganda," in: *Zeitschrift für Friedens- und Konfliktforschung* 5 (2016) 2: 189–220; Ulrike Krause, "'It seems like you don't have identity, you don't belong.' Reflexionen über das Flüchtlingslabel und dessen Implikationen," in: *Zeitschrift für Internationale Beziehungen* 23 (2016) 1: 8–37; Ulrike Krause, "Escaping Conflicts and Being Safe? Post-conflict Refugee Camps and the Continuum of Violence," in: *Gender, Violence, Refugees*, edited by Susanne Buckley-Zistel and Ulrike Krause (New York – Oxford: Berghahn, 2017): 173–196. (Studies in Forced Migration 37); Ulrike Krause, "Hegemonie von Männern? Flüchtlingslager, Maskulinitäten und Gewalt in Uganda," in: *Soziale Probleme* 27 (2016) 1: 119–145.

Refugee Camp: Humanitarian Actors, Structures, and Effects

Many of the recent studies about refugee aid and camps have focused on camp features and effects in countries in the global south, but refugee camps are neither new phenomena nor limited to these geographical regions.[6] In fact, they were used in various regions worldwide even during the First World War and the era of the Weimar Republic.[7] At the end of the Second World War, camps for displaced persons and refugees in Europe became a "standardized, generalizable technology of power [...] in the management of mass displacement".[8] Up until today, camps have constituted a key part of the protection of refugees.[9] Contemporary phenomena can be seen in large camp setups such as Dadaab in Kenya, but also the so-called hotspots on the Greek islands of Lesbos and Chios[10] or the *Erstaufnahmeeinrichtungen* (initial reception centres) in Germany[11] represent specific types of refugee camps with humanitarian structures.

In one of her early and seminal works, *Imposing Aid*, Barbara Harrel-Bond[12]

---

6 Kirsten McConnachie, "Camps of containment: A genealogy of the refugee camp," in: *Humanity: An International Journal of Human Rights, Humanitarianism, and Development*, 7 (2016) 3: 397–412.
7 Peter Gatrell, "Refugees and Forced Migrants during the First World War," in: *Immigrants & Minorities* 26 (2008) 1–2: 82–110; Jochen Oltmer, "Protecting Refugees in the Weimar Republic," in: *Journal of Refugee Studies* 30 (2 2017): 318–336.
8 Liisa H. Malkki, "Refugees and Exile: From 'Refugee Studies' to the National Order of Things," in: *Annual Review of Anthropology* 24 (1995): 495–523, 498.
9 An exact number of refugees in camps is not available; UNHCR estimates that 63.3 % of all refugees lived in 'individual accommodation' in 2016 (UNHCR, *Global Trends. Forced Displacement in 2016* (Geneva: UNHCR, 2017), 55), but this includes those in organised settlements which constitute a form of encampment (see Anna Schmidt, "Camps versus Settlements," *Forced Migration Online* (2003) http://repository.forcedmigration.org/show_metadata.jsp?pid=fmo:5134 (07.02.2019). UNHCR is increasingly seeking alternatives to camps for individual accommodation of refugees, also in urban areas (Jeff Crisp, "Finding Space for Protection: An Inside Account of the Evolution of UNHCR's Urban Refugee Policy," in: *Refuge* 33 (2017) 1: 87–96), but governments of host states remain reluctant to choose this option (Gaim Kibreab, "Why Governments Prefer Spatially Segregated Settlement Sites for Urban Refugees," in: *Refuge* 24 (2007) 1: 27–35). Moreover, the humanitarian approach to refugee protection has been adjusted to camp structures as well as the direct access to the people. This not only hinders effective change (settlement of refugees beyond camps), but also complicates the lives of refugees outside of camps as they often continue to live with insufficient or no humanitarian support.
10 Nora Markard and Helene Heuser, "'Hotspots' an den EU-Außengrenzen: Menschen- und europarechtswidrige Internierungslager," in: *Zeitschrift für Ausländerrecht und Ausländerpolitik*, (5–6) 2016: 165–172.
11 Melanie Hartmann, "Spatializing Inequalities: The Situation of Women in Refugee Centres in Germany," in: *Gender, Violence, Refugees*, edited by Susanne Buckley-Zistel and Ulrike Krause (New York – Oxford: Berghahn, 2017): 102–126. (Studies in Forced Migration 37).
12 Barbara E. Harrell-Bond, *Imposing Aid: Emergency Assistance to Refugees* (Oxford – New York – Nairobi: Oxford University Press, 1986). (Oxford Medical Publications).

illustrates the difficult conditions experienced by refugees in camps as well as the 'imposed' nature of the humanitarian structures present. But how is aid delivered in camps, and which conditions do refugees face there? These questions are addressed in the following sections which reveal the aforementioned forms of ambivalence typical for refugee camps.

Humanitarian Administration, Structures, and Setup

Although camps can be distinguished in different types, their setup, structures, and services are similar throughout the world.[13] Refugee camps generally constitute geographically and temporally limited spaces in host countries[14], which are purposefully established to accommodate, protect, and assist refugees until one of the three durable solution[15] has been found for them. Current camps are usually located close to national borders in rural regions. As a result, they are both physically and economically mostly isolated from the outside social world. While humanitarian actors have direct access to the people, governmental institutions of the host countries can maintain a certain control over them.[16]

The way in which refugee protection is provided in camps has been institutionalised over the course of the past decades: Based on global policies and norms of the refugee regime, aid is generally delivered through the approach of humanitarian relief aiming to meet the immediate basic needs of refugees, and projects are similar worldwide.[17] Camps are mostly administratively led by the host countries' governments and UNHCR. Operationally, NGOs[18] mainly deliver refugee aid and often act as implementing partners of UNHCR, thus carrying out

---

13 Agier, *Managing the Undesirables*. 37 ff; Karen Jacobsen, "The Forgotten Solution: Local Integration for Refugees in Developing Countries," in: *New Issues in Refugee Research* (2001): 45; Schmidt, "Camps versus Settlements."
14 As noted in the introduction, since refugees are in a territory of a host country, the respective country not only decides whether refugees have to live in designated spaces – i.e. camps – but also is responsible for protecting refugees. UNHCR and other humanitarian actors can only take action after being formally invited to do so by the country.
15 Three durable solutions exist: voluntary repatriation to the country of origin, resettlement to a third country, and local integration into a coutry of asylum.
16 Eric Werker, "Refugee Camp Economies," in: *Journal of Refugee Studies* 20 (2007) 3: 461–480; Rose Jaji, "Social Technology and Refugee Encampment in Kenya," in: *Journal of Refugee Studies* 25 (2012) 2: 221-238.
17 Jansen, *The Accidental City*; Hakim Chkam, "Aid and the Perpetuation of Refugee Camps: The Case of Dadaab in Kenya 1991–2011," in: *Refugee Survey Quarterly* 35 (2016) 2: 79-97.
18 Maja Janmyr, *Protecting Civilians in Refugee Camps: Unable and Unwilling States, UNHCR and International Responsibility* (Leiden: Brill, 2014), 310-344; Ulrike Krause, *Linking Refugee Protection with Development Assistance. Analyses with a Case Study in Uganda* (Baden-Baden: Nomos, 2013), 60-64.

measures under the supervision of and with funding from UNHCR. In addition, so-called operational partners implement their own projects, but in consultation with UNHCR and host government agencies. The latter include international organisations such as UN agencies like UNICEF.[19] Refugee protection and assistance consists of a great variety of projects in several thematic sectors, such as education, healthcare, nutrition, infrastructure, water, and sanitation. These are realised simultaneously and – ideally – with harmonised coordination among the actors.[20]

Physically, camps are divided into several sections, such as larger 'zones' demarcated into smaller 'blocks' or 'clusters', where refugees are settled and where markets, schools and other facilities are established. Tents and simple huts – or the communal rooms in the initial reception centres in Germany[21] – primarily provide accommodation for refugees. Offices of humanitarian and governmental institutions as well as hospitals, police stations, and so-called 'safe houses' for the short-term shelter and protection of immediately threatened people who run acute risks are often established close to each other. These can be located relatively central within a 'base camp' but can also be spread in different areas across the whole camp. Taking a geographical perspective of camp maps reveals the similar setups worldwide.[22]

How camps function and aid structures are organised can be exemplified by one of the refugee camps where I have carried out research, *Kyaka II* in Uganda. *Kyaka II* is a 'local rural refugee settlement' which essentially constitutes a form of encampment. Set up in the 1980s and coving an area of more than 80 km², the camp is structured in nine zones and 26 village-like clusters. Although *Kyaka II* is assumed to have a capacity for 17,000 refugees, the number has increased over the past years and reached 44,988 refugees in 2018.[23] During research, refugee protection and assistance in *Kyaka II* were generally delivered by a number of aid agencies working in diverse sectors. The camp was administered by the gov-

---

19 UNHCR, *Partnership: An Operations Management Handbook for UNHCR's Partners* (Geneva: UNHCR, 2003), 28–34.
20 Ibid., 37–39.
21 Melanie Hartmann, "Spatializing Inequalities: The Situation of Women in Refugee Centres in Germany," in: *Gender, Violence, Refugees*, edited by Susanne Buckley-Zistel and Ulrike Krause (New York, Oxford: Berghahn, 2017): 102–126. (Studies in Forced Migration 37).
22 A number of scholars refer to such maps in their works. See, among others, Katharina Inhetveen, *Die Politische Ordnung des Flüchtlingslagers. Akteure – Macht – Organisation: Eine Ethnographie im Südlichen Afrika* (Bielefeld: transcript Verlag, 2010), 63–70; Agier, *Managing the Undesirables*, 146–147; Jansen, *The Accidental City*, xiii, 66–73; Turner, *Politics of Innocence*, 14; Krause, *Linking Refugee Protection with Development Assistance*, 152–153.
23 UNHCR, "Kyaka II. Fact Sheet 2014," (2014) https://data2.unhcr.org/en/documents/down load/48486 (09.02.2019); UNHCR, "Uganda Refugee Response Monitoring Settlement Fact Sheet: Kyaka II, March 2018," (2018) https://reliefweb.int/report/uganda/uganda-refugee-response-monitoring-settlement-fact-sheet-kyaka-ii-march-2018 (09.02.2019).

ernmental institution responsible for refugees in Uganda, namely, the Office of the Prime Minister (OPM), and UNHCR. OPM was in charge of the overall management, security, and land-related issues, while UNHCR was responsible for the supervision, security, and protection measures for refugees. The Danish Refugee Council operated as the main implementing partner of UNHCR and covered several sectors such as child protection, livelihood, community services and development, and psychosocial support. Moreover, Windle Trust International was involved in offering educational programs, Samaritan's Purse was engaged in food distribution, and the Uganda Red Cross supported reunification processes for family members who had been separated during flight. The work conducted by these organisations was largely funded by UNHCR, while some others drew on additional sources. Among these, Africa Humanitarian Action implemented US-funded health projects that offered counselling for victims of sexual and gender-based violence, and the Finnish Refugee Council realised livelihood and adult education projects with funding from the Finnish government. After the refugees were registered and their status was determined, they received a ration card, some non-food items, two plots of land for residence and farming, and access to the measures provided by these aid agencies.

Such aid measures are offered in similar ways in other camps and are intended to reach all refugees. However, the idea of who 'all refugees' are was shaped in the past by a male paradigm in international refugee law and protection. This slowly changed as feminist studies in the 1980s and 1990s shed light on violence and other risks of women in refugee situations which were insufficiently regarded in humanitarian projects.[24] Reforms have taken place in refugee law and protection,[25] and UNHCR has published several strategies which establish protection standards for women in refugee aid.[26] In this way, gender has become a

---

24 See, among others, Linda Cipriani, "Gender and Persecution: Protecting Women under International Refugee Law," in: *Georgetown Immigration Law Journal* 7 (1993) 3: 511–548; Doreen Marie Indra, "Gender: A Key Dimension of the Refugee Experience," in: *Refuge* 6 (1987) 3: 3–4.

25 Despite reforms, recent studies still reveal a number of issues. See Ulrike Krause, "(Un)sichtbar und (un)sicher? Humanitäre Politiken und Praktiken um Frauen in Flüchtlingssituationen," in: *Feministische Perspektiven auf Sicherheit*, edited by Antje Daniel et al. (Opladen: Budrich), *forthcoming*; Nahla Valji, "Women and the 1951 Refugee Convention: Fifty Years of Seeking Visibility," in: *Refuge* 19 (2001) 5: 25–35; Georgina Firth and Barbara Mauthe, "Refugee Law, Gender and the Concept of Personhood," in: *International Journal of Refugee Law* 25 (2013) 3: 470–501.

26 Susan F. Martin, "UNHCR Policy on Refugee Women: A 25-Year Retrospective," in: *Gender, Violence, Refugees*, edited by Susanne Buckley-Zistel and Ulrike Krause, (New York – Oxford: Berghahn, 2017). (Studies in Forced Migration 37); see, e. g., UNHCR, *UNHCR Policy on Refugee Women* (A/AC.96/754; Geneva: UNHCR, 1990); UNHCR, *UNHCR Guidelines on the Protection of Refugee Women* (ES/SCP/67; Geneva: UNHCR, 1991); UNHCR, *Sexual and Gender-Based Violence against Refugees, Returnees and In-*

crucial category in the refugee aid system and processes. In spite of that, scholars have emphasised patronising language used to refer to women in policies[27] and criticised the prevalence of violence (despite protection measures) and the victimisation of women (due to the measures).[28] These aspects are further discussed below.

Humanitarian Power in Provisional Sites Despite Protracted Situations?

Within these highly regulated and confined camp spaces, the administrative procedures of humanitarian actors are manifested and reinforced. In connection with their organisational rules, institutional norms and values, strict power relations emerge which Katharina Inhetveen[29] describes as poly-hierarchical: Power structures evolve among and between members of the administration and the camp population in addition to hierarchies and hierarchisations among the refugees. Refugee camps, therefore, constitute powerful spheres of humanitarianism. Due to the globally produced setup, camps can be understood as humanitarian arenas with various actors, hierarchical decision-making processes, bureaucratic functions, and established practices of power, which transform humanitarian aid into everyday politics.[30]

Humanitarian services subsequently seem to become central which prompts questions about the roles of the social elements in camps – the refugees, the people. Despite refugees' access to aid and protection, authors of empirical studies have widely criticised that the humanitarian structures in camps create restrictive conditions with dependencies and limitations for the refugees.[31] Their

---

ternally Displaced Persons. Guidelines for Prevention and Response (Geneva: UNHCR, 2003); UNHCR, *UNHCR Handbook for the Protection of Women and Girls* (Geneva: UNHCR, 2008).

27 Alice Edwards, "Transitioning Gender: Feminist Engagement with International Refugee Law and Policy 1950–2010," in: *Refugee Survey Quarterly* 29 (2010) 2: 21–45, 32.

28 Awa M. Abdi, "In Limbo: Dependency, Insecurity, and Identity amongst Somali Refugees in Dadaab Camps," in: *Bildhaan: An International Journal of Somali Studies* 5 (2005) 7: 17–34; Ulrike Krause, "*Die* Flüchtling – der Flüchtling als Frau. Genderreflexiver Zugang," in: *Flüchtlinge: Multiperspektivische Zugänge*, edited by Cinur Ghaderi and Thomas Eppenstein (Wiesbaden: Springer, 2017), 79–93; ; Nahla Valji et al., "Where Are the Women? Gender Discrimination in Refugee Policies and Practices," in: *Agenda: Empowering Women for Gender Equity* 55 (2003): 61–72.

29 Inhetveen, *Die Politische Ordnung des Flüchtlingslagers*, chapter 11.

30 Dorothea Hilhorst and Bram J. Jansen, "Humanitarian Space as Arena: A Perspective on the Everyday Politics of Aid," in: *Development and Change* 41 (2010) 6: 1117–1139.

31 See, Jaji, "Social Technology and Refugee Encampment in Kenya,"; Tania Kaiser, "Between a Camp and a Hard Place: Rights, Livelihood and Experiences of the Local Settlement System for long-term Refugees in Uganda," in: *The Journal of Modern African Studies* 44 (2006) 4: 597–621; Harrell-Bond, *Imposing Aid*.

often difficult living conditions are thus not only caused by external factors such as the remote locations of camps but partly by the humanitarian politics and actors in camps.[32] These impose aid structures and decisions on refugees and often grant them insufficient space to participate.[33] The lives of refugees are, therefore, 'managed' by humanitarian agencies by applying what Foucault would describe as discipline and governmentality, through which control is exercised.[34] Due to the power asymmetries, aid actors have been criticised for posing as "humanitarian governments",[35] and camps for being "a form of human warehousing and 'storage of refugees who are simultaneously perceived as victims and agents of insecurity'."[36] As a consequence of their leadership and acquisition of governmental functions, humanitarian actors and camps have also been described as 'surrogate states' by UNHCR.[37]

Although these structures and practices affect the whole camp population in one way or another, this neither means that the people passively give in nor that the same humanitarian practices are used towards all refugees. While I will reflect on camps as social spaces and coping strategies of the people in the last part of this article, taking a gender-sensitive perspective reveals different humanitarian practices. The aforementioned trend to ensure better protection for women in refugee situations has led to the development of particular projects that place a focus on women's safety and prioritise their access to aid. This trend is certainly an achievement for women's security, but it also has drawbacks. For example, in Uganda's camp *Kyaka II*, 'safe houses' were set up in the base camp for people who were in need of immediate protection. Whereas potential victims remained undefined at the time of my research, I only saw women (mainly with children) receiving shelter there. One explanation for this may be that women were exposed to more risks in the camp and, thus, required more protection. However, another explanation is that decision-makers may not have been sufficiently aware of the risks experienced by men and other people and, for this reason, provided less, different or perhaps even no comparable protection measures for

---

32 Krause, "Wie bewältigen Flüchtlinge die Lebensbedingungen in Flüchtlingslagern", 213–214.
33 Turner, *Politics of Innocence*.
34 Jennifer Hyndman, *Managing Displacement. Refugees and the Politics of Humanitarianism*, in: Borderlines 16 (2000), edited by David Campbell and Michael J. Shapiro (Minneapolis – London: University of Minnesota Press, 2000) xv, 1–253; Jaji, "Social Technology and Refugee Encampment in Kenya"; Agier, *Managing the Undesirables*.
35 Agier, *Managing the Undesirables*, 196.
36 Jaji, "Social Technology and Refugee Encampment in Kenya," 227.
37 Sarah Deardorff Miller, *UNHCR as a Surrogate State: Protracted Refugee Situations* (London – New York: Routledge, 2018); Michael Kagan, "'We live in a Country of UNHCR': The UN Surrogate State and Refugee Policy in the Middle East," in: *New Issues in Refugee Research* (2011): 201; Jeff Crisp and Amy Slaughter, "A Surrogate State? The Role of UNHCR in Protracted Refugee Situations," in: *New Issues in Refugee Research* (2009): 168.

these groups. Either way, the example shows how aid projects materialise not only support mechanisms but also power structures within camps, as humanitarian agencies invest resources in assistance for specific groups but potentially neglect others.

Despite the provisional camp structures, such difficult environments tend to persist for a long time instead of demonstrating temporary circumstances. As durable solutions are rarely found quickly after refugees' arrival in host countries and thus also settlement in camps, protracted refugee situations arise.[38] The Executive Committee of UNHCR defines protracted situations as those where refugees live in exile "for five or more years after their initial displacement, without immediate prospects for implementation of durable solutions".[39] UNHCR also often uses the margin of at least 25,000 refugees of the same nationality being in the same situation.[40] An example for the scope of these protracted situations is revealed by a close reading of the current global trends: Of the 17.2 million refugees globally in 2016 (not including Palestinian refugees), only 552,200 repatriated to their home country, 189,300 resettled to safe third states, and 23,000 locally integrated in a country of asylum.[41] This indicates that the international community only found durable solutions for 4.4 percent of all refugees in this year. 11.7 million refugees and hence 67 percent were stuck in protracted situations in 2016,[42] which had lasted 17 years on average.[43]

These long-lasting developments contradict and oppose the provisional camp structures and temporary services, which rarely have long-term orientations. Instead, the typically interim and short-term nature of this system stands paradigmatically for refugee camps as spheres of transition and for refugee protection as transitional protection – but often for an unknown long duration.

Belonging vs. Isolation

As refugee camps constitute purposefully created and confined spaces, decisions are central of who is allowed to enter the camps, who is part of them, and who is able to influence specific spheres. The poly-hierarchical arrangement of camps

---

38 James Milner, "Protracted Refugee Situations," in: *The Oxford Handbook of Refugee and Forced Migration Studies*, edited by Elena Fiddian-Qasmiyeh et al. (Oxford: Oxford University Press, 2014), 151–162.
39 UNHCR, Conclusion on Protracted Refugee Situations, *Executive Committee of the High Commissioner's Programme No. 109 (LXI)* (Geneva: UNHCR, 2009).
40 UNHCR, *Global Trends: Forced Displacement in 2016* (Geneva: UNHCR, 2017), 20; Milner "Protracted Refugee Situations".
41 UNHCR, *Global Trends: Forced Displacement in 2016* (Geneva: UNHCR, 2017), 24–28.
42 Ibid., 20.
43 Calculation by author based on statistical details provided by UNHCR.

reveals that the humanitarian and governmental actors are principally in charge of making these decisions (top-down). However, questions of physical accessibility ultimately signify camps as places of limitation and isolation as well as of inclusion and exclusion.

From the perspective of nation states, camps primarily serve as means to control people who have been labelled as refugees. Thereby, their settlement in designated sites constitutes a legal, political and physical process for the separation and isolation of refugees from the ordinary citizens, i.e. from the people who appear to actually belong to the country.[44] These separation mechanisms seem to be an inherent part of the refugee concept,[45] since political and public discourses on refugees centre on their *flight from certain places* (and subsequently arising needs) but less on their *arrival in systems*. This can be clarified by taking a brief semantic excursion: Refugees are assumed to be *dis-placed, uprooted,* or *forced to flee* which is specified in the meaning of the words 'refugee' or 'displaced person'. The term *refugee* in English as well as, for example, *réfugié* in French, *refugiado* in Spanish, or *rifugiato* in Italian stem from the Latin noun *refugium*, referring to a space of refuge, as well as the verb *fugare*, meaning to expulse, chase away, and put to flight. The equivalent terms of *Flüchtling* in German, *flykting* in Swedish, *Vluchting* in Dutch, פליטים in Hebrew, or *беженец* in Russian signify the act of flight. The term 'refugee', therefore, connotes forced movement – not safe arrival or protection.

Refugees appear to be out of place, people in a new national or territorial context to which they have fled but lack to belong.[46] Their dislocation or deterritorialisation from a 'homeland' to a 'host country' or 'country of asylum' also symbolises a reterritorialisation, a construction of contexts of new affiliation. Following this logic, refugee camps distinctively illustrate the territorial component of their – lack of or new – affiliation to certain nation states. And by establishing camps, external humanitarian and governmental actors seem to create particular sites of belonging for refugees[47] in which these actors 'enable' refugees to be 'amongst their peers' – or rather, to be kept there.

Michel Agier argues that "[c]onfined in spaces that are out-places, they see their political existence depends no longer (or not only) on their origins, but on local contexts of identification, and particularly on the camps in which they

---

44 Jaji, "Social Technology and Refugee Encampment in Kenya," 224.
45 Dana Schmalz, "Der Flüchtlingsbegriff zwischen kosmopolitischer Brisanz und nationalstaatlicher Ordnung," in: *Kritische Justiz: Vierteljahresschrift für Recht und Politik* 48 (2015) 4: 376–389.
46 Krause, "It seems like you don't have identity, you don't belong," 22.
47 Cathrine Brun, "Reterritorilizing the Relationship between People and Place in Refugee Studies," in: *Geografiska Annaler: Series B, Human Geography* 83 (2001) 1: 15–25, 17.

live".[48] The notion that camps symbolise sites of belonging raises the question of the impact of such a 'camp membership' on the people. Stuck in massive refugee camps with thousands of others, the people are trapped in a discursive contradiction of "belonging (identity, community) and not belonging (uprooting, exile)" which essentialises their pasts and backgrounds, and leads to a dehistoricised and depoliticised portrait of the 'camp population'.[49] Indeed, within the humanitarian system, refugees are often treated as aid beneficiaries which anonymises them. With little or no regard to their individual features, hopes, or stories, refugees in camps are absorbed in and handled by the humanitarian system, a system that "induces the social and political non-existence of the recipients of its aid".[50]

Yet to determine whether refugees are perceived as being trapped in a sphere of non-existence, a time and gender-sensitive perspective is helpful. In political circles, refugees of the Second World War in Europe were initially seen as a "politico-moral problem" that could possibly jeopardise the national security of host countries.[51] This rhetoric of refugees as potential national 'problems' also found its way into the preamble of the 1951 Refugee Convention but it changed during the early stages of the Cold War, when many people fled the communist regime of the former Soviet Union. Western states, and especially the US, invoked the image of an ideologically shaped and almost heroic refugee figure,[52] portraying them as a strong-minded, politically active, white man with a past and history who fled for political reasons, possibly with close family members for whose safety he was responsible. "'[V]oting with his feet' by fleeing to the West"[53] became a core thesis of the courageous escape and refugee figure. As forced migration has increased in countries in the global south due to decolonisation struggles since the 1960s, a completely different identity construction of refugees has emerged. In political discourses, refugees were no longer portrayed as freedom fighters that belonged to one site or another, but as depoliticised and de-individualised victims in need of help. In contrast to the previous masculine, political figure in Europe, refugees in former colonies and decolonialised countries have been inflicted feminine attributes such as passiveness and

---

48 Agier, *Managing the Undesirables*, 17.
49 Malkki, "Refugees and Exile," 514.
50 Michel Agier, "Between War and City: Towards an Urban Anthropology of Refugee Camps," in: *Ethnography* 3 (2002) 3: 317–341, 322.
51 Liisa H. Malkki, "National Geographic: The Rooting of Peoples and the Territorialization of National Identity Among Scholars and Refugees," in: *Cultural Anthropology* 7 (1992) 1: 24–44, 32.
52 Peter Gatrell, *The Making of the Modern Refugee* (Oxford: Oxford University Press, 2013), 97.
53 Heather L. Johnson, "Click to Donate: Visual Images, Constructing Victims and Imagining the Female Refugee," in: *Third World Quarterly* 32 (2011) 6: 1015–1037, 1020.

weakness. These have contributed to a "feminization" of refugees and led to the people's marginalisation and invisibility.[54]

The question of 'camp membership' also indicates how refugee camps are associated with practices of inclusion and exclusion. A simplistic example of this is its physical distance from social circles of citizens or economically vibrant places in host countries. *Kyaka II* in Uganda where I carried out research is, for example, about one hour's drive from the next bigger city, Mubende. During my research, a man living in *Kyaka II* criticised the limitations in the camp and stated that, "this makes you feel like you are in a prison of some sort".[55]

As intensities and types of separation can vary among different camps, diverse forms of permeability also exist, such as trade of goods, modes of travel, or school attendance.[56] However, the remote locations of many refugee camps already exemplify their territorial delimitations. Camps are not always enclosed with fences, their borders remain invisible and areas blurrily blend into the national territory. Yet refugee camps constitute performative markers for the conditions of the people who live there and who are subject to the legally framed political discourses of exclusion, of non-belonging. Simon Turner[57] contrasts that a camp physically excludes but territorially includes people in host countries. It delimits refugees in geographical, social, political, economic, and legal senses, but it also locks them into certain patterns, while they are defined by the state that surrounds them. This translates into an included exclusion as well as an excluded inclusion, and Simon Turner further emphasises the nature of camps as contradictory spaces for refugees:

> "On the one hand, the camp is a means of maintaining order and removing impurity in society, rendering refugees invisible. On the other hand, refugees become highly visible by being placed in the camps and becoming the objects of state of the art humanitarian programmes."[58]

---

54 Jennifer Hyndman and Wenona Giles, "Waiting for what? The feminization of asylum in protracted situations," in: *Gender, Place & Culture* 18 (2011) 3: 361–379.
55 Male refugee, Dialogue, 27 March 2014, Base Camp, Kyaka II.
56 Werker, "Refugee Camp Economies," 467–473; Naohiko Omata and Josiah Kaplan, "Refugee livelihoods in Kampala, Nakivale and Kyangwali Refugee Settlements: Patterns of Engagement with the Private Sector," *RSC Working Paper Series* (2013), 16–17; Krause, "Wie bewältigen Flüchtlinge die Lebensbedingungen in Flüchtlingslagern," 208–209; Adam Ramadan, "Spatialising the Refugee Camp," in: *Transactions of the Institute of British Geographers* 38 (2013) 1: 65–77, 70.
57 Simon Turner, "What Is a Refugee Camp? Explorations of the Limits and Effects of the Camp," in: *Journal of Refugee Studies* 29 (2016) 2: 139–148, 141.
58 Ibid., 144.

(De)limitation and isolation, along with various questions about scopes of action, representation, and power, are also addressed through spatial theory.[59] Studies using spatial perspectives point out the general relevance of constructed spaces and sites of (non-)belonging to people in exile, and reveal the need for critical reflections about these sites in forced migration and refugee research. With a focus on encampment, spatial analyses shed light on the broad effects of camps on the diverse actors and actions. They elaborate on discursive border and boundary issues as moments of social segmentation, as well as the proactive engagement of refugees to challenge and break through such limitations.[60]

Refugees as Objects or Victims?

A critical part of the practices of humanitarian organisations is not only to choose which measures they implement to protect and assist refugees but also to decide for whom they are doing so. Many refugees not only escape violence and other threatening dangers, but are also exposed to various risks and precarious conditions in camps. In addition to structural insecurities, such as a lack of access to their rights (work, freedom of movement, etc.) in countries of asylum, refugees often remain in uncertainty about their future and are confronted with physical violence, such as robberies and assaults, as well as gender-specific risks. Men and boys can be exposed to militarisation and forced recruitment into conflict parties,[61] and women and girls can be confronted with sexual violence or domestic abuse.[62] Against this backdrop, it may seem to be understandable why humanitarian organisations strive to deliver aid to the 'vulnerable' refugees, but this perspective is problematic.

In general, vulnerability constitute one of many humanitarian categories, and has evolved into a key criterion in refugee aid. Whereas 'vulnerability assess-

---

59 See, among others, Hartmann, "Spatializing Inequalities"; Ramadan, "Spatialising the Refugee Camp"; Brun, "Reterritorilizing the Relationship".
60 Melanie Hartmann, "Contested Boundaries: Refugee Centers as Spaces of the Political," in: *Zeitschrift für Flüchtlingsforschung* 1 (2017) 2: 218–243.
61 James Milner, "The Militarization and Demilitarization of Refugee Camps in Guinea," in: *Armed and Aimless. Armed Groups, Guns, and Human Security in the ECOWAS Region*, edited by Nicolas Florquin and Eric G. Berman (Geneva: Small Arms Survey, 2005), 144–179. See also the conclusion for critical reflections on sexual and gender-based violence against men.
62 Rebecca Horn, "Exploring the Impact of Displacement and Encampment on Domestic Violence in Kakuma Refugee Camp," in: *Journal of Refugee Studies* 23 (2010) 3: 356–376; Krause, "Zwischen Schutz und Scham"; Katie McQuaid, "'There is violence across, in all arenas': listening to stories of violence amongst sexual minority refugees in Uganda," in: *The International Journal of Human Rights* (2017): 1–22; Karin Wachter, et al., "Drivers of Intimate Partner Violence Against Women in Three Refugee Camps," in: *Violence Against Women* 24 (2018) 3: 286–306.

ments' are used to deliver effective protection to those determined as vulnerable, humanitarian organisations differentiate between diverse types of vulnerable groups and intensities such as "'vulnerable' and 'highly vulnerable'" women.[63] Of course, particular groups and individuals can face specific risks in refugee camps as well as in other contexts. In a recent research project on sexual and gender-based violence with a case study in Uganda's *Kyaka II*, I found that women and girls have high risks of suffering acts, attempts, and threats of sexual abuse, domestic violence, denial of resources, and early/forced marriages.[64] However, the humanitarian vulnerability concept as well as similar categories (e. g., people 'at risk') are not only used to describe the threats of specific groups but also serve humanitarian purposes.[65] On the one hand, framing refugees as vulnerable justifies the imposed top-down power structures, as refugees seem incapable of making decisions due to their vulnerable states. On the other hand, it legitimises the need for immediate short-term relief to meet refugees' basic human needs – even long-term in protracted situations. This categorisation eventually produces material consequences as the vulnerable refugees are supposed to receive prioritised access to humanitarian measures.

Moreover, the meanings of humanitarian labels such as vulnerability have far-reaching implications for refugees: As victims, passive aid recipients and massive collectives, refugees seem to be detached from their various social, cultural, economic, and political interests and backgrounds.[66] Giorgio Agamben[67] refers to the reduction of the individual to its pure existence, "the bare life", and Liisa Malkki[68] compares the understanding of refugees in the humanitarian discourse with helpless infants. Humanitarian labels can thus victimise refugees, depriving them of agency and a sense of subjectivity.[69] Simon Turner[70] furthermore il-

---

63 UNHCR, *UNHCR Handbook for the Protection of Women and Girls* (Geneva: UNHCR, 2008), 172.
64 Krause, "Escaping Conflicts and Being Safe"; Krause, "Zwischen Schutz und Scham".
65 Stephen C. Lubkemann, *Culture in Chaos. An Anthropology of the Social Condition in War* (Chicago: University of Chicago Press, 2008), 16.
66 Ibid.; Turner, *Politics of Innocence*; Barbara E. Harrell-Bond, "The Experience of Refugees as Recipients of Aid," in: *Refugees: Perspectives on the Experience of Forced Migration*, edited by Alastair Ager (London: Continuum International Publishing Group Ltd, 1999), 136–168; Peter Nyers, *Rethinking Refugees: Beyond States of Emergency*, 2nd ed. (New York: Routledge, 2013).
67 Giorgio Agamben, *Homo Sacer: Sovereign Power and Bare Life*, trans. Daniel Heller-Roazen (Stanford: Stanford University Press, 1998).
68 Liisa H. Malkki, *Purity and Exile: Violence, Memory, and National Cosmology among Hutu Refugees in Tanzania* (Chicago, London: The University of Chicago Press, 1995), 11.
69 Agier, *Managing the Undesirables*, 150–151; Sewite Solomon Kebede, "The struggle for belonging: Forming and reformig identities 1.5-generation asylum seekers and refugees," *RSC Working Paper Series* (Oxford: RSC, 2010), 70; Lubkemann, *Culture in Chaos*, 16.
70 Turner, *Politics of Innocence*, 55, 20.

lustrates the contradiction between 'victims and troublemakers', 'good' and 'bad', 'needy' and 'dangerous' refugees. In a simplified manner, dichotomies are created; some refugees are portrayed as possible sources of insecurity and risks, others as a weak group in need of external help. And on this 'weak group', the category of "refugee-as-victim" is inflicted.[71]

A gender-sensitive view further reveals how the vulnerability concept in refugee aid is inseparably associated with the feminine.[72] Due to stereotypical identity ascriptions of women of innocence, purity, and peacefulness – as opposed to men's ascriptions of strength, dominance, and forcefulness – the humanitarian vulnerability designations seem to suit women refugees par excellence. However, this also imposes a label of submissive, powerless and helpless victims on women (in contrast to potentially violent male perpetrators).[73] It describes women as being unable of taking actions or making decisions,[74] and neglects their various individual histories, desires, and practices.[75] From a postcolonial view, the vulnerability label could even be criticised for institutionalising the correlation between victimhood, womanhood and refugeehood. Applying Gayatri Spivak's seminal critique of "white men saving brown women from brown men"[76] on the practices of refugee aid and camps in regions in the global south suggests that 'white' or 'western' humanitarian workers must step in (camps) to protect vulnerable 'brown' women refugee. If this is more broadly interpreted, it seems to indicate that the international community (i. e. the global north) must save the helpless masses of refugees, the 'brown refugees-as-victims' in camps in the global south.

This 'vulnerabilisation' and 'victimisation' ultimately pathologises and objectifies refugees, as they become 'objects of humanitarian protection' instead of subjects with agency. Peter Nyer[77] interprets the scope of the objectification of refugees as a state of animal-like imprisonment, because they have lost the means for political communication and "the capacity for reasonable speech [which] has

---

71 Ibid., 45–50.
72 Elena Fiddian-Qasmiyeh, "Gender and Forced Migration" in: *The Oxford Handbook of Refugee and Forced Migration Studies*, edited by Elena Fiddian-Qasmiyeh et al. (Oxford: Oxford University Press 2014), 395–408, 398.
73 Jane Freedman, *Gendering the International Asylum and Refugee Debate* (Basingstoke, Hampshire: Palgrave Macmillan, 2015), 119 ff.
74 Erin K. Baines, *Vulnerable Bodies: Gender, the UN and the Global Refugee Crisis* (Aldershot: Ashgate, 2004), viii; Katarzyna Grabska, "Constructing 'Modern Gendered Civilised' Women and Men: Gender-Mainstreaming in Refugee Camps," in: *Gender & Development* 19 (2011) 1: 81–93, 90.
75 Hyndman and Giles, "Waiting for what?"; Valji, "Women and the 1951 Refugee Convention".
76 Gayatri Chakravorty Spivak, *A Critique of Postcolonial Reason: Toward a History of the Vanishing Present* (Cambridge: Harvard University Press, 1999), 284.
77 Peter Nyers, *Rethinking Refugees: Beyond States of Emergency*, 2nd ed. (New York: Routledge, 2006).

historically been deployed to discursively establish an animal quality of refugeeness".[78] Nyers reasons that refugees lack authenticity and, although they are labelled as humans, "they are discursively and visually cast as animal".[79] Liisa Malkki notes that "[t]he term refugee denotes an objectified, undifferentiated mass that is meaningful primarily as an aberration of categories and an object of 'therapeutic interventions'" while refugee camps turn into powerful tools for "the management of space and movement – for peoples out of place."[80]

Refugees' actual living conditions and experiences before flight and whilst in camps, which are unmistakably often very difficult, become covered by humanitarian strategies, practices and labels and hidden in plain sight. Of course, aid is supposed to protect and assist the refugee, but the approach translates into 'aid' for 'people in need of help' in a top-down fashion. This focus legitimises and reinforces the imposed power asymmetries, as humanitarian actors hierarchically outrank the 'people in need' and appear to 'have to' make wide-ranging decisions for them. And even when humanitarian agencies employ participatory approaches and speak of refugees as "active and creative agents",[81] "agents of development"[82] or "helping displaced people transition from aid recipients to self-reliant agents of change, able to contribute to the peace, stability and prosperity of the communities that offer them asylum",[83] humanitarian domination and control are still present. The scopes and means of refugees' participation and actions remain to be defined in humanitarian norms. In addition, the powerful actors appear to be necessary in that they 'have to' help the vulnerable 'refugees-as-victims' participate in the first place. This constellation essentially makes it possible for humanitarian actors to blame refugees if they do not fit into the humanitarian categories or disobey the regulations.

---

78 Ibid., xvii.
79 Ibid., 74, 92.
80 Liisa H. Malkki, "National Geographic: The Rooting of Peoples and the Territorialization of National Identity Among Scholars and Refugees," in: *Cultural Anthropology* 7 (1992) 1: 24–44, 34.
81 UNDP and UNHCR (2014), *Regional Refugee & Resilience Plan 2015–2016 in Response to the Syria Crisis: Regional Strategic Overview* (New York: UNHCR, UNDP, 2014), 17.
82 UNHCR, *Livelihood Programming in UNHCR: Operational Guidelines* (Geneva: UNHCR, 2012), 106.
83 UNHCR, *Global Strategy for Livelihoods: A UNHCR Strategy 2014–2018* (Geneva: UNHCR, 2014), 8.

Refugee Camps as Social Space of Refugees

Thus far, a focus was placed in the article on the diverse effects of camps on refugees, but what about the people? How do they handle the hardships and cope with the conditions? How do they contribute to camps as social spaces?

As a part of her understanding of poly-hierarchical structures in camps, Katharina Inhetveen[84] also sheds light on the roles of refugees and how interaction patterns and power structures have developed among Angolan refugees in Zambian camps. She distinguishes between formal and informal hierarchisation and hierarchies that are formed by elected representatives and traditional – or as she calls them, 'imported' – hierarchies. She describes the latter as hierarchies that the people had already used prior to their flight and re-established in the camp. In a similar vein, Clara Lecadet[85] differentiates among the power structures for Togolese refugees in Benin, referring to them as hybrid forms of politics. In addition to 'councils' or 'commissions' that are supported by humanitarian actors, political authority figures emerge among the refugees. Thereby, the refugees' autonomous establishment of a political life in camps becomes visible. This representation process and constellation emphasises the fact that refugees can shape the campsites and contribute to the formation of order or establish order themselves.

Like all social spaces, refugee camps are influenced by and influence social transformations; they change dynamically and are constituted jointly. Because the people have fled, changed locations, and entered the regulated conditions in the camps, they cannot maintain the social structures that they knew in their homes. The roles and relations are locally rooted and bound to specific contexts, forcing women and men to (re-)negotiate and (re-)define roles and relations.[86] Empirical studies have shed light on how women often (have to) take on new and additional responsibilities due to the lack or disruption of social cycles and support networks.[87] This can be overwhelming but also empowering for women.[88] For men, life in refugee camps can be associated with a loss of status,

---

84 Inhetveen, *Die Politische Ordnung des Flüchtlingslagers*, chapter 11.
85 Clara Lecadet, "Refugee Politics: Self-Organized 'Government' and Protests in the Agamé Refugee Camp (2005–13)," in: *Journal of Refugee Studies* 29 (2016) 2: 1–21.
86 Krause, "Zwischen Schutz und Scham"; Asha Hans, "Gender, Camps and International Norms," in: *Refugee Watch* (2008) 32: 64–73.
87 Alice Szczepanikova, "Gender Relations in a Refugee Camp: A Case of Chechens Seeking Asylum in the Czech Republic," *Journal of Refugee Studies* 18 (2005) 3: 281–298; Deborah Mulumba, *Women Refugees in Uganda: Gender Relations, Livelihood Security, and Reproductive Health* (Kampala: Fountain Publishers, 2010); Horn, "Exploring the Impact of Displacement and Encampment".
88 Freedman, *Gendering the International Asylum and Refugee Debate*, 34–40; Deborah Mulumba, "Gender Relations, Livelihood Security and Reproductive Health among Women

since the restrictions and hardships keep them from maintaining their traditional roles as decision-makers and bread-winners for their families.[89]

While this shows that forced migration and the life in refugee camps constitute gendered processes,[90] these social changes are not detached from humanitarian structures. Aid agencies rather intervene in negotiations among refugees with their projects. The aforementioned vulnerability concept or specific projects for women's empowerment and participation, among others, contribute to new imbalances or inequalities by preferentially providing assistance to women. This simultaneously neglects or diminishes the formerly powerful roles of the men.[91] In fact, humanitarian organisations supersede as decision-makers and providers, taking on the role of the patriarch.[92]

Although refugees are confronted with structural limitations, power asymmetries, and physical risks such as sexual and gender-based violence, which can also be caused by humanitarian actors,[93] refugees do not passively give in, obey, and comply with restrictions but strive to deal with these conditions. They cope with the hardships by using individual and collective strategies,[94] they protest restrictions,[95] and they contribute to the local economy.[96] Moreover, refugees use the imposed humanitarian structures for their advantage. By providing incorrect

---

Refugees in Uganda. The Case of Sudanese Women in Rhino Camp and Kiryandongo Refugee Settlements," (Wageningen University, 2005), 230.

89 Simon Turner, "Angry Young Men in Camps: Gender, Age and Class Relations Among Burundian Refugees in Tanzania," in: *New Issues in Refugee Research* (1999): 9; Barbra Lukunka, "New Big Men: Refugee Emasculation as a Human Security Issue," in: *International Migration* 50 (2011) 5: 130–141; Krause, "Hegemonie von Männern".

90 Hans, "Gender, Camps and International Norms".

91 Elisabeth Olivius, "Displacing Equality? Women's Participation and Humanitarian Aid Effectiveness in Refugee Camps," in: *Refugee Survey Quarterly* 33 (2014) 3: 93–117; Elena Fiddian-Qasmiyeh et al., "'Faithing' Gender and Responses to Violence in Refugee Communities: Insights from the Sahrawi Refugee Camps and the Democratic Republic of Congo," in: *Gender, Violence, Refugees*, edited by Susanne Buckley-Zistel and Ulrike Krause (New York, Oxford: Berghahn, 2017), 127–151. (Studies in Forced Migration 37).

92 Turner, "Angry Young Men in Camps"; Krause, "Hegemonie von Männern".

93 Elizabeth G. Ferris, "Women in Refugee Camps. Abuse of Power: Sexual Exploitation of Refugee Women and Girls," in: *Signs: Journal of Women in Culture and Society* 32 (2007) 3: 584–591.

94 Jessica Gladden, "Coping Strategies of Sudanese Refugee Women in Kakuma Refugee Camp, Kenya," in: *Refugee Survey Quarterly* 32 (2013) 4: 66–89; Susan Thomson, "Agency as Silence and Muted Voice: The Problem-solving Networks of Unaccompanied Young Somali Refugee Women in Eastleigh, Nairobi," in: *Conflict, Security & Development* 13 (2013) 5: 589–609; Krause, "Wie bewältigen Flüchtlinge die Lebensbedingungen in Flüchtlingslagern".

95 Lecadet, "Refugee Politics"; Carolina Moulin and Peter Nyers, "'We Live in a Country of UNHCR': Refugee Protests and Global Political Society," *International Political Sociology* 1 (2007) 4: 356–372.

96 Alexander Betts et al., *Refugee Economies: Forced Displacement and Development* (Oxford: Oxford University Press, 2017).

or incomplete information, they try to negotiate personal improvements through humanitarian structures.[97] Or by reproducing the 'humanitarian speak' of vulnerability or empowerment, they aim to obtain sympathy and claim more aid.[98] This may be interpreted as a type of refugees' entrepreneurship[99] or "as evidence of the re-development of 'solidarity' among these populations" in camps.[100]

As a basic principle, these observations reveal how millions of people worldwide who have been legally determined and politically labelled as refugees practice agency rather than passively submitting to humanitarian domination in camps. They eke out their own scopes for actions within and beyond the humanitarian boundaries and borders.[101] Hence, refugee camps are also especially strongly shaped by the various practices of refugees, who obviously have daily routines, raise families, bear children, cook, sleep, eat, play, and work. It would be insufficient to only look at camp features through humanitarian lenses or from the perspective of the social formation of humanitarian order, because these camp settings constitute living spaces for many people worldwide. Whereas this statement may almost seem trivial, the diversity of this everyday life is placed at risk of being pushed into the background or even into oblivion by only focusing on humanitarian structures and deficits.

As refugee situations often last longer, and protracted situations arise, the daily social structures are being reinforced. Among others, Michel Agier[102] notes various coffee shops, video stores, hairdressing salons, and photo studios that have been set up by refugees in *Dadaab Refugee Camps* in Kenia. Katharina Inhetveen[103] describes wedding ceremonies that have taken place in Zambian refugee camps, and Bram Jansen[104] writes about people watching football together in *Kakuma Refugee Camp* in Kenya. Pia Jolliffee[105] explains what refugees from Myanmar in camps in Thailand do after dark, how some people meet in the

---

97 Gaim Kibreab, "Pulling the Wool over the Eyes of the Strangers: Refugee Deceit and Trickery in Institutionalized Settings," in: *Journal of Refugee Studies* 17 (2004) 1: 1–26; Bram Jansen, "Between Vulnerability and Assertiveness: Negotiating Resettlement in Kakuma Refugee Camp, Kenya," in: *African Affairs* 107 (2008) 429: 569–587.
98 Katharina Inhetveen, "'Because we are Refugees': Utilizing a Legal Label," in: *New Issues in Refugee Research* (Geneva: UNHCR, 2006), 11; Turner, *Politics of Innocence*, 58.
99 Martha Kuwee Kumsa, "'No! I'm Not a Refugee!' The Poetics of Be-Longing among Young Oromos in Toronto," in: *Journal of Refugee Studies* 19 (2006) 2: 230–255.
100 Barbara E. Harrell-Bond, "Weapons of the Weak," in: *Journal of Refugee Studies* 17 (2004) 1: 27–28, 28.
101 Hartmann, "Contested Boundaries".
102 Agier, "Between War and City," 326.
103 Inhetveen, *Die Politische Ordnung des Flüchtlingslager,* 188, 351.
104 Jansen, *The Accidental City,* 123.
105 Pia Jolliffee, "Night-Time and Refugees: Evidence from the Thai-Myanmar Border," in: *Journal of Refugee Studies* 29 (2015) 1: 1–18.

early-evening hours, and how others only leave their homes in the 'shelter of the darkness'.

In the context of my empirical research with Congolese refugees in *Kyaka II* in Uganda, I not only learned a great deal about violence and hardships by talking to the people, but also about their social dynamics. They sold crops on the markets, helped each other, and met up with friends at religious centres or bars. They talked about their worries, that their children might have the wrong friends, would imitate bad behaviour, and insult adults. Others explained how they established economic cooperation with refugees in the Western part of Uganda to resell fish in the camp.[106] A crucial part of the people's coping strategies turned out to be their social structures; they used these to create spheres of belonging. Some women joined women's groups to speak about their experiences and help each other; young people decided to walk to school together to protect each other but also to spend time with each other; and both women and men created economic networks to generate income, which also contributed to social support.[107]

To establish a 'daily routine' and a sense of belonging, it is important to create a 'home'[108] which not only reflects a certain normality but also a "site of nurture, stability, reliability, and authenticity".[109] Due to their uncertainty about the future as well as the prevalent domestic violence, they may feel as though creating a home is initially an impossible task. For example, during my research in *Kyaka II*, a woman said that she was beaten by her husband 'like a drum',[110] illustrating the intensity of violence. Moreover, a man noted that "a man has no power [in the camp], has no property and [...] some women have taken over".[111] The challenges of creating a home in such fragile social spheres not only affect refugees in camps in Uganda but worldwide. However, Catherine Brun[112] explains the dif-

---

106 Krause, "Wie bewältigen Flüchtlinge die Lebensbedingungen in Flüchtlingslagern," 205–214.
107 Ulrike Krause and Hannah Schmidt, "'Being beaten like a drum' Gefahren, Humanitarismus und Resilienz von Frauen in Flüchtlingssituationen," in: *GENDER. Zeitschrift für Geschlecht, Kultur und Gesellschaft*, 2018 2: 47–62.
108 A special edition of the journal *Refuge* deals with the question of how refugees create homes and which meanings they have for refugee situations; see Giorgia Doná, "Making Homes in Limbo: Embodied Virtual 'Homes' in Prolonged Conditions of Displacement," in: *Refuge* 31 (2015) 1: 67–73.
109 Malathi De Alwis, "The 'Purity' of Displacement and the Reterritorialization of Longing: Muslim IDPs in Northwestern Sri Lanka," in: *In Sites of Violence: Gender and Conflict Zones*, edited by Wenona Giles and Jennifer Hyndman (Berkeley: University of California Press, 2004), 213–231, 215.
110 Discussion with women, 12 March 2014, Base Camp, Kyaka II.
111 Discussion with religious leaders, 19 March 2014, Base Camp, Kyaka II.
112 Cathrine Brun, "Home as a Critical Value: From Shelter to Home in Georgia," in: *Refuge* 31 (2015) 1: 43–54.

ference between accommodation and home for displaced people in Georgia and highlights the critical value of acquaintances and relatives, buildings, and their surroundings for the creation of a home. Naohiko Omata[113] furthermore describes how Lebanese refugees found and established homes which were meaningful to them and eventually influenced their decisions to repatriate to their country of origin.

Quo Vadis? From an Urban Interpretation of Camps Reverting to Confinement

By analysing the contradiction between the exercise of humanitarian power and the establishment of a home and a routine, a place of normality, and even a vibrant economy, as well as everyday facilities such as schools, shops, markets, bars, hospitals, and meeting places, researchers have gained an understanding of 'urban' refugee camp architecture. Refugee camps have been described as 'accidental cities'[114], 'city-camps', as a 'naked city', 'city as camp',[115] and 'camp as city'[116], or even 'urban enclaves'.[117] As such, they unite political, social, economic, and cultural infrastructures. With an urban reading, humanitarian power structures could be reinterpreted as a 'city council' or 'administration'; humanitarian services, as 'municipal social services'; and the demarcated areas in camps, the zones and clusters, as 'districts'. Similar to the idea of an 'urban jungle', camps represent human-made and defensible systems as well as sites of unpredictability, chaos, and risk-taking.[118] In the midst of these confined, at times crowded spheres, people vindicate their positions but can also disappear in the crowd, merge into the group, or remain unnoticed. The urban interpretation of refugee camps is not only persuasive from a social sciences perspective but also from geographical and architectural points of view. In this way, the chequered or loose rural arrangements of residential areas become identifiable from an aerial perspective.[119]

---

113 Naohiko Omata, "Home-making during protracted exile: Diverse responses of refugee families in the face of remigration," :*Transnational Social Review* 6 (2016) 1–2, 26–40.
114 Jansen, *The Accidental City*.
115 Agier, "Between War and City".
116 Peter Grbac, "Civitas, polis, and urbs: reimagining the refugee camp as the city," *RSC Working Paper Series,* No. 96 (2013).
117 Marc-Antoine Perouse De Montclos and Peter Mwangi Kagwanja, "Refugee Camps or Cities? The Socio-economic Dynamics of the Dadaab and Kakuma Camps in Northern Kenya," in: *Journal of Refugee Studies* 13 (2000) 2: 205–222.
118 Bülent Diken, "From Refugee Camps to Gated Communities: Biopolitics and the End of the City," in: *Citizenship Studies* 8 (2004) 1: 83–106, 98.
119 Schöpfer, Elisabeth et. al., "Temporäre Siedlungen: Wenn aus Flüchtlingslagern Städte

Such different perspectives and theoretical approaches contribute to a better understanding of the setup, functioning, and effects of camps on refugee all over the world. As this article drew on the growing body of research about refugee camps, developments can be revealed. However, the problematic conditions for the 'camp population' do not seem to have changed greatly during the past years; scholars in the 1980s were already criticising poverty, violence, and lack of opportunities to generate a livelihood in camps.[120] Moreover, despite the variety of studies, some fields have received insufficient attention from scholars. From my research focus on violence and gender, a prominent example of neglected issues is violence that occurs against men in camps. Violence against men is rarely considered as a kind of sexual and gender-based violence, the issue of the rape of men remains taboo, and the gender-specific dangers they face are often trivialised and thought of as 'everyday problems'.[121] By focusing on sexual and gender-based violence as a 'women's issue', scholars are in danger of (re-)-producing dichotomies of 'victim-women' and 'perpetrator-men'.[122] Additionally, although this article has mostly referred to women, men, and 'others', LGBTI* people also constitute an important group. How LGBTI* people experience life in camps, which risks they are exposed to, and how they cope with the conditions requires further research.

Finally, if we examine the multiple actions of the people, we can see that refugee camps not only signify humanitarian spaces but that the people shape the social space of camps. They create a social environment, economic opportunities, and political structures.[123] They operate individually and help each other, not only within the defined humanitarian limits but also beyond. They challenge humanitarian structures rather than passively giving in.[124] If scholarly work aims to shed light on the impact and complexity of refugee camps, we have

---

werden," in: *Globale Urbanisierung: Perspektive aus dem All*, edited by Hannes Taubenböck et al. (Berlin – Heidelberg: Springer, 2015), 71–81; Alain Beaudou et al. "Geographical Information System, Environment and Camp Planning in Refugee Hosting Areas. Approach, methods and application in Uganda," (Bondy: Institut de recherche pour le développement (IRD), 2003).

120 See, among others, Harrell-Bond, *Imposing Aid*.
121 Cathrine Brun, "Making Young Displaced Men Visible," *Forced Migration Review* 9 (2000), 10–12; Shayne Henry et al., "Promoting Accountability for Conflict-Related Sexual Violence Against Men: A Comparative Legal Analysis of International and Domestic Laws Relating to IDP and Refugee Men in Uganda," *Refugee Law Project Working Paper Series* (Kampala: Makerere University, 2013), 1–83; Krause, "Hegemonie von Männern".
122 Crit. Krause, *"Die Flüchtling – der Flüchtling als Frau"*.
123 Jansen, *The Accidental City*; Betts et al., *Refugee Economies*; Inhetveen, *Die Politische Ordnung des Flüchtlingslagers*.
124 Kibreab, "Pulling the Wool over the Eyes of the Strangers"; Inhetveen, "'Because we are Refugees'"; Krause, "Wie bewältigen Flüchtlinge die Lebensbedingungen in Flüchtlingslagern".

to continue to reveal these heterogenous practices as well as direct and indirect forms of resistance – actions that exist not only despite but also because of humanitarian structures and adversities.

Acknowledgements

This article draws on research carried out in three research project, *Global Refugee Protection and Local Refugee Engagement* (Gerda Henkel Foundation, Centre for Conflict Studies, Marburg University as well as Institute for Migration Research and Intercultural Studies (IMIS), Osnabrück University, 2016–2019), *Gender Relations in Confined Spaces* (Deutsche Stiftung Friedensforschung, Centre for Conflict Studies, Marburg University, 2013–2016) and *Development-oriented Refugee Aid* (Magdeburg University, 2009–2012). I am grateful to the funding institutions for their support, and I sincerely thank all refugees and aid workers for their time and trust to speak with me.

Robert Jan van Pelt

Labour Service Barrack-Huts in Germany and the United States, 1933–45

Introduction

The following pages present a micro-history of the basic architectural element of the labour service camps created during the Great Depression in Germany and the United States.[1] Both the German *Freiwillige Arbeitsdienst* (FAD; Voluntary Labour Service), which in 1934 became the *Reichsarbeitsdienst* (RAD; Reich Labour Service), and the American Civilian Conservation Corps (CCC) used the *Baracke* (German) or "barrack," "hut," or "barrack-hut" (English) to house young men put to work in rural and remote areas.[2]

This essay seeks to extend the literature on the architecture of total institutions, as articulated by sociologist Erving Goffman. More than a half century ago, Goffman defined a total institution as "a place of residence and work where a large number of like situated individuals, cut off from the wider society for an appreciable period of time, together lead an enclosed, formally administered round of life."[3] Goffman distinguished five kinds of total institutions: (1) those established to care for persons felt to be both incapable and harmless, such as orphanages; (2) those established to care for persons felt to be incapable of looking after themselves and a threat to the community, albeit an unintended

---

1 I thank Victor Tulceanu and Mark Clubine for their drawings of the RAD and CCC barrack-huts, Amy Hughes for fine-tuning the text, and Dr. Antje Senarclens de Grancy, Miriam Greenbaum, and the anonymous peer reviewer for their constructive criticism.
2 The English noun *barrack-hut* addresses the tricky and at times confusing reversal of the meanings of *barrack* and *casern* in English. Both are loanwords from French: *baraque* normally refers to a single-storey wooden building and *caserne* to an often multistorey brick or stone military building. In standard English, however, the plural form *barracks* denotes what the French call a *caserne*, while the English noun *casern* denotes a small, temporary building for housing troops.
3 The Canadian sociologist Erving Goffman created the concept of the *total institution*. He defined it as "a place of residence and work where a large number of like-situated individuals, cut off from the wider society for an appreciable period of time, together lead an enclosed, formally administered round of life." Erving Goffman, *Asylums: Essays on the Social Situation of Mental Patients and Other Inmates* (London: Penguin, 1961), 11.

one, such as mental asylums; (3) those that are organised to protect the community against those who are seen to present an intentional danger to it, such as prisons; (4) those that are designed as retreats from the world, such as abbeys; (5) those that are purportedly established to improve the pursuit of some work-like tasks, such as boarding schools. The labour service camps belong to the fifth category. However, at an institutional level the boundaries between these categories are not absolute: a workhouse that accommodates the allegedly "unproductive" and "lazy" poor has characteristics of the second, third, and fourth types, and a reformatory for wayward boys shows aspects of a boarding school and a prison. Historically, one of the types has easily morphed into another one: for example, Russian Orthodox monasteries *also* served as prisons under the czars and *exclusively* served as prison camps under the Bolsheviks.[4] Likewise in Germany, some of the camps that were created to house civilian labourers engaged to build the *Reichsautobahn* were easily transformed into forced labour camps for Jews during the Holocaust.[5]

In particular, this paper aims to augment Kiran Klaus Patel's *"Soldaten der Arbeit": Arbeitsdienste in Deutschland und den USA 1933–1945* (2003), published in English as *Soldiers of Labor: Labor Service in Nazi Germany and New Deal America, 1933–1945* (2005). Exploring similarities and differences in the way these labour services were conceived and operated, as well how they were perceived by the public, Patel gave considerable attention to the purpose and form of the labour service camps. Both RAD and CCC camps reflect military models in the grouping of buildings and the hierarchy amongst them, creating a spatial framework of social discipline. Yet, at the same time, the apparent similarity between the camps created in 1930s Germany and the United States camouflaged a significant difference between them. The RAD camps were part of a totalitarian organisation in which the appearance of strict hierarchy and absolute unity, and the political and social symbolism that came with it, mattered more than economic realities and individual well-being, while the CCC camps had a broader horizon. Created and run by a pragmatic organisation that promoted efficiency in its operations and the psychological welfare of each enrollee, the American camps also promoted engagement with civil society.[6] A detailed architectural-historical analysis of the RAD and CCC barrack-huts both confirms and extends Patel's conclusions about the substantial differences between

---

4 Daniel H. Shubin, *Monastery Prisons* (Philadelphia: Xlibris, 2001).
5 Hermann F. Weiss, "From Reichsautobahnlager to Schmelt Camp: Brande, a Forgotten Holocaust Site in Western Upper Silesia, 1940–1943," in: *Yad Vashem Studies* 39, no. 2 (2011): 81–119.
6 Kiran Klaus Patel, *Soldiers of Labor: Labor Service in Nazi Germany and New Deal America, 1933–1945* (Cambridge: Cambridge University Press, 2005), 205, 267, 285, 399, 401.

the RAD and CCC camps in terms of standardisation, adaptability, and social and ideological ambition.

The analysis I will present also continues the trajectory of investigation on the history of barrack-huts initiated by Manfred Seifert in his *Kulturarbeit im Reichsarbeitsdienst* (1996). Seifert's study pioneered an analysis of the design and technology of the RAD barrack-hut and its arrangement in camps in terms of the practices and ideology of the RAD as an organisation.[7] And it is inspired by the work of Axel Dossmann, Jan Wenzel, and Kai Wenzel, who, in their *Architektur auf Zeit: Baracken, Pavillons, Container* (2006), not only provided the groundwork for a comparative approach to the history of the barrack-hut but also demonstrated that the barrack-hut is *a*, if not *the*, key architectural type of the modern age, and that the study of its rise and fall adds a component both exciting and profitable to our quest for an understanding of the twentieth century.[8] Seifert, Dossmann, and the Wenzel brothers have shown that there are more nuanced ways to look at the barrack-hut, which, in too many writings on camps as total institutions, has become a single-meaning metaphor for the spatial condition of the regimented life of inmates robbed of the basic freedoms, such as the freedom to act.

In a wider sense, the following case study of a key element of the camp as a total institution is set against the horizon of parallel investigations into the apparently commonplace elements that allowed such places to be quickly erected and pulled down as the need arose. The work of Olivier Razac, Alan Krell, and Reviel Netz on the history and meaning of barbed wire provided general inspiration.[9] The barbed wire fence, developed to control cattle on the American prairies, became in the twentieth century the main tool to define the perimeter of the total institutions established to protect the community against those who are seen to present an intentional danger to it. Barbed wire has no place in defining the boundaries of total institutions that are purportedly established to better the pursuit of some work-like task. And indeed, RAD camps typically were not surrounded by barbed wire, and CCC camps never were. Yet, under conditions of total war, such camps came to be used to imprison people, and the barrack-huts developed for those camps became standard-issue shelter in newly established

---

7 Manfred Seifert, *Kulturarbeit im Reichsarbeitsdienst: Theorie und Praxis nationalsozialistischer Kulturpflege im Kontext historisch-politischer, organisatorischer und ideologischer Einflüsse* (Münster and New York: Waxmann, 1996), 238–69.
8 Axel Dossmann, Jan Wenzel, and Kai Wenzel, *Architektur auf Zeit: Baracken, Pavillons, Container* (Berlin: B Books, 2006).
9 Olivier Razac, *Histoire politique du barbelé: La prairie, la tranchée, le camp* (Paris: La Fabrique Editions, 2000); Alan Krell, *The Devil's Rope: A Cultural History of Barbed Wire* (London: Reaktion Books, 2002); Reviel Netz, *Barbed Wire: An Ecology of Modernity* (Middletown, CT: Wesleyan University Press, 2004).

concentration camps that have become symbolic for the twentieth century, defined by Zygmunt Bauman as "the Age of Camps."[10] It is clear that a comparative study that considers the adaptive reuse *casu quo* metamorphosis of all the architectural elements that became the building blocks of the concentration camp – barbed wire fence, guard tower, gate, barrack-hut, latrine, delousing shed, and so forth – and dynamic interrelation between those elements in the camp, will make an interesting dissertation on the history of modern architecture. Perhaps this essay might provide, together with the works mentioned earlier, another foundation piece for such a study.

A Very Short History of the Barrack-Hut

The barrack-hut traces its ancestry to the soldier's hut, cobbled together in the field from available material when the weather did not allow for bivouacking under the open sky, and when neither tents nor billets were available. In the seventeenth century the soldier's hut became an object of prescription, and in the eighteenth century the barrack-hut was first recognised as a useful tool by the emerging army-medical and prisoner-of-war services. During the Crimean War (1853–56), British builders who specialised in making prefabricated huts for settlers in Australia designed a simple, sturdy military version and, with great publicity, shipped it in quantity to the Black Sea, saving the expeditionary forces.[11] At that same time, both the British and French governments decided to create large hut-furnished camps – at Aldershot, England; the Curragh, County Kildare, Ireland; and Châlons-en-Champagne, France – to provide realistic military-training conditions in the field.[12]

During the American Civil War (1861–65), the U.S. Army made the barrack-hut the backbone of a system for managing both mass casualties and prisoners of war.[13] Building on the experience of the Civil War, the German military medical

---

10 Zygmunt Bauman, "A Century of Camps?," in: *Life in Fragments: Essays in Postmodern Morality* (Oxford and Cambridge, MA: Blackwell, 1995), 192–206.
11 See [Royal] Sanitary Commission, *Report to the Right Hon. Lord Panmure, G. C. B., &c., Minister at War, of the Proceedings of the Sanitary Commission Dispatched to the Seat of War in the East, 1855–56* (London: Harrison & Sons, 1857); Gilbert Herbert, *Pioneers of Prefabrication: The British Contribution in the Nineteenth Century* (Baltimore and London: Johns Hopkins University Press, 1978), 75–96.
12 Henry W. Lugard, *Narrative of Operations in the Arrangement and Formation of a Camp for 10,000 Infantry on the Curragh of Kildare* (Dublin: Alex. Thom and Sons, 1858).
13 Joseph Janvier Woodward, "Hospital Organization and Construction," in: U.S. Surgeon General's Office, *Reports on the Extent and Nature of the Materials Available for the Preparation of a Medical and Surgical History of the Rebellion* (Philadelphia: Lippincott & Co., 1865), 152–66.

system made the barrack-hut a basic element of its infrastructure. In the decades that followed the Franco-Prussian War (1870–71), prefabricated panelled barrack-huts came to be used as quarantine hospitals for epidemic diseases, colonies for children infected with tuberculosis, temporary settlements for construction workers in faraway places, housing at spas, inner-city schools, instant settlements in the colonies, and emergency shelters after the 1908 earthquake and tsunami in Messina, Italy.[14]

The adoption of the barrack-hut as a major piece in the toolkit of emergency relief had been stimulated by the advocacy of the International Committee of the Red Cross, which in 1885 had run a competition inviting designs for a barrack-hut that could be not only prefabricated, easily transported, and quickly assembled but also easily taken apart and reconstructed elsewhere. Danish tent-maker Johan Gerhard Clemens Døcker won the first prize with a patented design that was something of a cross between a rigid hut and an army tent. The German-Danish firm Christoph & Unmack bought Døcker's patent, initiated a sales campaign in which they obtained the endorsement of prominent physicians and powerful generals, and began the large-scale production of what the firm called the *Döcker'sche Baracke*, marketed in the English-speaking world as the Doecker Barrack, at its plant in Niesky, Upper Lusatia (Saxony).[15]

The optimism that propelled the simple barrack-hut onto the public stage as a practical tool to take the sting out of war and the contagion out of epidemics turned into its opposite when, in the first days of World War I, it became clear that barrack-huts, surrounded by barbed wire fences, would make cheap and secure camps for prisoners of war, civilian enemy aliens, and refugees. Despite the fact that barrack-huts also provided much appreciated shelter for soldiers when on temporary leave from front-line duty in the trenches, the reputation of this building type never fully recovered from its use in prison camps. It also did not help that barrack-huts did not age well: built without proper foundations, these makeshift structures had the tendency to shift, sag, and slump on-site, which made them particularly prone to rot and infestation. Only with the highest level of maintenance could they be kept in an acceptable state of repair, and when resources were tight, maintenance was usually postponed. Thus most barrack-huts became eyesores as seen from the outside and either too hot or too cold,

---

14 See Bernhard von Langenbeck, Alwin Gustav Edmund Coler, and Friedrich Emil Otto Werner, *Die transportable Lazareth-Baracke*, 2nd ed. (Berlin: Hirschwald, 1890).

15 Henry Menger, *Transportabeles Baracken-Lazareth für 200 Kranke* (Niesky: Christoph & Unmack, 1895); Christoph & Unmack, *Ein Vierteljahrhundert im Dienste der Gesundheitspflege und Volkswohlfahrt in Krieg und Frieden, 1882–1907: Festschrift zum 25 jährigen Bestehen der zerlegbaren transportablen Döcker-Bauten* (Niesky: Christoph & Unmack, 1907).

often fungus-prone, and always vermin-filled environments as experienced from the inside.

On the Origin of European Labour Service Camps

Ideas to create labour camps for young people had been in circulation since 1850, when British writer Thomas Carlyle proposed the formation of "industrial regiments [...] to fight the bogs and wildernesses at home and abroad" and to make arable and habitable "a country of savage glaciers, granite mountains, of foul jungles, unhewed forests, quaking bogs."[16]

Sixty years later, American psychologist William James reflected on the deeply ingrained need for war and the way camp life could provide a societally and culturally harmless psychological "equivalent" to war. "The earlier men were hunting men, and to hunt a neighbouring tribe, kill the males, loot the village and possess the females, was the most profitable, as well as the most exciting, way of living," James observed. Pacifism offended against the natural desire to understand human life as a large, collective drama. This explained the desire of so many young men to submit themselves to the austerity of military life in the barracks, to unconditional duty in the field, and to the self-abnegation brought by a camaraderie that arises in shared suffering. It was no use to fight this tendency by pointing out the horrors and cost of war. "The horror makes the thrill." Hence it made sense to create, within conditions of peace, places where young people could experience what James called "the moral equivalent of war" and face the order and discipline of army life, with its ideals of service and devotion, its focus on physical fitness and constant exertion, and its message of mutual respect and trust. Of course, there were many occupations, mostly at the lowest end of the socioeconomic scale, that offered much toil and pain and require much hardiness. These were generally taken up by those who, because of the accident of their birth, were poor. James believed that all young men ought be drafted into an army of labour, where they could engage in "the immemorial human warfare against nature." Conscription of young men into labour camps would help to preserve in a world at peace the masculine virtues celebrated in war. James had little doubt this could be achieved: "It is but a question of time, of skillful propagandism, and of opinion-making men seizing historic opportunities."[17]

---

16 Thomas Carlyle, "Latter-Day Pamphlets," in: *Thomas Carlyle's Works*, 17 vols. (London: Chapman and Hall, 1885–88), 5: 37.
17 William James, "The Moral Equivalent of War," in: *Memories and Studies* (London: Longmans, Green and Co., 1911), 269–92.

Yet events intervened before such historic opportunities presented themselves. Three years after James's reflections, a young Bosnian Serb nationalist shot the heir to the Austrian throne in Sarajevo, and within weeks, the Austrians, Serbs, Germans, French, Russians, and English were at war – all eager to demonstrate the greatness of their nation and to experience the unity of their people.

Thirty-seven million civilian and military casualties later, the idea of a labour service gained a new foothold, first with the idealists who believed that armies of young volunteers might repair, both physically and spiritually, what armies run by politicians and generals had destroyed. In 1920 the Swiss engineer Pierre Cérésole established the *Service Civil International* (SCI), which brought together Swiss, German, Dutch, American, and English volunteers in a work camp in Esnes-en-Argonne, a village destroyed during the Battle of Verdun. They cleared rubble, repaired roads, cleaned gardens and fields, and constructed five houses. In the years that followed, the SCI and similar organisations helped out in the aftermath of natural disasters.[18]

The German academic and World War I veteran Eugen Rosenstock-Huessy had experienced in the trenches the collective instinct of men and the pleasure of being engaged in common service. During the Weimar years he tried to create a structure in civilian life that provided a symbol of our humankind's struggle with nature, and he organised regular labour service camps that brought together, for a month at a time, young workers, farmers, and students, both employed and unemployed. Key to this initiative was the spiritual dimension embodied in the shared effort of young people of different backgrounds and prospects to live in an autonomous, self-governing community, in which they learned to work together and to understand one another. Rosenstock believed that the primary beneficiaries of this collaboration were not the young workers and farmers, who already knew the social dimension of common manual labour, but the young participants who belonged to the middle and upper classes. "No wages were paid them for their work, and labor therefore ceased to be a means of financial gain. Thus freed it took its rightful place as a necessary ingredient of a well-balanced life, as an outlet for energy as natural as other vital impulses."[19]

The camps created in the 1920s by Cérésole, Rosenstock-Huessy, and others were small experiments in isolated places. The volunteers that participated in them were normally housed in whatever accommodation was available. In 1920s Bulgaria, however, labour camps proliferated as an integral part of a nationwide mobilisation of young people. An ally of Germany and Austria-Hungary in World

---

18 Kenneth Holland, *Youth in European Labor Camps: A Report to the American Youth Commission* (Washington, D.C.: American Council on Education, 1939), 20–38.
19 Eugen Rosenstock-Huessy, "The Army Enlisted against Nature," in: *Journal of Adult Education* 6, no. 3 (June 1934): 272–73.

War I, Bulgaria was forbidden by the terms of the Treaty of Neuilly to maintain a standing army. In January 1920 the country's prime minister, Aleksandŭr Stamboliyski, declared: "Bulgaria will be the first to give to the world a good example of replacing a military army which absorbs, without profit for anyone, the best years of youth, with a labor army developing the idea of brotherhood and solidarity of social classes and producing materially useful and tangible results for the economy."[20] The new labour service embraced men of twenty years and older, and women of fifteen years and older, and enrolled them for eight months (men) or four months (women). Most of the men were put to work to build roads, lay railway tracks, log timber, and maintain forests, and they were housed in camps. In principle the government provided them with canvas tents, but in practice the men lived in huts with wattle-and-daub walls. A German observer noted that the huts were adequate in view of the general level of accommodation in Bulgaria. "The simplicity of the accommodation is in accordance with the very primitive living conditions in the country as a whole."[21]

From FAD to RAD

In the wake of the Wall Street crash of 1929, millions of young men found themselves unemployed in the Americas and Europe, and political leaders feared that those who came of age without prospects were destined to lead a life of crime or become political radicals. In response, the German government established the FAD, in 1931, to deal with this generation at risk. All unemployed between eighteen and twenty-five could join "open camps" (which offered only a place of work), "half-open camps" (which offered work and one or two meals), and "closed camps" (which offered work, room, and board). By the end of 1931, some 4,000 camps were in operation, conscripting some 285,000 men. Most camps were very small.

In general the closed camps used as dormitories whatever was available: an empty factory, a youth hostel, a castle, a barn, or a gymnasium. "In case fixed abodes cannot be obtained, then one must buy, rent, or build a barrack – the last option is especially appropriate if the sponsor of the work owns a forest," stipulated instructions issued to camp leaders in late 1932. "One should negotiate with him that, in compensation for the work done, one is allowed to cut appropriate wood that can be exchanged in sawmills, without costs for the

---

20 As quoted in Holland, *Youth in European Labor Camps*, 42.
21 Hans Raupach, *Arbeitsdienst in Bulgarien: Studienergebnisse der Schlesischen Jungmannschaft* (Berlin and Leipzig: Walter de Gruyter, 1932), 41.

sponsor of the work or the sponsor of the service, for lumber that can be used to build a barrack."[22]

By 1932 the FAD had become the focus of a culture war. The government saw it as a practical tool to combat youth unemployment. Liberal thinkers like Rosenstock-Huessy saw it as a democratic, autonomous society in which young men of different backgrounds could get to know each other and learn the art of critical thinking. At the far right, National Socialists did share the liberal view that the labour service might provide an environment of social unification but fundamentally disagreed with the idea that labour camps would be autonomous. They considered a compulsory labour service organised on the basis of military principles a necessary step to condition the young in a National Socialist manner, and prepare for the reintroduction of the military draft. A key element of the Nazi proposal, articulated by retired colonel Konstantin Hierl, was a uniformity of approach. Every camp was to be subject to an absolute hierarchy that found its apex in the government, and it was be identical in its structure, discipline, and operation to every other camp. This implied the adoption of a standardised camp design and the use of standardised prefabricated barrack-huts as accommodation.

On 30 January 1933, the National Socialists came to power. In March, Hierl became state secretary in the Reich Ministry of Labour. On 1 May, Reich chancellor Adolf Hitler announced a compulsory labour service. "It remains our firm decision to lead every single German, be he who he may, whether rich or poor, whether the son of scholars or the son of factory workers, to experience manual labor once in his lifetime so that he can come to know it, so that he can here one day more easily take command because he has learned obedience in the past." The labour service was to destroy the breeding ground of class hatred and hence Marxism. Hitler was a man in a hurry: "This year for the first time we will turn this great ethical concept, which we connect with the *Arbeitsdienst*, into reality."[23] A few days later Hierl provided a more detailed schedule in an interview with the Nazi Party newspaper. "From 1 October there will be no volunteers of the current kind left, but at their place will be a labour service army of 120,000 men [...]. At the beginning of January we plan to have a labour service army of 350,000 men."[24]

---

22 Hermann Bues (ed.), *Deutscher Arbeitsdienst, Methode und Technik: Leitfaden für den Lagerleiter und Gruppenführer* (Bernau: Grüner, 1932), 56.
23 Adolf Hitler, speech given on the Tempelhof airfield, 1 May 1933, in: Adolf Hitler, *Speeches and Proclamations, 1932–1945*, edited by Max Domarus, 4 vols. (Wauconda IL: Bolchazy-Carducci, 1990–2004), 1:314–15.
24 Konstantin Hierl, "Unterredung mit dem 'Völkischen Beobachter,'" in: Konstantin Hierl, *Ausgewählte Schriften und Reden*, edited by Herbert von Stetten-Erb, 2 vols. (Munich: Franz Ehere Nachfolger, 1941), 2:101–2.

By July Hierl was in full control of the FAD, which was to be known, from 1934 onwards, as the RAD.

The RAD Barrack-Huts

Hierl had ordered that all camps were to be "closed camps," and that, as a matter of principle, they would be established to support betterment work in thinly populated rural areas, in the moors, heaths, forests, tidal flats, and so on – in other words, in places that did not offer any existing accommodations. The executives of Christoph & Unmack and smaller companies that produced barrack-huts, which had been cultivating relations with the FAD, began to prepare for the request for tender that the Reich Ministry of Labour was bound to issue in the near future.

The 1 June 1933 issue of *Deutscher Arbeitsdienst* carried an illustrated article written by architect Will Kämper on the barrack-huts to be built. Kämper noted that the service had few resources, but with new, steep discounts offered by the Reichsbahn for the transport of goods, it had become feasible to buy underused or abandoned prefabricated barrack-huts wherever they might be found, transport them to wherever they might be needed, and repair them. Kämper also considered alternatives such as constructing barracks from logs, yet he quickly dismissed this construction method: it was too expensive, and it offered too little protection. He then proceeded to propose his own design for prefabricated barrack-huts, based on a grid of 1.25 metres.[25]

Kämper had opened a door, and within days manufacturers of barrack-huts began to approach the FAD with their products. Overwhelmed, the FAD made a statement in the 15 June 1933 issue of *Deutscher Arbeitsdienst*, in which it confirmed that the FAD camps would be hutted and that it was at work to develop a standard hut type that, at some future date, might be produced by different firms. Yet it also stressed that the design development had not come yet to a close and hence, "it is useless for suppliers to attempt at this time to obtain firm orders."[26] The statement did not articulate whether the FAD was developing the new standard hut in-house, or if it had commissioned an established firm to do so. But attentive readers of the 15 June issue certainly noticed that an article on the Reich agricultural show in Berlin contained photos not only of prize cattle but

---

25 Will Kämper, "Errichtung von billigen Arbeitslagern mit Holzbaracken und Einrichtungen sowie wirtschaftliche und zweckmässige Aufteilung derselben," in: *Deutscher Arbeitsdienst* 3, no. 11 (1 June 1933): 232–34.
26 "Zur Frage der Unterkünfte im Arbeitsdienst," *Deutscher Arbeitsdienst* 3, no. 12 (15 June 1933): 245.

also of five images of the construction and completion of a labour-service model barrack-hut "exhibited by Christoph & Unmack, Niesky, Upper Lusatia."[27]

Six weeks later it became clear that the labour service had indeed turned to Christoph & Unmack to help it develop the standard barrack-hut. In the 1 August issue of *Deutscher Arbeitsdienst*, Friedrich Abel, head of the prefabricated-home section of the enterprise that had brought the world the Doecker Barrack, took ownership of the issue with an article entitled, "The New Types of the Standard Dwelling for the Labour Service!" Showing photos of a new barrack-hut type under construction in one of the firm's factory halls in Niesky, and accompanied by detailed plans for four different barrack types, Abel predicted that the current practice to house labour service troops in empty buildings would cease to be an option as the economy gained track again. Key issues were the creation of a standardised shelter that could be used for all troops and one that could be erected quickly. "It must be avoided that a part of the camp workforce are kept engaged for weeks and even months with the construction of such buildings, as this will actually mean a deflection from the actual job to be done at the expense of the Reich."[28]

Abel reported on the development of three barrack types that were based on a grid of 1.1 metres, allowing for corner elements of 0.7 metres at the gables. "The floor, walls, and roof consist of standardised panels, which allows unskilled labourers to put such a building together with playful ease."[29] The standard width of the barrack was 8 metres, and the length was to be a multiple of that standard structural bay, defined by the distance between the truss beams, of 3.3 metres. Abel showed the plans for a barrack-hut for the administration, one for housing men, and one for the mess and the kitchen. They were designated with the numbers I, II, and III.

Type II, the dwelling barrack (Fig. 1: Worm's-eye view and perspective drawing of a RAD three-room barrack-hut), was the most important. In the first version illustrated in Abel's article is a building of twelve bays, of which eight bays consisted of four rooms of 6.6 by 8 metres, one bay of rooms for officers, one bay a washing room and a drying room, and two bays for tool storage. The two-bay room was to house a *Trupp* (troop) of sixteen labour service men and one *Truppführer* (troop leader), giving each person 3.1 square metres and 9.2 cubic metres. These rooms were very crowded at night. Nine years after its conception, one of the architects involved, Georg Pöthke, explained that the need to make the barracks as cheap as possible had led to the very tight measurements, reducing

---

27 "Bilder von der grossen Reichslandwirtschaftsschau Berlin," in: *Deutscher Arbeitsdienst* 3, no. 12 (15 June 1933): 249.
28 Friedrich Abel, "Die neuen Typen der Einheitsunterkünfte für den Arbeitsdienst," in: *Deutscher Arbeitsdienst* 3, no. 15 (1 August 1933): 320.
29 Ibid.

the floor and air space per man to below a minimum standard set by the public health authorities. "With justification one assumed that, during the day, in the field the young men would pump themselves full of air and oxygen."[30]

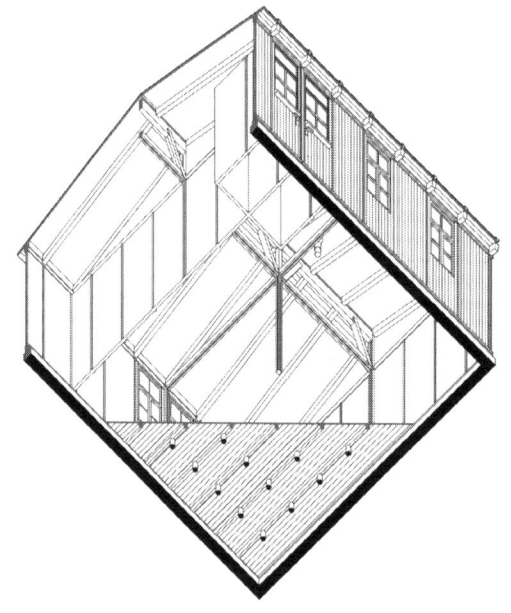

Fig. 1: Worm's-eye view and perspective drawing of a RAD three-room barrack-hut housing forty-eight men and three troop leaders. (Drawings: Victor Tulceanu and Mark Clubine)

Neither Abel nor Pöthke ever claimed authorship for the overall design. In 1944, eleven years after the development of the FAD barrack-hut, a German magazine dedicated to barrack-hut construction credited its own publisher, Alfred Künzel, as the inventor of the new barrack-hut. The article praised Künzel's barrack-hut

---

30 Georg Pöthke, "Zur Entwicklung einer neuen Konstruktion für Lagerunterkünfte," in: *Der deutsche Holzbau* 2 (1942): 243.

as something that had "in its scope and significance hardly any parallel in other fields of human endeavour."[31]

To stress the point, the article was illustrated by an alleged facsimile of Künzel's initial sketch, framed by drawings of all the different barrack types that had evolved from it.

Neither Abel nor Pöthke discussed what was the key innovation of the proposal, and which was very likely conceived not by Künzel but by Christoph & Unmack: the fact that the structures proposed by the firm were not barrack-huts as such but a system of modular, standardised, and cost-effectively produced parts that was to be universally adopted in all of Germany and that would allow not only factories but also smaller workshops to produce construction elements that could be mixed and matched at any building site.[32] In other words, they introduced the so-called American system – which organised the manufacturing process by separating the production of standardised, identical, and interchangeable parts – into the German construction industry.[33]

The general principle of the construction had been established by June 1933, but the most practical arrangement of the elements was still a topic of debate. In September 1933 Abel published a second article, in which he reported that while the types he had published earlier were undoubtedly the most efficient – and this suggests that, indeed, Künzel might have been the author, because they could not be dismissed without some formality – considerations of costs had led to the development of three new types aimed to provide eating facilities, administration, and the accommodation of senior staff.[34]

By the fall of 1933 the system was in place. By establishing a good relationship with the FAD early on, and by keeping Künzel happy, Abel had made Christoph & Unmack a key partner to a regime that, many thought, would need many barrack-huts. In order to ensure the future dominance of Christoph & Unmack, Abel used his position as co-founder of the Deutsche Holzbau Konvention (DHK; German Wooden Construction Convention), a trade organisation of all barrack producers in Germany, to establish a new research and design institute in Niesky, in which DHK, representing the manufacturers of barracks, and the RAD, which was the biggest client at the time, participated as equal partners. The *Forschungs- und Konstruktionsgemeinschaft der Reichsleitung des Reichsarbeitsdienstes und der Deutschen Holzbau Konvention* (FOKORAD; Research and Construction

---

31 "Generalarbeitsführer Alfred Künzel 49 Jahre alt," in: *Der deutsche Holzbau* 4 (1944): 127.
32 See Karl Gabriel, "Zerlegbare Holzbauten," in: *Der deutsche Holzbau* 1 (1941): 4–5.
33 David A. Hounshell, *From the American System to Mass Production, 1800–1932: The Development of Manufacturing Technology in the United States* (Baltimore, MD: Johns Hopkins University Press, 1984).
34 Friedrich Abel, "Die neuen Typen der Einheitsunterkünfte für den Arbeitsdienst," in: *Deutscher Arbeitsdienst*, 3, no. 17 (1 September 1933): 382.

Community of the Reich Leadership of the Reich Labour Service and the German Wooden Construction Convention) ensured that Christoph & Unmack would control barrack construction in the Third Reich. Karl Gabriel, who was an experienced designer of farms, was in charge of FOKORAD, while the architects Georg Pöthke, Paul Heinze, Helmuth Kipke, Hermann Strohmaier, and Willi Wüstehoff perfected the kit of parts for the RAD barracks and began to design other barrack types.[35]

By 1935 the catalogue issued by the RAD (Fig. 2: Sheet from the 1935 catalogue published by the RAD showing the single-*Truppstube* version of the standard RAD barrack-hut) listed barracks that were organised by type: dormitories, administration building, mess hall and kitchen, wash house, barrack-hut dwelling for a married officer and his family, latrine barrack, bicycle shed, and engine house. They all came at different sizes. Pricing was transparent: there was a base price for each type, with extra charges for add-ons and upgrades. Delivery within 500 kilometres of Niesky was included, and standard surcharges were added for greater distances.[36] Development of new types continued after 1935. By 1942 the RAD series included: a sentry box; an improved administration building containing a mini jail and a sick bay; a general-purpose storage and workshop building; barrack-huts for single officers; a wash house that included a disinfection unit, undressing room, wash room, showers, and drying room; a wash house that also included a laundry; and finally an equipment-storage shed.[37]

At that time a typical RAD camp housed either nine or twelve troops. To create a camp, one needed only to have the RAD building catalogue at hand and to place an order for one mess hall, two latrines, one sentry box, one administration building, one general-purpose barrack, one single leader's barrack, one wash house, one equipment-storage shed, and three or four three-room dwelling units. The three-room barrack-hut became the preferred dwelling barrack in RAD camps because three troops formed one *Zug* (platoon), led by an *Obertruppführer* (senior troop leader). Thus, in the same way that each single room embodied the organisational unit of the *Trupp*, the three-room barrack-hut itself represented a *Zug*.

Only the barrack-huts made available through the RAD and produced either

---

35 See Kai Wenzel, "Die FOKORAD in Niesky: Eine Planungsbehörde für den Barackenbau," in: *Führerschule, Thingplatz, "Judenhaus": Topografien der NS-Herrschaft in Sachsen*, edited by Konstantin Hermann (Dresden and Leipzig: Sächsische Landeszentrale für Politische Bildung, 2014), 198–201.
36 Reichsarbeitsdienst, *10. Preisliste vom 16. Juni 1935 betreffende Baracken* (Berlin: Reichsleitung des Arbeitsdienstes, 1935), 5, 23–24.
37 Karl Gabriel, "Beschreibung der beweglichen Unterkünfte des Reichsarbeitsdienst," pt. 1, *Der deutsche Holzbau* 2, no. 1 (1942): 3–5; pt. 2, no. 3 (1942): 36–39.

DER REICHSKOMMISSAR FÜR DEN FREIWILLIGEN ARBEITSDIENST
REICHSLEITUNG DES ARBEITSDIENSTES   BERLIN N 24   FRIEDRICHSTRASSE 110—112

Typ RL IV/1
Mannschaftsbaracke

(Baubeschreibung siehe Seite 26 und 27)

Zeichnung Nr. 18019/1

Preise bei Abnahme von:	1—5	6—8	9—11	12— aufwärts Stück
	RM	RM	RM	RM

Kosten der Baracke frachtfrei Bestimmungsbahnhof bis
zu einer Entfernung von 500 km vom Lieferwerk . . 2140,— 2110,— 2075,— 2035,—

Zuschlag für Fracht bei einer Entfernung von:
    500—600 km . . . . RM 15,—
    600—700 km . . . . RM 25,—
    700—800 km . . . . RM 30,—
    800—900 km . . . . RM 35,—

Gewicht der Baracke rund 6000 kg

Bei einem Transport der Bauteile durch Lastkraftwagen werden benötigt 2 Lastkraftwagen je 3 to

Mehrkosten für zusätzliche Lieferungen:

(Baubeschreibung der zusätzlichen Lieferungen sowie Hinweise auf die betreffenden Technischen Mitteilungsblätter siehe Seite 28).

Pos. 1) Pfahlrostfundament, bestehend aus Rundpfählen und äußerer Sockelverbreiterung	RM 65,—
Pos. 2) 1 Blech-Schornstein	RM 22,—
Pos. 3) Doppelfußboden, als Fehlboden zwischen den Lagerhölzern mit einer Abdeckung aus teerfreier Pappe	RM 115,—
Pos. 4) Isolierplatteneinlage in den Umfassungswänden	RM 110,—
Pos. 5) Isolierplatteneinlage in den Dachflächen	RM 85,—
Pos. 6) Doppelfenster für alle Räume	RM 98,—
Pos. 7) 2 Fliegenfenster	RM 6,—
Pos. 8) Fensterläden für alle Fenster	RM 90,—
Pos. 9) Lignatbekleidung für die Innenseite der Umfassungswände	RM 220,—
Pos. 10) Lignatbekleidung für Dachuntersichten	RM 165,—
Pos. 11) Beiderseitige Lignatbekleidung für alle Scheidewände . .	RM 35,—
Pos. 12) Durchlaufende Dachrinnen mit Abfallrohren	RM 45,—

(Die nebenstehenden Mehrkosten für zusätzliche Lieferungen verstehen sich bei Lieferung für 1—5 Stück Baracken. Es treten Ermäßigungen ein: Bei Lieferung für 6—8 Baracken . . . 1,5 Prozent / Bei Lieferung für 9—11 Baracken . . . 3 Prozent / Bei Lieferung für 12 und mehr . . . 5 Prozent)

3   10. Preisliste vom 16. 6. 1935

Fig. 2: Sheet from the 1935 catalogue published by the RAD showing the single-*Truppstube* version of the standard RAD barrack-hut. (Collection Berlin State Library)

by Christoph & Unmack or under the company's license could be used as accommodations in the labour service camps. This monopoly was justified not only by the desire to project a uniformity of purpose and appearance in all the corners of the Reich. It also had a practical dimension: the hope that it would transform the issuance of building permits into a routine procedure. The strategy worked: from March 1936 onwards RAD barracks were pre-approved for construction in the territory of Prussia, which covered 60 per cent of the German Reich.[38]

From their early days, the designers of barrack-huts had never considered the aesthetic integration of this building type into the landscape. Yet as the RAD adopted the barrack-hut as its symbol, the question of the relationship between barrack-hut and landscape became urgent. Nazism promoted a perverse kind of environmentalism that was based on the idea that a healthy *Volk* (people) exists in an almost mystic union with its *Volksboden* (the soil of the people) and that the result was a particular, partly natural and partly man-made *Kulturlandschaft* (cultural landscape) in which the people were *verwurzelt* (rooted).

In 1935 the RAD was the subject of exhibitions in Dortmund and in Wiesbaden.[39] The first exhibition presented two full-scale RAD barrack-huts, and its building type now became the object of connoisseurship. A review noted the economy and rationality of the design, and reflected on the way the buildings of this type lent, "in their unique form that, at the same time, was grown together with the soil, a totally new character to the German landscape." The barrack-hut allowed Germans to live amidst nature, and hence close to nature, and thus became itself an expression of this relationship. It meant a kind of redemption for a building type that carried many negative associations. "The 'barrack' has become the standard form of accommodation in the *Arbeitsdienst*, and it has removed the ugly aftertaste that came with the word."[40]

In a review of the second exhibition, architect Wilhelm Schlaghecke also reflected on the role of the RAD hutted camps. They created, he claimed, "places of culture, born from the spirit of the community within, in the same way as culture emanated from the old monasteries." He compared the mess hall not only to a Pomeranian farmer's home, but also to the world-famous refectory in the Grand Master's Palace at the Castle of the Teutonic Order in Marienburg, in East Prussia (now Malbork, Poland). "And then the exhibition showed how a [RAD] dwelling that is in its location adjusted to the terrain can conquer a landscape, and how the handsome shapes of the individual parts of the dwelling add up to a

---

38 J. Stangelmayer (ed.), *Hilfsbuch 1 für die Aufstellung und Errichtung ortsveränderliche Unterkünfte* (Berlin: Der Bevollmächtigte für den Holzbau, 1942), 34–36.
39 *Reichsarbeitsdienst, Sein Wollen, sein Erfolg: Ausstellung Landesmuseum Wiesbaden 7. bis 14. Juli 1935* (Mainz: Zaberndruck, 1935).
40 "Zur Ausstellung 'Schule der Nation' in der Westfalenhalle zu Dortmund," in: *Deutscher Arbeitsdienst* 5, no. 21 (1935), 669.

general appearance that is both cheerful and cultural."⁴¹ Having given some thought the relationship between barrack and landscape, Schlaghecke decided to make it the subject of a more intensive study. In 1937 he published the heavily illustrated *Das Heim im Reichsarbeitsdienst* (The Home in the Reich Labour Service). Its central idea was simple: "Our camps are castles in the land."⁴² Two years later, after the annexation of Austria, which had expanded the territory of the RAD, Schlaghecke published a second book on the subject, in which he made the case that the RAD barrack-hut was a perfect complement to the Tyrol mountainscape.⁴³ It was the first and the penultimate time that the barrack-hut was charged with so much symbolic significance.

The Civilian Conservation Corps

In the United States the Great Depression began in 1930 when, a year after the Wall Street crash, many banks began to fail. Unemployment rose from 5 to over 20 per cent. Young men especially were affected. In 1931 New York governor Franklin D. Roosevelt supported the creation of a temporary emergency relief administration, which hired these unemployed youth to work in the reforesting of barren lands, thinning of growing forests, building of fire lines, trails, and roads, and so on. Putting the unemployed to work proved an electoral trump card. On 2 July 1932, Roosevelt declared in his acceptance speech for the Democratic nomination for president: "We know that a very hopeful and immediate means of relief, both for the unemployed and for agriculture, will come from a wide plan of the converting of many millions of acres of marginal and unused land into timber land through reforestation [...]. Economic foresight and immediate employment march hand in hand in the call for the reforestation of these vast areas. In so doing, employment can be given to a million men."⁴⁴ President Herbert Hoover's secretary of agriculture, Arthur Mastick Hyde, mocked Roosevelt's idea as "chimerical" and, after some kitchen-table arithmetic, suggested that a maximum of 27,900 jobs could be generated at the cost of incredible dislocation that "would throw more people out of their homes than the New York

---

41 Wilhelm Schlaghecke, "Rückblick auf die Ausstellung 'Reichsarbeitsdienst, Sein Wollen – Sein Erfolg,'" in: *Deutscher Arbeitsdienst* 5, no. 33 (1935): 1113–14.
42 Wilhelm Schlaghecke, *Das Heim im Reichsarbeitsdienst* (Frankfurt am Main: Bechhold, 1937), 12.
43 Wilhelm Schlaghecke, *Holzhaus im Landschaftsraum* (Innsbruck: Gauverlag und Druckerei Tirol G.M.B.H., 1939).
44 As quoted in "Forestry as Relief Aid to the Unemployed Takes Limelight," in: *American Forests* 38 (1932), 468.

Governor could employ."⁴⁵ Hyde's response politicised the issue, turning it into a key element of Roosevelt's election platform.

On 8 November 1932, Roosevelt routed President Hoover in a landslide victory. In his inauguration speech, on 4 March 1933, Roosevelt declared, "Our greatest primary task is to put people to work. This is no unsolvable problem if we face it wisely and courageously. It can be accomplished in part by direct recruiting by the Government itself, treating the task as we would treat the emergency of a war, but at the same time, through this employment, accomplishing greatly needed projects to stimulate and reorganise the use of our natural resources."⁴⁶ Roosevelt had obviously taken a page from William James's writings. Seventeen days after his inauguration, President Roosevelt sent a proposal to Congress. "I have proposed to create a civilian conservation corps to be used in simple work, not interfering with the normal employment, and confining itself to forestry, the prevention of soil erosion, flood control, and similar projects [...]. It is not a panacea for all the unemployed but it is an essential step in this emergency."⁴⁷

Congress responded quickly, and ten days later passed a law that allowed Roosevelt to establish a new agency, which was formally known as the Emergency Conservation Work but became famous as the Civilian Conservation Corps. Led by Robert Fechner, a national labour union leader, the CCC mobilised the resources and expertise of the Department of Labor, which enrolled fit, unemployed single men ages eighteen to twenty five; the Department of War, which constructed and administered labour camps and conditioned the men; the Department of Agriculture, which oversaw the work in the national forests; and the Department of the Interior, which dealt with state, county, and local park lands. Enlistment was for six months. In return, each person received food, clothing, shelter, and an allowance of thirty dollars per month, of which twenty-five dollars was to be sent home. The plan was to enrol 275,000 men by 1 July.⁴⁸

Fechner was a remarkable organiser: by 5 April, 25,000 men already had been enlisted, and a few days later sites for fifty camps, each holding 200 men, had been approved. By the beginning of June, 80,000 men were working in 400 camps, while 155,000 were enrolled in conditioning camps, and each day 9,000 of these

---

45 As quoted in Ibid.
46 Inaugural address of President Franklin D. Roosevelt, 4 March 1933, in: *Congressional Record*, vol. 77, pt. 1: 4 March–3 April 1933 (Washington D.C.: Government Printing Office, 1933), 5.
47 Message of President Franklin D. Roosevelt to the Congress, 21 March 1933; *Congressional Record*, vol. 77, pt. 1, 4 March–3 April 1933 (Washington D.C.: Government Printing Office, 1933), 650.
48 On the CCC, see Perry Henry Merrill, *Roosevelt's Forest Army: A History of the Civilian Conservation Corps, 1933–1942* (Montpelier, VT: Merrill, 1981).

trainees were transferred to forest camps. A total of 1,437 camps had been approved, of which 573 were to be located in national forests, 321 in state forests, 202 in private forests, 1,010 in state parks, and 62 in national parks.[49]

The CCC Barrack-Huts

In the summer of 1933 all the CCC camps were using tents. The men had been given only a six-month contract, and work was to stop in the winter. But the CCC had caught the public imagination, and in August, Fechner capitalised on this when he proposed that the contracts of the men be extended by another six months when they expired in November. Now the CCC faced the challenge of providing the men with suitable winter accommodations.[50]

Organisation, layout, and construction of the camps had been entrusted to the army, and in its initial planning it had counted on tents to provide shelter. When it became clear that the CCC would also operate in winter, the army had to quickly come up with plans. It settled on a simple, framed structure with board-and-batten or clapboard siding and a roof covered with shingles or tarpaper. The design followed the vernacular of the bunkhouse, which was in wide use to house men who worked in remote conditions, chopping trees, mining ore, building railways, and so on. The huts could be built by local carpenters using locally sourced lumber. In Germany, Christoph & Unmack and the RAD had developed the barrack-huts as a monopoly. The CCC, however, was determined to spread the wealth by ensuring that the construction program would not only bring money into the local economy but would also be seen to do so. In contrast with the enrolees of the RAD, those enrolled in the CCC camps were, as a matter of principle, not to build their own camps.[51] "Forty thousand carpenters, working in 46 states and utilizing 300 million feet of lumber, are rushing to completion a record-breaking camp construction program for the Civilian Conservation Corps," a press release issued in early November 1933 announced. "On over 1,400 camp sites, a total of nearly 15,000 buildings are being constructed to take care of housing and recreation needs of the 300,000 men of the CCC for the winter and spring months."[52]

---

49 "With the Civilian Conservation Corps," in: *American Forests* 39 (1933): 302–3.
50 "Plans Shaping to Continue Emergency Forestry Work through Winter," in: *American Forests* 39 (1933): 402.
51 Major General McKinley, War Department, "Memorandum to commanding generals, all corps areas," 5 February 1934, 1–4, Records of the Civilian Conservation Corps, grp. 35–6, vol. 2, item 239, National Archives, College Park, MD.
52 Press release, 3 November 1933, 1–2, Official File 268, 2, Franklin D. Roosevelt Presidential Library, Hyde Park, NY.

The CCC had been created as an emergency measure, but by the middle of 1934 it was recognised as a great success. In early 1934 the magazine *American Forests*, published by the nonprofit conservation organisation of the same name, issued a call to the 300,000 formerly unemployed young men living in more than 1,400 hutted forest camps, asking them to write a short essay on the topic "What the Civilian Conservation Corps Has Done for Me." It received hundreds of contributions, and most of them told a similar story about despair that came with unemployment and homelessness, and personal redemption that came with a rediscovery of one's individual dignity. All the essays were highly individualistic in tone and character, none stressed the idea of comradeship, and none adhered to any propaganda line that extolled, for example, preset ideas of the camp community or the national community – because unlike the RAD, the CCC was not a platform for either indoctrination or the forced sociability of comradeship. Unlike the German RAD men, the CCC enrolees had ample free time to spend as they desired: alone under a tree, hiking with a friend, sharing a drink or two in the saloon of a nearby town, or taking classes offered in the camp itself.

Conceived as a temporary emergency measure, the organisation and goals of the CCC never transcended the relaxed, pragmatic, and typically American standard of "good enough for now." But by 1934 there was a consensus amongst policymakers and CCC officials that it might be needed as a tool of unemployment relief for at least five years. This implied that once work had been completed at the existing sites, new projects would be developed at new locations. Providing the CCC with prefabricated demountable barracks began to make sense, for this reason and also because too many of the barrack-huts constructed in the fall of 1933 by local builders had turned out to be shoddy. Prefabrication would ensure quality control.[53] In September 1934, Fechner ordered the development of a portable model that might be brought into production in 1935 if the CCC continued to be funded.[54]

The design job ended on the desk of Captain Andre L. Violante of the Quartermaster Corps. Unlike his German colleagues at Christoph & Unmack, who had forty years of experience and the resources of a large corporation at their disposal when they set out to design what became the RAD barrack, Violante had to work from scratch. With Yankee inventiveness, he decided to pursue a simple design with interchangeable parts that could be easily transported and easily put

---

53 Major General McKinley, "Report to all corps area commanders on supply plans for the CCC," 24 April 1935, 3–5, Records of the Civilian Conservation Corps, grp. 35–6, vol. 3, item 336, National Archives, College Park, MD.
54 Robert Fechner, letter to Ferdinand A. Silcox, USDA Forest Service, Washington, D.C., 7 September 1934, 1–2, Records of the Civilian Conservation Corps, grp. 35–6, box 908, item 788. National Archives, College Park, MD.

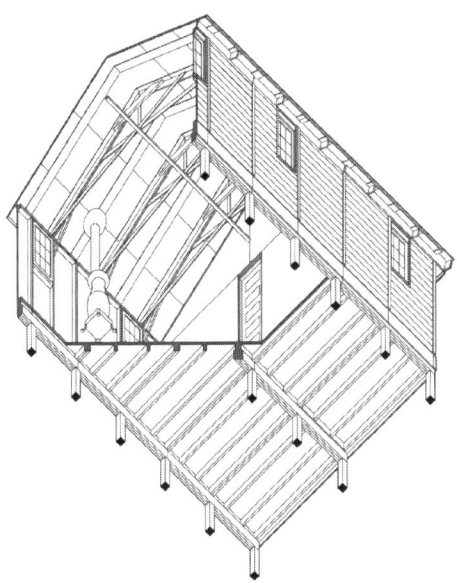

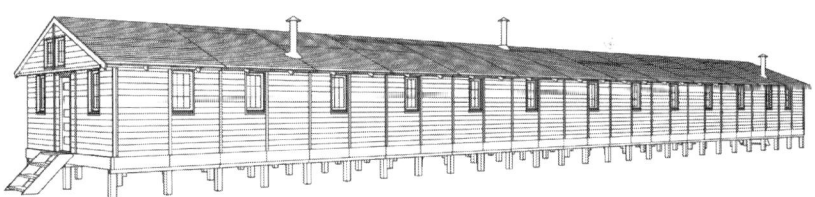

Fig. 3: Worm's-eye view and perspective drawing of a CCC barrack-hut housing fifty men. (Drawings: Mark Clubine)

together to provide a cheap, weathertight hut that was appropriate for different climates (Fig. 3: Worm's-eye view and perspective drawing of a CCC barrack-hut).[55] "Many panel assemblies were tried, but most were discarded," an article published five years later reported. "The design had to be worked out largely by the application of intelligent engineering judgment, since the combination of stresses developed in the unique arrangement of structural members was not

---

55 John Guthrie and C. H. Tracy, "Portable Camp Buildings," 1943. Records of the Civilian Conservation Corps, grp. 35–6, box 908, item 788, National Archives, College Park, MD.

subject to simple rational analysis."⁵⁶ In early 1935 the CCC decided that it would adopt Violante's barrack-hut, but that it would also continue the construction of locally sourced buildings and compare the cost of each.⁵⁷ In the background of the decision to continue with a double-pronged approach might have been the fact that in April, Roosevelt had ordered the CCC to be doubled in size within sixty days, growing to 600,000 men at work in almost 3,000 camps.⁵⁸

In the fall of 1935, Colonel Duncan K. Major, the War Department's representative on the CCC advisory council, made an inspection of portable-building camps. Colonel Major reported that most local camp commanders did not favour the barrack-huts, and that it was not clear yet that dismantling and re-erection would be easy.⁵⁹ Nevertheless, the issue of costs proved decisive: a report issued in early 1936 suggested that portable barracks were cheaper in the long run, and now they became the preferred choice. In addition, it had become clear that the prefabricated hut offered greater protection against twisters and hurricanes. "There are numerous recorded instances of portable structures, with men inside, having been lifted by wind off foundation posts with absolutely no resultant damage except for the labour incidental to dismantling and re-erecting on foundations."⁶⁰ At the same time, the need to continue to provide work for local builders put a brake on the use of the prefabricated huts, which could be put together by the CCC men themselves.⁶¹

The RAD and CCC Barrack-Huts Compared

Compared to the RAD barrack-huts, the CCC huts were simple if not crude. The two represent two different design cultures: the first was the product of the proverbial highly qualified German architect, and the second of the stereotypical Yankee mechanic (albeit with an army commission) who was guided by the desire to produce something that conformed to an utterly pragmatic standard. Yet, while less sophisticated in its concept and technology than the RAD barrack-

---

56 C. R. French, "A Workable Plan for Prefabricated Housing," in: *American Forests* 46 (1940): 512–13.
57 Guthrie and Tracy, "Portable Camp Buildings."
58 "President Orders the Civilian Conservation Corps Doubled," in: *American Forests* 41 (1935), 232.
59 Duncan K. Major, "Memorandum for Chief of Staff, War Department, Washington, DC, concerning visit to CCC camps in the IV, VI, VII, VIII, and IX Corps Areas," 1935, 1–15. Records of the Civilian Conservation Corps, grp. 35–6, vol. 3, item 404, National Archives, College Park, MD.
60 French, "A Workable Plan for Prefabricated Housing," 513.
61 *CCC Procedural Manual*, supplement no. 21, 23 November 1938, 433–34, Records of the Civilian Conservation Corps, grp. 35–11, 927, National Archives, College Park, MD.

hut, the standard CCC hut came with three key advantages. First: it could be built by any locals who knew how to drive a hammer onto a nail. Second: at 14 cubic metres per person, compared to the 8.7 cubic metres provided by the RAD barrack-hut, the CCC hut offered 1.6 times more space per enrolee, which meant that the CCC men did not have to sleep in bunk beds but enjoyed a single cot each. In fact, the space available to CCC men was even larger, because in the RAD barrack-hut the troop room served as both dormitory and as a day room, while in the CCC the two functions were separated in different buildings. If we compare only the dormitory parts of the two barrack-hut types, the CCC hut offered more than 2.2 times the amount of space per enrolee. Third: it offered this much more generous and healthful shelter at between one-quarter and one-fifth the cost of the FOKORAD product.[62]

More important, however, is the difference between the RAD and CCC barrack-huts as symbolic structures. Until 1933, no major organisation or institution was exclusively tied to the barrack. The wooden barrack had been developed for soldiers, but even if it acquired, at times, a high visibility as an architectural representation of the idea and reality of military life, it always competed with other building and shelter types: the fortress, the arsenal, the blockhouse, the casern, the multistorey brick or stone barracks, the tent, the bivouac. The same goes for the barrack-hut used in a medical context or as accommodation for labour involved in big infrastructure projects. Of course, during World War I the barrack-hut got a particularly strong association with prisoner-of-war and civilian internment camps. Yet these camps were, by their very nature, only temporary installations and did not represent the highest aspirations of the nations that built and maintained them. In addition, these camps consisted of many different kinds of barrack-huts, and as a matter of course the public was kept physically distant from these places, and the press did not print many photos of the physical environment within the barbed wire fences.

The CCC barrack-hut continued in the tradition of being first and foremost a tool to provide shelter, and it never acquired significance within the CCC as a symbol of the organisation itself, which, within the United States, never transcended its purpose of providing a temporary solution to the problem of mass unemployment of young men. The CCC never published books, articles, or pamphlets extolling the virtues of its barrack-huts as representations of its own – or for that matter, more general "democratic" or even "American" – values. Also, the CCC barrack-hut did not aim to provide in its architecture or interior arrangement an exact match to its organisational structure; sleeping, working, and

---

62 The typical portable CCC fifty-person barrack cost $510 (U.S.); the equivalent RAD barrack, a noninsulated Type IV/3, housed fifty-one men for a price of 5,671 Reichsmark or $2,270.

socialising were kept separate in the CCC. Men who worked together by day might not socialise together in the evening or share the same dormitory at night.

The RAD was, in that sense, radically different from the CCC. The RAD was key to the self-representation of the German Reich as a National Socialist state – made clear, for example, in the participation of thousands of RAD men in the annual Nuremberg rallies. Its camps presented the idea of a social harmony that transcended the struggle between classes, and also made manifest the idea that the National Socialists had put a nation back to work. The image of an early-morning assembly of troops of healthy-looking, blond men in a hutted camp, followed by a cheerful march to a moor, where they engaged in a day of constructive work, followed by a communal sing-along around an evening campfire, proved very enticing to the propagandists. Each *Zug*, consisting of three *Trupps*, occupied one barrack-hut, and the troop, housed in its *Truppstube* (troop room), was an inviolable unit. The sixteen men, led by the *Truppführer*, worked together in the field and lived together in the same room. This room was, as a handbook for enrolees in the RAD made clear, not only the place of the troop in the camp but also its embodiment as a living community. Labour service men were encouraged to make it into a communal home by drawing and framing pictures to put on the wall, providing the room with one or more meaningful quotes that expressed "a great thought," and to have vases with fresh flowers. "One is able to recognise in the presence or lack of domestic comfort of the troop room if the troop is structured in a spirit of collaboration and comradeship."[63] Thus the barrack-hut developed by Christoph & Unmack had become, by the end of 1934, the one and only architectural form, and it not only housed the labour service men but also represented the very idea of the labour service as the basic building block of a series of embedded communities, from troop to state.

The way the CCC and the RAD barrack-huts were assembled into camps also showed a different attitude. The American camp was not separated by a fence from the larger environment in which it stood, allowing men to wander off into the countryside whenever they were not at work. The German version, which ideologically was meant to be integrated into the landscape, was often defined by a clearly defined and fenced-in compound, and always marked with a gate that was guarded, around the clock, by an armed RAD labour service man – both suggesting and actually enforcing around-the-clock discipline and a sharp separation from the larger world around it.

---

63 Rolf von Gönner (ed.), *Spaten und Ähre: Das Handbuch der deutschen Jugend im Reichsarbeitsdienst* (Heidelberg: Kurt Vowinckel, 1938), 215.

The Labour Camps as Symbolic Structures

In 1937 the main author and director of the CCC program, Robert Fechner, wrote an article in which he considered the various achievements of his organisation. He also noted that the "big picture" full of statistics wasn't that meaningful, because the true meaning of the CCC was not to be found in its size or the scope of its activities, or even the benefits it did to society at large, but in the impact it had on each and every individual who participated it. "It has produced men who have retained and increased their own initiative and ability to think and to act independently," Fechner proudly observed. "The individual enrollee has been made to feel responsibilities and his worth as a person, rather than to regard himself as a cog in some great organization."[64] In the CCC the individual was more important than the collective because, in the end, the CCC was not burdened with the task to radically renew society. In the United States, the Constitution adopted exactly 150 years earlier provided a stable foundation for the life of the nation, and the great institutions of the state and the way they worked were, despite the many innovative aspects of the New Deal, not subject to a revolutionary transformation.

In the Third Reich things were different – at least in the official ideology. In 1933 the Nazis claimed that the revolution they had begun had transformed Germany into a country *im Aufbruch* (figuratively, "in a state of renewal"; literally, "in a state of decampment"). Camps located outside of the bounds of civil society were to be the key sites in the social revolution that Hitler had promised. In 1934 the publicist Albrecht E. Günther evoked the variety of these camps. "There are camps in tents and houses, camps for thirty and for several hundred, even 1,000 participants; there are camps that concentrate on physical labour and others that concentrate on mental training; camps that hardly last one week and permanent camps whose members change every six weeks or every six months; camps with a full-time permanent staff and others that cope with a minimum of fixed organisation." Günther lauded the "great multitude of purposes" of these camps and noticed that they created "an incalculable variety of special communities." And he noted that, at sunset, "camp teams fall in for evening colours all over Germany."[65]

Three years later the concept of a society in a state of decampment was still strong, at least in the self-representation of the German nation. "The camp as a place of training and as a place of spiritual resurrection has conquered the whole of Germany in an incomparable triumphal progress," educator Adolf Mertens

---

64 Robert Fechner, "The Civilian Conservation Corps Program," in: *Annals of the American Academy of Political and Social Science* 194 (November 1937): 140.
65 Albrecht E. Günther, "Das Lager," in: *Deutsches Volkstum* (1934): 809.

observed. "The current camp form is a unique phenomenon. No nation and no epoch can show something similar. In the past, no state of society would have been able to grasp the idea of the camp and to realise it in the modern sense." The camp was the tool that transformed a civilian into a National Socialist comrade. It was the location where the ideal – from a Nazi perspective – social form of the *Lagerkameradschaft* (camp comradeship) could arise, a society in which all shared the same rhythm of life and in which social standing, financial prosperity, professional reputation, bourgeois manners, and carefully cultivated personal eccentricities not only were utterly irrelevant but also were mocked. A key element in the reduction of each multifaceted individual to a typical specimen of the German man was a strict hierarchy. "Marching in step and keeping in line are the foundations on which the camp is based," Mertens acknowledged, and he added: "The truly free person approves of this constraint through intrinsic conviction and follows it willingly." Thus the camp forges a sense of comradeship. "The miraculous experience of community embraces all like an inseverable bond. It carries the certainty of togetherness into daily life, into the community of the nation. In this manner the camp fulfils one of its purposes: we become a single people."[66] Of all the camps Günther and Mertens had described, the RAD camps were to remain at the core of the Third Reich. "We can no longer imagine doing without you," Hitler told the RAD men at the 1937 Nuremberg rally. "It is an edifying thought to know that, long into the most distant future, generation after generation will shoulder the weapon of peace – the spade – and report for duty at the service of our community and thus for our *Volk*."[67]

Because the RAD camps provided the largest, most consistent, and most visible core of the camp universe suggested by Günther and invoked by Mertens, and because they were to remain at the core of Germany "into the most distant future," they became symbolic of all the others. And the RAD barrack-hut defined the appearance of the RAD camp.

Conclusion

The CCC was abolished in 1942, when the United States began to draft healthy young men into the armed forces. Many CCC camps were dismantled, but some found a new use as places where conscientious objectors could perform "work of national importance" in lieu of military service. Other camps were taken over by

---

66 Adolf Mertens, *Schulungslager und Lagererziehung* (Dortmund and Breslau: Crüwell, 1937), 3, 15–16.
67 Adolf Hitler, speech given to the men of the *Reichsarbeitsdienst*, 8 September 1937, in: Hitler, *Speeches and Proclamations*, 2: 928.

programs established by the U.S. Army's Western Defense Command to intern not only "enemy aliens" but also American citizens of Japanese ancestry. The CCC barrack-huts never became deathtraps for these involuntary occupants, yet their role in a squalid chapter of American history provides its otherwise upbeat trajectory with a sad and shameful shadow.

The legacy of the RAD barrack-hut is one of utter darkness. By the time Hitler spoke at the 1937 Nuremberg rally, the RAD barrack-hut had also become the standard shelter in another kind of camp – one that came to define Nazi Germany in the collective memory of the world: the SS-run concentration camp. There is an old curse: "May you get what you wish for." Konstantin Hierl had hoped the RAD would become a symbol of the Nazi state as a folkish community, and the inventors and builders of the RAD barrack-hut had worked hard to elevate the barrack-hut, until then a weed in the garden of architectural types, into the primary architectural embodiment of the RAD. But when the government asked FOKORAD to design versions for use in forced labour camps, camps for Soviet prisoners of war and others it called "subhumans," and camps for non-Soviet prisoners of war, it complied. And by cramming more bunks into the troop room with a few strokes of their pens, the architects easily increased the barrack-huts' capacity. In the 1942 version designated for Soviet prisoners of war, also to be used in concentration camps, bunks were replaced by superimposed sleeping platforms, and now a troop room was meant to house thirty-six prisoners.[68]

In the concentration camps, the density of occupation was often twice or thrice the official maximum. Prisoners were packed together in each space, and the still healthy were forced to share whatever portion of bunk assigned to them with the sick, the very sick, and the dead. "It is man who kills, man who creates or suffers injustice; it is no longer man who, having lost all restraint, shares his bed with a corpse,"[69] Primo Levi wrote in 1946, recalling the last days of his imprisonment in Auschwitz-Monowitz, in a RAD barrack modified for use in prison camps.

When units of the British Army entered the Bergen-Belsen concentration camp on 15 April 1945, they encountered a catastrophe: everywhere, they saw sick and dying prisoners – mostly Jews – sharing space with corpses in filthy RAD barrack-huts. The British soldiers made a heroic effort to bury the dead and move the living to a nearby army base. On 19 May, the last of the survivors left the Belsen compound. Immediately thereafter, an armoured vehicle, the Vickers-Armstrong Mk. II Universal Carrier, drove towards the now abandoned wooden barrack-huts and used a flamethrower to set them ablaze.

The burning of the last barrack-hut happened on 21 May, with a bit of staging

---

68 Stangelmayer, *Hilfsbuch 1*, 18.
69 Primo Levi, *If This Is a Man*, trans. Stuart Woolf (New York: Orion Press, 1959), 204.

Fig. 4: The burning of the last barrack-hut of the Bergen-Belsen concentration camp. (Photo: Bert Hardy. Collection Robert Jan van Pelt)

orchestrated by the British commanding officer, Colonel H. W. Bird. He arranged for a 1933 model of the war ensign, the Reich flag carrying an image of the Prussian iron cross, to be nailed to the structure, along with a large portrait of Hitler. And he ordered the erection of a large stake in front of the barrack-hut, to serve as a flagpole. Sergeant Bert Hardy, who had been photographing in Belsen for a month, carefully arrayed the rest of the scene for posterity. The barrack-hut itself was soaked in gasoline and, after a few words from Colonel Bird and volley shots fired as a salute to the dead, set on fire. The crowd of soldiers and some survivors cheered, the Union Jack fluttered from the top of the flagpole, and the shutter of Sergeant Hardy's Leica clicked (Fig. 4: The burning of the last barrack-hut of the Bergen-Belsen concentration camp).[70]

---

70 See Ian Bevan, "Union Jack Raised over Ruins of Belsen," in: *Sydney Morning Herald*, 23 May

That defiant auto-da-fé ended a relatively limited act of physical erasure – sixty barrack-huts burned – and began a larger process of forgetting, at least where it concerned the barrack-huts. Sergeant Hardy's picture suggests that this barrack-hut, and by implication all the RAD barrack-huts, *deserved* to disappear from human memory. And this implication may be just: the Allied discovery of the horrors contained within the RAD barrack-huts of Bergen-Belsen and the other German camps continues to mark a moment of truth from which the imagination has not yet recovered.

1945, 1; Michael John Hargrave, *Bergen-Belsen 1945: A Medical Student's Journal* (London: Imperial College Press, 2014), 68–69.

Heidrun Zettelbauer

Unwanted Desire and Processes of Self-Discipline. Autobiographical Representations of the *Reichsarbeitsdienst* Camps in the Diary of a Young Female National Socialist

She fell "right in love"[1] with her camp leader – this is how the young female National Socialist, hereafter referred to as Gerta Zaczek, retrospectively described the relationship with her superior in a camp for the *Reichsarbeitsdienst für die weibliche Jugend* (RADwJ) [*Reich* labour service for young females] in her diary. Considering the absolute compliance with heterosexual gender norms which characterised Zaczek's self-narrations elsewhere, this choice of words is astonishing. It is generally known that the National Socialist regime established living environments for youth as gender specific and homosocial spaces, and the extent to which they did so was unprecedented. At the same time, homosexuality was considered a criminal offense and grounds for persecution in the so-called *Ostmark*, which allowed people to be brought to court, jail or concentration camps during the 'Third Reich' period. In the following text, the records in Zaczek's diary serve as a starting point and objects of analysis, which raise the question of how narrow the gap was between the desired homosociality and the unwanted/forbidden homoerotic/homosexual desire in camps for *Volksgenossinnen* [national comrades]. I will specifically deal with this question in the context of the *Reichsarbeitdienst* (RAD)[2] and discuss it from perspectives of contemporary history and in its dimensions of life writing. The analysis focuses on the autobiographical representation of 'the camp space', which is revealed in Gerta Zaczek's diary.

---

1 Cf. [Gerta Zaczek], Diary, in: Universitätsbibliothek Graz (UBG), Sondersammlungen (SoSa), bequest [Dr. Gerta Zaczek], Mar 13, 1943, 85 (quoted subsequently as: [Zaczek], Diary). I cordially thank Stefan Benedik for fruitful discussions on this case study and for his very helpful feedback.
2 Cf. Jill Stephenson, "Der Arbeitsdienst für die weibliche Jugend," in: Dagmar Reese (ed.), *Die BDM-Generation. Weibliche Jugendliche in Deutschland und Österreich im Nationalsozialismus* (Berlin: Verlag für Berlin-Brandenburg 2007), 255–288, here 270. (Potsdamer Studien 19).

Introduction and Research Questions

Until now, most research on female homosexuality in National Socialist camps has been conducted on the living conditions and the experiences of women who were persecuted by the regime. Comparatively few studies have been done on women, however, who were considered to be members of the Aryan *Volksgemeinschaft* or who advocated National Socialism and supported its ideologies with conviction. Since the 1990s, historians who have dealt with the topic of female homosexuality during the period of National Socialism[3] have consistently pointed out that the analysis of the living conditions of lesbian women during this period has had to integrate research on female (co-)perpetrators, sympathisers, fellow runners, informers or resistance fighters.[4] When referring to the work of Ulrike Janz, we have to assume that lesbian women, on the one hand, were oppressed in the camps on all levels and in every possible way and, in turn, potentially were in the position to suppress others as well. On the other hand, 'lesbian behaviour' in camp contexts can be interpreted as "a multitude of possible actions that have to be judged as ranging from absolutely positive kinds of behaviour (indicating affection, love, care, tenderness, indicating the aim of survival or solidarity) to absolutely negative ones (coercion, forced prostitution,

---

3 Cf. the pioneer studies of Claudia Schoppmann, *Nationalsozialistische Sexualpolitik und weibliche Homosexualität*. 2nd ed. (Pfaffenweiler: Centaurus Verlag, 1997). (Frauen in Geschichte und Gesellschaft 30); Claudia Schoppmann, *Zeit der Maskierung. Lebensgeschichten lesbischer Frauen im "Dritten Reich"* (Berlin: Orlanda Frauenverlag, 1993). Also: Gudrun Hauer, "Lesben und Nationalsozialismus: Blinde Flecken in der Faschismustheoriediskussion," in: *Que(e)rdenken. Weibliche/männliche Homosexualität und Wissenschaft*, edited by Barbara Hey et al. (Innsbruck – Wien: Studienverlag, 1997), 142–156 (Simul: lambda nachrichten, June 2001, 46–52); Ilse Kokula, "Zur Situation lesbischer Frauen während der NS-Zeit," *nirgendwo und überall. Lesben. Beiträge zur feministischen Theorie und Praxis* 12 (1989) 25/26: 29–36. As an overview and concerning research desiderata, cf. Claudia Schoppmann, "Lesbische Frauen und weibliche Homosexualität im Dritten Reich. Forschungsperspektiven," in: *Homosexuelle im Nationalsozialismus*, edited by Michael Schwartz (Oldenburg: Oldenburg Wissenschaftsverlag, 2014), 85–91. (Zeitgeschichte im Gespräch 18). Concerning Austria cf. Angela H. Mayer, "'Schwachsinn höheren Grades'. Zur Verfolgung lesbischer Frauen während der NS-Zeit," in: *Nationalsozialistischer Terror gegen Homosexuelle. Verdrängt und ungesühnt*, edited by Burkhard Jellonek and Rüdiger Lautmann (Paderborn – München – Wien – Zürich: Ferdinand Schöningh, 2002), 83–96. Concerning theoretical debates on the problem of homogenised victimisation, cf. Gudrun Hauer, "Nationalsozialismus und Homosexualität: Anmerkungen zum 'lesbischen Opferdiskurs,'" in: *l[i]eben und Begehren zwischen Geschlecht und Identität*, edited by Maria Froihofer et al. (Wien: Löcker, 2010), 132–138; Elisa Heinrich, "Marginalisierte Erinnerung. Auseinandersetzungen um homosexuelle NS-Opfer in Nachkriegsösterreich," in: *zeitgeschichte* 43 (2016) 2: 101–115; Corinna Tomberger, "Homosexuellen-Geschichtsschreibung und Subkultur. Geschlechertheoretische und normativitätskritische Perspektiven," in: Schwartz (ed.), *Homosexuelle im Nationalsozialismus*, 19–26.
4 Cf. Schoppmann, "Lesbische Frauen."

violence)".[5] Janz, who has studied the evidence of female homosexuality in Nazi concentration camps for a long period of time, has convincingly referred to the problem of historical sources and explained that "being lesbian" always has to be interpreted as a "cultural sign" in the autobiographical documents of survivors. In a similar way, Insa Eschebach interpreted representations of female homosexuality in the autobiographical and literary testimonies of survivors from the Ravensbrück women's concentration camp by referring to theories of othering.[6]

Unlike its treatment in the works of Janz and Eschebach, the question of gender, self-representation and homosociality/homoeroticism/homosexuality will be examined in the following text by placing a focus on so-called "inclusion camps"[7]. These were camps that were set up to integrate the *Volksgenossinnen*[8]

---

5 Originally Janz: Andererseits bezeichnet "lesbisches Verhalten" dort "eine Vielzahl von Handlungen, die von absolut positiv (Zuneigung, Liebe, Fürsorge, Zärtlichkeit, überlebensnotwendig, solidarisch) bis absolut negativ (Nötigung, Zwangs-Prostitution, Gewalt) zu beurteilen sind." Cf. Ulrike Janz, "Das 'Zeichen lesbisch' in den nationalsozialistischen Konzentrationslagern," in: Schwartz (ed.), *Homosexuelle im Nationalsozialismus*, 77–84, here 82.

6 Cf. Insa Eschebach, "Homophobie, Devianz und weibliche Homosexualität im Konzentrationslager Ravensbrück," in: idem (ed.), *Homophobie und Devianz. Weibliche und männliche Homosexualität im Nationalsozialismus* (Berlin: Metropol Verlag, 2012), 65–78. (Forschungsbeiträge und Materialien der Stiftung Brandenburgische Gedenkstätten 6).

7 Cf. Kiran Klaus Patel, "Volksgenossen und Gemeinschaftsfremde. Über den Doppelcharakter der nationalsozialistischen Lager," in: *Lager vor Auschwitz. Gewalt und Integration im 20. Jhdt.*, edited by Christoph Jahr and Jens Thiel (Berlin: Metropol Verlag, 2013), 311–334.

8 Dealing with the differentiated situation of women under the NS regime, gender historians have presented research on female protagonists of the Aryan *Volksgemeinschaft* in the last 20 years, emphasizing the highly complex positions and positionings of women as (co)perpetrators, sympathizers, supporters and profiteurs of the NS regime and broadly examining the NS organisations which explicitly adressed female 'national comrades'. Cf. Sybille Steinbacher (ed.), *Volksgenossinnen. Frauen in der NS-Volksgemeinschaft* (Göttingen: Wallstein Verlag, 2007), 9–16, here 13. Cf. Ingrid Bauer, "Eine frauen- und geschlechtergeschichtliche Perspektivierung des Nationalsozialismus," in: *NS-Herrschaft in Österreich. Ein Handbuch*, edited by Emmerich Tálos et al., 1st. ed. (Wien: Verlag für Gesellschaftskritik, 2000), 409–445, here 418. Exemplarily cf. Johanna Gehmacher and Gabriella Hauch (eds.), *Frauen- und Geschlechtergeschichte des Nationalsozialismus. Fragestellungen, Perspektiven, neue Forschungen* (Innsbruck – Wien – Bozen: StudienVerlag, 2007). (Querschnitte. Einführungstexte zur Sozial-, Wirtschafts- und Kulturgeschichte 23); Marita Krauss (ed.), *Sie waren dabei. Mitläuferinnen, Nutznießerinnen, Täterinnen im Nationalsozialismus*, 2nd ed. (Göttingen: Wallstein Verlag, 2009). (Dachauer Symposien zur Zeitgeschichte 8). – Concerning Austria cf. especially the works of Johanna Gehmacher, i. e. "Selbstdarstellungen und Allianzen. 'Völkische' Frauen in Österreich," in: *Gebrochene Kontinuitäten? Zur Rolle und Bedeutung des Geschlechterverhältnisses in der Entwicklung des Nationalsozialismus*, edited by Ilse Korotin and Barbara Serloth (Innsbruck – Wien – München: StudienVerlag, 2000), 216–233; idem, "'Ostmarkmädel'. Anmerkungen zum Illegalen Bund Deutscher Mädel in Österreich (1933–1938)," in: *TöchterFragen: NS-Frauen-Geschichte*, edited by Lerke Gravenhorst and Carmen Tatschmurat (Freiburg in Breisgau: Kore Verlag, 1990 [2nd ed. 1995]), 253–269 (in the following, the pages refer to the edition of 1990). Particularly dealing with the aspect of individual participation, processes of (self) mobilising for and integration into the *Volksgemeinschaft* cf. Sybille Steinbacher. "Einleitung," in: Steinbacher (ed.), *Volksgenossin-*

and especially young adults into the imagined National Socialist Aryan community. Zaczek's diary documents how strongly her processes of growing up and self-discovery were connected to the structural and ideological conditions of National Socialism. This socio-political context limited her potential to act and think, but she also profited personally as member of the National Socialist *Volksgemeinschaft*.

I analyse the life history and autobiographical narration of Zaczek as a member of the specific "BDM generation",[9] who were born in the early 1920s. Their individual detachment from the parental home occurred in parallel to the political and cultural socialisation process within Nazi youth organisations. Historian Johanna Gehmacher attested a "particularly high and difficult-to-solve degree of identification with National Socialism" to this generation.[10] A few biographical cornerstones support such positioning: According to the prescribed extension of the RADwJ duration from six to twelve months that occurred in mid-1941[11], Gerta Zaczek spent a full year on duty for the RAD up until the end of March 1942. In her case, the relevant convocation office was in Breslau/Wrocław (*RAD-Heimatamt* No. 215),[12] where she had been born in 1923. She grew up with two younger brothers in a prosperous bourgeois household, living in the small town of Chrzanów/Krenau[13] in the Polish voivodeship of Krakow in an idyllic countryside and multilingual German-Czech-Polish environment. Her mother was born (and grew up) in Graz, her father, who was a graduate from the University of Leoben, headed a large mining company in Chrzanów. We can

---

nen, 13–14. Steinbacher especially deals with the aspect of individual bonding towards the NS regime, which is also at the center of the following case study on [Gerta Zaczek].

9 Cf. Dagmar Reese, "Einleitung," in: Reese, *Die BDM-Generation*, 9–39.

10 Cf. Johanna Gehmacher, "Biografie, Geschlecht und Organisation. Der nationalsozialistische 'Bund Deutscher Mädel' in Österreich," in: Tálos et al. (ed.), *NS-Herrschaft in Österreich*, 467–493, here 489.

11 Cf. Christina Altenstraßer, "Zwischen Ideologie und ökonomischer Notwendigkeit. Der 'Reichsarbeitsdienst für die weibliche Jugend'," in: *Frauen im Reichsgau Oberdonau. Geschlechtsspezifische Bruchlinien im Nationalsozialismus*, edited by Gabriella Hauch (Linz: OÖLA, 2006), 107–108. (Oberösterreich in der Zeit des Nationalsozialismus 5).

12 She had to "swear her oath to the Führer" as usual on April 20. Zaczeks ID card from the RADwJ listed the following positions: "15/224/7/5, am 2.4.41 eingestellt als Amd. [recruited as labour maiden] Vz. zu 15/224 Kärntnerhof [sent to Kärntnerhof]; 15/224/1/8F, am 1.8.41 B apl. Kam. Älteste [comrade elder]; 15/224/1/8, am 1.10.41 B Kam. Älteste [comrade elder]; 15/224/1/8, am 4.10.41 Av. z. 16/224; 16/224/9/8, am 5.10.41 Zv. V. 15/224 Kärntnerhof; 16/224/9/8, am 3.3.42 Av. n. 8/221 Rosegg; 8/221/8/6, am 4.3.42 Zv. v. 16/224 Faak; 8/221/8/6, 31.3.1942 entlassen als K.Ä. [dismissed as comrade elder]; Führung: vorzüglich; Entlassendes RAD-Meldeamt: L.p. [qualification certificate very good, unreadable signature]; Eignung: RAD-Führerin [qualified as RAD leader]; gez. E. Jakob". ID card from the RADwJ, [Gerta Zaczek], UBG, SoSa, bequest [Gerta Zaczek].

13 1939 occupied by the German Wehrmacht, the region then was named "Krenau" by the NS authorities.

reconstruct a strong German nationalist socialisation tendency within the family.[14] After her father lost his job in 1933, the mother decided to return to Austria with her three small children without her husband. Gerta Zaczek, who had been educated by private tutors up until then, started school in fall 1933 in the private High School of the Ursulines for girls. Her academic achievements were outstanding; her class teacher attested several times that she had an "above-average talent" and "mental agility"[15].

We can prove, at latest in April 1937, that Zaczek was taking part illegally in the Nazi *Jungmädelbund* (JMB) [Young Girls' Association] – at that time, she was 14 years old. She quickly ascended the ranks within the organisational hierarchy:[16] At the age of 16, she had assumed the position of a *Ringführerin* [ringleader] in the city of Graz and, by gaining this position, had already attained the highest level for a *Führerin* [leader] in the Styrian *Untergau*, maintaining close contacts with the area leadership and the upper-level management of the local *Hitlerjugend* (HJ) [Hitler Youth]. Her commitment to the JMB was already characterised by her participation in regular weekend training sessions and in various camps as well as by her personal pursuit of political education. For instance, she attended public political lectures in the context of the HJ-*Obergauführung* [Obergau leader corps], undoubtedly at the expense of her school performance.[17] The Styrian leading corps of the *HJ-Obergau* at least saw a future for Zaczek as a professional full-time leader in the *Bund Deutscher Mädel* (BDM) [League of German Girls].[18] From December 1940 and on, Zaczek was engaged with the *Notdienstverpflichtung* [Emergency Services], and she worked as a camp leader in the *Umsiedlerlager* [resettlement camp] in Graz-Liebenau. This camp was built for members of the so-called *Buchenlanddeutsche*, who voluntarily returned *Heim ins Reich* [home to the German realm] from the summer of 1940 and on in compliance with the Hitler-Stalin-Pact. Zaczek directed the female pupils' home there.[19] Immediately afterwards, she began her so-called

---

14 Cf. *The life story of [Erna Zaczek]*, brochure published in 2003, bequest [Gerta Zaczek], UBG, SoSa, 10–28, 31.
15 Cf. School certificate of [Gerta Zaczek], student of the 7th class Oberschule for Girls, Language Branch, school year 1939/40, July 6 1940, UBG, SoSa, bequest [Gerta Zaczek]. – Certificate for the first third of the current school year [Gerta Zaczek], student in the 7th class of Oberschule for Girls, 20.12.1939, UBG, SoSa, bequest [Gerta Zaczek].
16 In March 1938 [Zaczek] was named a "JM-Scharführerin", in November 1939, named a "Jungmädelringführerin". She afterwards switched from the *Untergau* city of Graz to the *Untergau* surroundings of Graz, became a "JM-Gruppenführerin" and was occupied from the winter of 1940 to April 1941 as "Jungmädelhauptgruppenführerin".
17 Cf. Heidrun Zettelbauer, *Sich der Nation ver|schreiben. Politiken von Geschlecht und nationaler Zugehörigkeit in autobiographischen Selbstzählungen von Akteurinnen des völkischen Milieus*, unpublished habilitation thesis (Graz 2016) (forthcoming), 265–270.
18 Cf. [Zaczek], Diary, Jan 2, 1941, 40.
19 Concerning the resettlement camp at Graz-Liebenau, cf. Barbara Stelzl-Marx, *Das Lager*

Pflichtjahr [compulsory year of service] in the RAD, and was assigned to the camp *Kärntnerhof* in the *Arbeitsgau Klagenfurt*,[20] where she achieved the rank of a comrade elder [*Kameradschaftsälteste*] four months later.[21] In her post-war narration in the context of the denazification, Zaczek retrospectively constructed an alienation from National Socialism that had increased since her school graduation (in the spring of 1941). Despite this construction, she still noted in her diary in December 1941 that she had begun to sympathize intensely with the NS labour service during her compulsory year of service. At the end of December of that year, she voluntarily signed a renewal of her RADwJ commitment for another three years. Although she withdrew this request for renewal only 10 days later and decided to refrain from performing professional full-time activity as a RADwJ leader, this decision was hardly because she was distancing herself from National Socialism. On the contrary, up until the end of the war, her commitment to the NS regime was as obvious as her integration into various National Socialist organisations. After leaving the RAD in the spring of 1942, Zaczek began to study at Heidelberg University where she was active in the *Arbeitsgemeinschaft nationalsozialistischer Studentinnen* (ANSt.) [Association for National Socialist Female Students].[22] Thus, the entangled influences of different NS youth organizations, members of which tried to access the young National Socialist, prove to be significant for her biography. Zaczek's personal testimonies and especially her diary records simultaneously document scopes of action, which she used to pursue her personal interests as a committed adherent to National Socialism. These sources also indicate how she was able to evade the regime's attempts to access to her as individual subject.

Zaczek's (personal) integration into the NS *Volksgemeinschaft* prototypically

---

Graz-Liebenau in der NS-Zeit. Zwangsarbeiter–Todesmärsche–Nachkriegsjustiz (Graz: Leykam Verlag, 2012), 15. (Veröffentlichungen des Ludwig-Boltzmann-Instituts für Kriegsfolgen-Forschung 20). Stelzl-Marx regrettably only deals with the history of the early resettlement camp in a side note, but focusses primarily on its following function and reuse as camp for forced labourers, respectively, as a layover during the death marches of Hungarian jews. The latter were forced by the regime to march to the concentration camp in Mauthausen at the end of war. Cf. Steiermärkisches Landesarchiv (StLA), Contemporary History Collection (ZGS), Karton 177, Volksdeutsche Mittelstelle, Umsiedler, VOMI 1, 1940/44.

20 The RADwJ-camp *Kärntnerhof* can presumably be identified as camp 3/221 in the *Arbeitsgau Klagenfurt*, located in the district of Müllnern in today's municipality of Finkenstein. The camp was housed in an existing building, a former forging hammer, in which the young working women lived (Warmbaderstraße 38, Finkenstein). The building belonged to the property of the pasta factory Finkenstein, in which they worked. It is listed currently as a landmarked building, cf. Kärntner Denkmalschutzgebäude Nr. 74527, https://de.wikipedia.org/wiki/Liste_der_denkmalgesch%C3%BCtzten_Objekte_in_Finkenstein_am_Faaker_See (3 October 2018).

21 Cf. ID card of the RADwJ, [Gerta Zaczek], UBG, SoSa, bequest [Gerta Zaczek].

22 Cf. Zettelbauer, *Sich der Nation ver | schreiben*, 274.

took place in camps[23]: These included those of the JMB, the BDM, weekend training and education camps for (aspiring) leaders and functionaries, who had already advanced far within the administration or the NSDAP and, last but not least, in the RADwJ camps. The camp as a physical as well as a socio-cultural space determined Zaczek's individual political-ideological socialisation process. She spent the period between December 1940 and March 1942 almost entirely in NS inclusion camps with only a few, short interruptions. This camp experience structured her later life concept in spatial as well as temporal terms; in particular, the compulsory year of service in the RADwJ represents a significant biographical caesura. Zaczek's self-narration in her diary documents – as will be shown in the following – the strict gender segregation that occurred in the RAD camps as well as the significant spatial narrowness of the described sites, continual disciplinary efforts and daily attempts by members of the administration or leader corps to make the camp inmates feel insecure. At the same time, however, the individual way she handled these political-cultural and spatial requirements will become clear. In the context of the thematic description of 'the camp', positive aspects of close social relationships as well as homoerotic desire become clearly visible. The initial hypothesis being explored in the present paper is that the daily life in the camp allowed social practises to become established which hardly fit into the politically desired (and also affirmed by Zaczek), heteronormatively anchored, National Socialist image of the *neuer Mensch* [new human being], who should be prototypically created in the camps. This discrepancy apparently led the young National Socialist frequently to the limit of what she could describe or note in her diary records.

In order to contextualise Zaczek's autobiographical representation of the camp and discuss the reflections that appear in her diary on the relationship with 'her camp leader' adequately with respect to historical aspects of the time and gender images, several relevant aspects will be addressed here: The strict gender segregation in the context of inclusion camps, its connex to homosociality and homosexuality as well as the RAD(wJ)-camp as a prototype for camps for *Volksgenossinnen*. I will discuss these aspects in the second section of the article. The results of the present study show that the *Reichsarbeitsdienst* – unlike hardly any other National Socialist organisation – attempted to completely, and even totally, include the working men and young women through the *Lagerdienst* [labour service]. Nevertheless, it would be inadequate to quickly contrast the ideological goals and hegemonic political discourse with diverging or converg-

---

23 Patel warns against essentializing or homogenizing 'the camp' as it is defined in NS contexts. Cf. Patel, "Volksgenossen und Gemeinschaftsfremde," 313. Nevertheless, I suggest in this context to work with a broadly defined term of the camp, specifically understanding the camp as a social structure that – as will be shown – functioned not only in terms of a space, but also (without spatially considerations) as a sociocultural configuration.

ing 'social practices' that occurred during the daily life in the camps. In accordance with the concept of this present volume, however, the following sections also include a focus on forms of agency and the ways in which the addressed young female adults could assume the roles of protagonists with specific scopes of action. The analysis of 'the Zaczek case study' outlines how and with what motives the subjects that were addressed by the regime could control the process of the intended ideological subordination – at least up to a certain extent. The focus of the autobiographical representations discussed here is not only placed on the norms that structured the 'space of the camp', but also on the processes of attachment between the self and the ideological guidelines that took place in the camp context.

In particular, I want to investigate distortions along the matrix of desired homosociality and forbidden homosexuality. If the term "homosociality", according to Michael Meuser, can be understood as "reciprocal orientation [...] toward members of the same sex",[24] the National Socialist camp communities can be described as living environments in which wo/men mutually confirmed their 'normality' and their sense of 'being adequate' regarding their own world views or understandings of society, politics and culture.[25] Moreover, the concept of space applied in this context primarily implies that the 'social production of space' is a multi-layered and often contradictory process. It implies a localisation of cultural practices, which points to the dynamics of social relationships as well as the changeability of space. Analyses that position themselves within the context of the *spatial turn* allow researchers to examine processes of politicisation/depoliticization, naturalisation and the symbolisation of space in the widest sense. They also permit examinations of the social constitution of spatial areas and (conversely) the importance of space in the process of creating social relations.[26] From the standpoint of researchers working in the field of Gender Theory, however, power relations that occur in different spaces prove to be of particular relevance as do processes of exclusion/inclusion or appropriation of space.[27] Within such a theoretical framework, socio-cultural spaces are understood as contradictory, ambiguous or unclear assignable categories of human

---

24 Cf. Michael Meuser, "Männerwelten. Zur kollektiven Konstruktion hegemonialer Männlichkeit," in: *Schriften des Essener Kollegs für Geschlechterforschung* 1 (2001) 2, 13. Quoted after Martin Dröge, *Männlichkeit und 'Volksgemeinschaft'. Der westfälische Landeshauptmann Karl Friedrich Kolbow (1899–1945): Biografie eines NS Täters* (Paderborn: Ferdinand Schöningh, 2015), 51. (Forschungen zur Regionalgeschichte).
25 Cf. Dröge, *Männlichkeit*, 51.
26 Cf. ibidem, 289, 291, 292–302.
27 Gerald Lamprecht, Ursula Mindler and Heidrun Zettelbauer, "Zonen der Begrenzung. Aspekte kultureller und räumlicher Grenzen in der Moderne," in: idem (eds.), Zonen der Begrenzung. Aspekte kultureller und räumlicher Grenzen in der Moderne (Bielefeld: [transcript]-Verlag, 2012), 11. (Edition Kulturwissenschaft).

order. When conducting a gender-sensitive historical analysis, taking such approach is of interest as well as the emphasis placed on the 'lack of agreement' concerning spatial/border concepts – particularly regarding a given gender order.[28] Accordingly, the focus here is placed on defining conflicts related to (gender) spaces, their ambivalence, shifts and transgressions that take place in different socio-cultural spaces or the individual/collective strategies that are used to cope with discrepancies between the mentioned aspects.[29] The following sections of the article do not address the material dimensions of space in RAD camps as strongly as they address its socio-cultural dimensions, inherent hierarchies and the im/possible performance of inmates living and acting in such contexts. How did Zaczek portray the homosocialism demanded by the regime while excluding and ultimately 'weeding out' the unwanted homoerotic desire and forbidden homosexuality? How did she depict mutual attraction, physical closeness and/or desire in the camp context in her diary records? Which power relations are inscribed into the camp space, and in which way were these aspects constitutive for the social relations among the *Arbeitsmaiden* [young working women] as well as with their superordinate leaders? What did a committed young female National Socialist like Zaczek make of the gestures of personal subjugation that occurred in the context of the camp? What sorts of symbolic capital, in the sense of Pierre Bourdieu, did she negotiate for?

Contextualisation

Ultimately, it turns out to be irrelevant whether Gerta Zaczek, in the throes of an adolescent crush, imagined having a homoerotic relationship with 'her camp leader', only hinted at such a relationship in her diary or actually had a love affair with the woman. Zaczek's diary entries are too vague and ambiguous to come to a clear conclusion about this. Instead, I am interested in conducting an analysis of the cultural perceptions of 'the self' and 'the other', which are expressed in Zaczek's personal reflections in her diary. These reflections develop against the backdrop of various historically relevant parameters. I would like to examine three of these in detail here: First, the strict gender segregation that occurred in the RADwJ camps and – associated with this – the relation between homosociality and homosexuality. Second, I will examine basic discourse strategies on

---

28 Ibid.
29 Concerning the term space that I use here, cf. Heidrun Zettelbauer, "Das fragile Geschlecht der Kriegsheldin. Diskursivierungen weiblicher Heilungs- und Verletzungsmacht im Ersten Weltkrieg," in: *Heroes. Repräsentationen des Heroischen in Geschichte, Literatur und Alltag*, edited by Johanna Rolshoven et al. (Bielefeld: [transcript] Verlag, 2018), 91–126. (Edition Kulturwissenschaft).

'being a lesbian' in the context of Nazi camps and, third, I will study the RAD camp as a prototype of the camp for national comrades. From the perspective of the regime, this type of camp was created to ideally re/produce the 'new National Socialist human being'.

The RADwJ Camp as a Gender-Segregated Space. Fine Lines between the Desired and the Forbidden

National Socialism organised those institutional policies that addressed the German youth and young adults in gender-segregated spaces to an unprecedented extent. This was particularly the case in the camps, which brought the young national comrades together. Such structural conditions draw the attention fundamentally toward the connection between the desired gender segregation and the supposedly concomitant homosociality and unwanted/forbidden homoeroticism/homosexuality. In general, it is useful to reflect on the relationship between homosociality and homosexuality in National Socialism from the perspective of the hegemonic culture and dominant social debates of the time and consider the negotiation of sexuality in the context of national (socialist) concepts and processes of nation building. It is well-known that the fears concerning the "purity of the German national body" and the National Socialist obsessions about the intended production of "racial purity" or the intended elimination of "social degeneration" – which were clearly expressed also in debates on homosexuality[30] – reveal not only the contradictory and inconsistent nature of the cultural images of sexuality propagated by National Socialism, but also refer to a racialisation of homosexuality. However, in light of this knowledge, the culturally constructed 'otherness' of homosexuality – which appears in various contemporary sources with regard to national citizens as well as persecuted people[31] – should by no means be maintained as part of a critical historical research process. Instead, the mechanisms of constructing 'the other' as processes involved in constituting the NS *Volksgemeinschaft* must be investigated. In hegemonic debates, these usually function as the 'centre' of culture and society, even if they are not explicitly designated. Regardless of the heteronormative political discourse, sexuality in National Socialism was neither homogeneous nor "unaffected by its margins", but has to be regarded – according to W. Spurlin – in principle as "fluid

---

30 Cf. Dagmar Herzog, *Die Politisierung der Lust. Sexualität in der deutschen Geschichte des 20. Jahrhundert*s (München: Siedler Verlag, 2005); William J. Spurlin, *Lost intimacies. Rethinking Homosexuality Under National Socialism* (New York: Peter Lang, 2009), 6. (gender, sexuality & culture 4).
31 Cf. Eschebach, "Homophobie, Devianz", 65.

and tenuous".³² In addition, it appears important to consider the relationship between homosociality and homoeroticism/homosexuality as a continuum and a historically variable relation, referring to Eve Kosowsky Sedgwick (1985). It is, therefore, not as important to explain that eroticism was an integral part of homosocial relationships in the gender-segregated inclusion camps, but to explain how the boundary between homosociality and homosexuality was drawn in this specific historical constellation.³³

Fig. 1: The *RAD* published many propagandist, illustrated books which communicated idyllic sceneries of the camps and thematised their homosocial character. The sujet of bodily closeness and intimacy among the *Arbeitsmaiden* was persistently present in the portrayed photographs and advertising art, although the NS organisation tried to reject any homoerotic meanings. This was not always successful, as this example shows. (Source: Bezirksleitung XX. des Reichsarbeitsdienstes für die weibliche Jugend (ed.), *Helfende Hände bei den Bergbauern*, bearb. Rosemarie Pierer (Innsbruck: Deutscher Alpenverlag Ges.m.b.H. 1942), 132.)

---

32 Cf. Spurlin, *Lost intimacies*, 6.
33 Cf. Wiebke Backhaus, *Bergkameraden. Soziale Nahbeziehungen im alpinistischen Diskurs (1860–2010)* (Frankfurt am Main: Campus Verlag, 2016), 140 (Geschichte und Geschlechter 67).

In fact, National Socialism sharply defined this boundary: While homosocial organisations represented a core element of the regime, homosexual people were repressed and persecuted. While male bonding structures within the NDSAP certainly integrated ideals of enhanced masculinity and constructions of a close cohesion among men, homoerotic elements were under no circumstances allowed to develop into homosexuality.[34] Consequently, homosexuality was rigorously prosecuted.[35] Together with homosexual men, lesbian women had to witness the destruction of their subculture and infrastructure, as well as live within a repressive cultural environment that forced many to live a double life – although there were more remaining scopes of action for women than for men. Female homosexuality was considered to be "less socially harmful" and, in the sense of the population policy, "less threatening". At least in the *Altreich* no systematic prosecution of lesbian women took place. *Gestapo* and criminal police concentrated strongly on the persecution of male homosexuals, whom the regime had declared to be "enemies of the state and the people".[36] At the same time, extremely different conditions existed in specific regions. In Austria section §129Ib of the hitherto valid criminal law was upheld after 1938, whereby homosexual relationships between women were penalised, unlike in Germany. Austrian historian Angela H. Mayer argues convincingly that, in fact, the criminalisation and prosecution processes applied to homosexual women in Austria at that time can be analysed as equivalent to those of men.[37]

---

34 Herzog, *Politisierung*. 8. Quoted after Backhaus, *Bergkameraden*, 141.
35 Cf. Hauer, "Lesben und Nationalsozialismus," 145. – Concerning Austria cf. Albert Müller and Christian Fleck, "'Unzucht wider die Natur'. Gerichtliche Verfolgung der 'Unzucht mit Personen gleichen Geschlechts' in Österreich von den 1930er bis zu den 1950er Jahren," in: *Österreichische Zeitschrift für Geschichtswissenschaften (ÖZG)* 9 (1998) 3: 400–422; Niko Wahl, *Verfolgung und Vermögensentzug Homosexueller auf dem Gebiet der Republik Österreich während der NS-Zeit* (Wien–München: Oldenburg Verlag, 2004). (Veröffentlichungen der österreichischen Historikerkommission 25); Johann Karl Kirchknopf, "Die umfassende Aufarbeitung der NS-Homosexuellenverfolgung in Wien," in: Schwartz (ed.), *Homosexuelle im Nationalsozialismus*, 121–128.
36 Claudia Schoppmann, "Zwischen strafrechtlicher Verfolgung und gesellschaftlicher Ächtung: Lesbische Frauen im 'Dritten Reich'," in: Eschebach (ed.), *Homophobie und Devianz*, 35–52, here 49. In the *Altreich* lesbians were registered by the police, and different NS authorities collected information about them, i. e. in the *Rassepolitisches Amt*, but most of the time – according to the impunity of female homosexuality in Germany at the time, this information was not used against individual women. According to Schoppmann, the situation was thus different from to politics in the *Ostmark*.
37 Cf. Mayer, "Schwachsinn höheren Grades," 83. The persecution and conviction of lesbian women proceeded in the context of highly complex measures of the prevailing criminal law. Mostly women were sentenced in line with §129Ib, but beyond this, the courts applied several other paragraphs to persecute lesbians. Cf. Kokula, "Zur Situation," 29. Gertrude Baumgartner and Angela H. Mayer, *Arbeitsanstalten für sog. "asoziale Frauen" im Gau Wien und Niederdonau. Endbericht zum Forschungsprojekt des Bundesministeriums für Wissenschaft und Forschung* (Wien 1990).

On the other hand, the National Socialist regime created gender-segregated spaces to an unprecedented extent – especially in the central NS youth organisations of the *Hitler-Jugend* or in the context of the employment of young workers in RAD camps. Young wo/men often spent months in the latter, initially usually completely isolated from their families and their previous social relationships. In the area of present-day Austria, the compulsory labour service was introduced for young males in October 1938; scarcely a year later, in September 1939, the compulsory labour requirement for young women was established, first for a half and – after 1941 – for a full year.[38] More than any other National Socialist organisation, the RAD was ideologically charged in terms of its political and educational significance: Work which was referred to as "German quality work" and an "honourable task" in the service of the *Volksgemeinschaft* was meant to integrate people from different social and class backgrounds. The repressive downside of such an employment strategy was clearly evident, in that the so-called *Arbeitsscheuen*, *Asozialen* and *Fremdvölkische* were excluded and prosecuted and the forced labourers were exploited. Even those who were considered members of the German *Volksgemeinschaft* and were correspondingly integrated in the RAD were confronted with obligatory regulations, a restrictive registration requirement, monitoring and an extensive authority to wield power over individuals.

From the perspective of a gender historian, it proves to be significant that the NS decision-makers did not formulate any gender-specific regulation with respect to the RAD. The guidelines for female education sometimes argued for seemingly "greater modesty" of the addressed *Volksgenossinnen*. On the one hand, female employment was imbued with a higher status, attention and significance in that it appealed to the women's senses of commitment and responsibility. On the other hand, irrational maternal biologistic ideologies as well as the regime's economic and war-related interests in the female labour resources remained in place.[39] Nonetheless, the same labour service concept, the same

---

38 Cf. Altenstraßer, "Zwischen Ideologie", 107–130, here 107–110.
39 Ibid., 107–130, here 107–110. Cf. Patel, "Volksgenossen", 323. In his studies Patel discussed central results concerning the history of the RAD (dealing with constructions of masculinity and other topics), but he presents the history of the male RAD units as the 'general history' of the organisation. By doing so, he ignores not only the phases that shaped the labour service idea in the context of the first women's liberation movement (cf. accordingly the pioneer study of Stefan Bajohr, "Weiblicher Arbeitsdienst im 'Dritten Reich'. Ein Konflikt zwischen Ideologie und Ökonomie," in: *Vierteljahrshefte für Zeitgeschichte* 28 (1980) 3: 331–357), but he also prolongues the contemporary interpretation of the RADwJ as an 'unpolitical' organisation. Thus, Patel relativises the significance of the RADwJ as one crucial instance of socialisation for a whole generation of female young adults between 1939 and 1945. – Concerning the current state of research from a gender history perspective, cf. Stephenson, "Der Arbeitsdienst für die weibliche Jugend," 255–288. Concerning the Austrian situation, cf.

political goals and the same ethical foundations applied to both genders. As in other NS organisations, the male and the female RAD formed strictly gender-segregated organisational structures that were inseparably intertwined units in their reciprocal relations.[40]

Regarding the previously posed question of the desired homosociality and forbidden homosexuality, historian Ilse Kokula already generally referred at the end of the 1980s to the fine line divided between promoting the enthusiasm of the young women for 'their leaders' in NS youth organisations and preventing the proximity from becoming *too* close. Individual criminal proceedings show that the scope for discretion in this respect was large. Young women who were accused of having a lesbian relationship – from the perspective of the responsible superior – could be warned or dragged before an *Ehrengericht* [court of honour], while others remained unmolested. The criminal proceedings in the context of the *Reichsarbeitsdienst* which were investigated by Kokula, Mayer or Nicole Gisch document that denunciation in the camp context – unlike what has previously been assumed in research[41] – could also initiate a prosecution process in

---

Siglinde Trybek, *Der Reichsarbeitsdienst in Österreich 1938–1945* (Phil. Diss. Wien 1992). Trybek, as the first historian to study the subject in Austria, concluded a broad organisational history of the RAD in the 'Ostmark' and has dealt not only with the prehistory of the labour service idea since World War One, but also its legal contexts since 1938 as well as the different phases in its development up until outbreak of war, also focusing in detail on single RAD camps on the Austrian territory. In particular, she dedicates herself to the gender specific development and the RADwJ. – Cf. also Karoline Blankosegger, *Im Spannungsfeld individueller und "gleichgeschalteter" Erinnerungen. Frauen im Reichsarbeitsdienst für die weibliche Jugend* (Phil. Dipl. Salzburg 2003). Blankosegger focusses on the field of tension between individual and 'homogenised' memories of Austrian women in the RADwJ, working innovatively with video and oral history approaches. Examing individual biographies, she thus advanced the analysis on common patterns of remembrance concerning the terms *Dienst*, duty, *Volksgemeinschaft* and comradeship, has dealt with the mechanisms of social levelling and instrumentalisation of work in the *Volksgemeinschaft* and has reconstructed individual experiences concerning i.e. taboo subjects in narrations or audience-related discourses.

40 Cf. Manfred Seifert, *Kulturarbeit im Reichsarbeitsdienst. Theorie und Praxis nationalsozialistischer Kulturpflege im Kontext historisch-politischer, organisatorischer und ideologischer Einflüsse* (Münster–New York: Waxmann, 1996), 181–182. (Internationale Hochschulschriften 196). Encodings of 'male' and 'soldier-like' elements are also visible in the education program of the RADwJ, particularly in the morning roll-call or in the *Ordnungsübungen* [disciplinary exercises] and 'military games' conducted by the *Arbeitsmaiden*. Thus, the hegemonic concepts of feminity, on the one hand, served to demarcate them from constructions of manliness and, on the other hand, the regime offered the women possibilities of integration via the gender-neutral term of 'comradeship'.

41 Cf. Eschebach, "Homophobie, Devianz", 76–77. The Austrian cases analysed by Gisch, Mayer and Baumgartner/Mayer document the opposite. Cf. Nicole Gisch, *Anklagen nach §129Ib des ÖStGb während der NS-Herrschaft. Fallstudien zur Konstruktion weiblicher Homosexualität anhand der Gerichtsakten der Wiener Land(es)gerichte I und II* (Phil. Dipl. Wien 2012); Mayer, "Schwachsinn höheren Grades;" Baumgartner and Mayer, *Arbeitsanstalten*.

the case of (actual or alleged) female homosexuality if the criminal law allowed such prosecution (as in Austria).[42] The camp authorities also had the far-reaching power to punish (alleged) homosexual relationships: It was apparently their duty to report possible crimes. Even interrogations of women who were suspected to practise homosexual relations could take place in the camp context. Finally, the cases analysed so far prove that there was no 'private sphere' in the RAD camp: Camp leaders searched through the personal belongings of the young working women or started criminal proceedings on the basis of incriminating material they discovered (such as letters or diaries) as a matter of course.[43] The almost unlimited quality of 'publicity', which affected all social relations in the camp context, played a crucial role.[44] The responsible leaders made efforts to completely eliminate any privacy or hidden spaces in which same-sex love could develop or sexual relationships could take place.

Ultimately, the quoted research also shows that criminal records can only allow us to draw limited conclusions about the true life situations of lesbian women or about homoerotic relationships in camp contexts and grant only a limited amount of insight into individual perceptions.[45]

Homophobia and Attributions of Deviance in the Camp Context

Current research shows that female homosexuality in the camp context can hardly be reconstructed as a "space of experience"[46], but rather as a space of discourse. Insa Eschebach, for instance, presented an illuminating study on the political-cultural use of the category 'being lesbian' in camps by analysing the written memories of survivors of the women's concentration camp in Ravensbrück. In this study, Eschebach examines homophobia and attributions of deviance in representations of female homosexuality under the extreme conditions of NS concentration camps. She emphasizes that the discursive figure of 'the lesbian' that coincides with hegemonic interpretive patterns especially represents a version of the "sexualized woman", a model of "deviant sexuality" and, in

---

42 Cf. Kokula, "Zur Situation," 29–36, 32; Gisch, Anklagen, 103–105.
43 Cf. Gisch, Anklagen, 121.
44 Cf. Hauer, "Nationalsozialismus und Homosexualität," 135–136; Eschebach, "Homophobie, Devianz," 74. The retrospective quality of her journal entries during her time in the RADwJ could be a consequence of the fact that she did not bring the diary into the camp. The camp knew – as mentioned above – no 'private sphere', and the camp leaders could gain access even to the lockers of the Arbeitsmaiden in (allegedly) needed.
45 Cf. Schoppmann, "Lesbische Frauen," 85–91.
46 Concerning current debates on the term 'experience' in gender history cf. Andrea Griesebner, Feministische Geschichtswissenschaft. Eine Einführung (Wien: Löcker 2005), 143–153.

general, a "category of being different".[47] The attribution/thematisation of 'being lesbian' had the function, "to make the profile of one's own group stand out as a positive". At the same time, the stigmatisation of female homosexuality served to emphasize differences within the prisoners' community and justify demarcations. Under the compulsory conditions to maintain uniformity in concentration camps, the act of heteronormative distancing oneself from the figure of 'the lesbian' (as well as 'the prostitute') made it possible to simultaneously express a desire for moral superiority or proof of moral integrity. The attribution of 'being lesbian' as a desired distinction also often interlocked with national criteria or the determination of power positioning within the prisoners' community.[48] Referring to Judith Butler, Eschebach notes that female homosexuality in this type of interpretative framework nearly always represents a scene of "disorder, error, confusion, and discomfort".[49] At the same time, the sexualised representations testify the attempts to distance oneself, as a way to banish the horrors and the unbearable effects of the concentration camps, and to position them in a space outside of the normal. Eschebach concludes that one common feature in women's written memories is that "all forms of homosexuality are wiped out, reduced", and then "reconstructed as sites of radical homophobic fantasies". The "reality of female homosexuality in the camp" is expressed "if at all, only as a trace and reminiscence in the texts".[50] The interpretation of female homosexuality as 'abnormal' also serves to externalize it, while individuals are simultaneously recruited to represent differences between collectives. Homophobic constructions in the camp context support the establishment of social

---

47 Cf. Sander L. Gilman, *Rasse, Sexualität und Seuche. Stereotype aus der Innenwelt der westlichen Kultur* (Reinbek b. Hamburg: Rowohlt Verlag, 1992), 13. Quoted after Eschebach, "Homophobie, Devianz," 66.
48 Homophobia and debasement expressed in the contexts of complex social relations among the prisoners community as splitting: Relationships among women who were considered to be part of the 'own prisoner's group' were remembered positively as 'platonic' (and nonsexual) and were symbolised in most memory texts by solidarity, mutual care and support. In contrast to this, sexual relations among women (actual and attributed ones) were assigned to 'the others' (other groups of prisoners, functionaries out of the prisoners' group or NS supervisors). They were connected with constructions of "depravation" and "reprobacy" and marked over all "deviance". Cf. Eschebach, "Homophobie, Devianz," 68–70, 76–77.
49 Cf. Judith Butler, "Imitation und die Aufsässigkeit der Geschlechteridentität," in: *Grenzen lesbischer Identitäten. Aufsätze*, edited by Sabine Hark (Berlin: Querverlag, 1996), 15–37, here 20. Quoted after Eschebach, "Homophobie, Devianz," 72–74.
50 Eschebach: Deren Gemeinsamkeit besteht darin, dass "alle Formen der Homosexualität ausgelöscht, reduziert" und anschließend "als Schauplätze radikaler homophober Phantasien rekonstruiert werden." Die "Realität weiblicher Homosexualität im Lager" kommt "wenn überhaupt nur als Spur und Reminiszenz in den Texten zum Ausdruck." Cf. Eschebach, "Homophobie, Devianz," 76.

differences such as the strengthening of group identities or the expression of moral superiority over another group of individuals.⁵¹

In her study, Eschebach points out an interesting aspect which also structures Gerta Zaczek's personal narratives about the RAD camp: the discursive negotiation of belonging. Even though these negotiations were encoded differently in inclusion camps for *Volksgenossinnen*, the discussion about homosexuality in the RAD camp or the inclusion camps permits only a limited number of conclusions to be drawn about the actual presence and form of homoerotic or homosexual relationships. Instead, the signifier of 'being lesbian' illuminates the political use of the categories of body and sexuality in the representations of power relations and belonging within the communities in the camps. The decision about who 'truly' belonged to the Aryan *Volksgemeinschaft* and who did not was already made at the entrance to the camps.⁵²

RADwJ Camps as Prototypical Inclusion Camps

In his New Year's speech of 1941,⁵³ RAD *Reichsführer* Konstantin Hierl invoked what the regime expected of young working women: to be economic helpers for "mothers in the *Volksgemeinschaft*", to provide "spiritual support" in "faith", in "community spirit and cheerfulness". He focused exclusively on the employment of young women in agriculture, despite the fact that the young women were being used less and less in agriculture, but being increasingly settled in the war-related industries, agencies of the *Wehrmacht*, hospitals or social institutions. By 1942/43 at the latest, many young working women were serving in the army as air force assistants and anti-aircraft gun assistants, and they were often involved in these functions directly in military battles.⁵⁴

The placement of young working women in closed camps was considered by the regime as eminently important. Since the fall of 1936, the so-called *Einheitslager* [camp units] included 40 persons, comprising 32 *Arbeitsmaiden*, three

---

51 Cf. Eschebach, "Homophobie, Devianz," 76–77. At the same time, survivors do not use homophobic strategies in all recollections, and such reports do not always correlate directly to experiences of sexual violence in the camp context.
52 In the context of the *Pflichtjahr*, many young German adults had to submit for the first time to applying for an 'Aryan certificate' [*Ariernachweis*] and, with this, had to document that they 'belonged' to the German *Volksgemeinschaft* by presenting a piece of evidence. Cf. Patel, "Volksgenossen," 322.
53 Reichsarbeitsdienstführer Konstantin Hierl in seiner Neujahrsbotschaft an die Arbeitsmaiden, 1 January 1941. In: Bezirksleitung XX. des Reichsarbeitsdienstes für die weibliche Jugend (ed.), Helfende Hände bei den Bergbauern, bearb. Rosemarie Pierer, Innsbruck 1941, 7.
54 Cf. Altenstraßer, "Zwischen Ideologie," 107–108.

Kameradschaftsälteste (KÄ) [comrade elders], three assistants to the camp leader, a 'health assistant' and the camp leader. The latter and her assistants were employed full-time, while the young working women and comrade elders received a daily allowance. These kinds of camp units were the smallest organisational units in the RAD, but their sizes were in fact highly variable. At the beginning of the war, an order was given to reach a number of 100,000 active young working women, which led to a reorganisation of camp structures. After the reorganisation, instead of the usual camp units, 'small', 'medium' and 'large camps' existed with staffs of 41, 54 and 81 persons, respectively. The staff numbers increased even more during war, so that camps with up to 300 women were no longer exceptions at the time of later *Wehrmacht* deployment.[55]

Many of Zaczek's diary records refer indirectly or directly to the time span that she spent in the RADwJ camps. The social and physical spaces described by Zaczek prototypically illustrate the intentions that the National Socialist regime had for the *Lagerdienst*. The *closed* camps – which had constituted the typical camp form in the RAD since 1933 – can be classified as "total institutions" in the sense of Erving Goffman respectively Michel Foucault.[56] They attempted to function as a means of educating, controlling and disciplining *Volksgenossinnen* whose daily routines were rigidly regulated. These routines were characterised by precise planning, by the separation of work, leisure, privacy and publicity as well as a complete subordination of everyday life to achieve ideological-educational objectives.[57] The prototype of the 'new human being' [*neuer Mensch*] in

---

55 Cf. "Jugend in Deutschland 1918–1945", NS-Dokumentationszentrum der Stadt Köln. "In 'Einheitslagern' – Der Reichsarbeitsdienst der weiblichen Jugend," http://www.jugend1918-1945.de/thema.aspx?s=1796&m=1610&v=1796; "Vom 'Einheitslager' zum 'Großlager' – Die Einführung der Arbeitsdienstpflicht," http://www.jugend1918-1945.de/thema.aspx?s=1797&m=1610&v=1797 (Nov 16, 2015).

56 Cf. Erving Goffman, "Über die Merkmale totaler Institutionen," in: idem, *Asyle. Über die soziale Situation psychiatrischer Patienten und anderer Insassen* (Frankfurt am Main: Suhrkamp, 1973), 13–123 (edition suhrkamp); Michel Foucault, *Überwachen und Strafen. Die Geburt des Gefängnisses*, 7th ed. (Frankfurt am Main: Suhrkamp, 1987); concerning debates about the definition and the ambivalence of 'total institutions' in the Modern, cf. Martin Scheutz, "'Totale Institutionen' – missgeleiteter Bruder oder notwendiger Begleiter der Moderne? Eine Einführung," in: *Totale Institutionen. Wiener Zeitschrift zur Geschichte der Neuzeit* 8 (2008) 1: 3–19, here 3–10.

57 The motto of Hierl – "Im Arbeitsdienst darf keine Viertelstunde vertrödelt werden" ["Not a quarter-hour is to be piddled away in the RAD"] (Verlautbarung RAD 1937, nr. 378, 179. Quoted after Trybek, *Der Reichsarbeitsdienst*, 96) – was applied to make it impossible for people to find forms of privacy. Thus, most of the evenings were fully planned, and the young women were only able to keep in touch with the 'outer world' during the few leisure hours (cf. written note of the former *Arbeitsmaid* Lore E. to Siglinde Trybek, 30 January 1992, quoted after ibid., 97.). Two out of four Sundays were scheduled for hiking or common excursions in order to strengthen the mutual comradeship among the young women. After the initial (lasting a few weeks) enclosure phase, the camp leaders allowed the young women to spend

the sense of the Nationalist Socialist ideology would be shaped in the camp.[58] The authorities methodologically sought to establish an experiential education: During the highly ritualised everyday life, a kind of National Socialist consciousness would be provided as well as ideological patterns of thinking, reasoning and causal relations would be deeply internalised. Indoctrination was specifically supposed to be carried out in three phases: demonstration – practice – imitation. One aimed to achieve a structure of reflection or imitation. Time was an extremely important factor during this process; this is mirrored by the debates that took place among the *Reichsführung* concerning the appropriate duration of the RAD labour service. Especially at the beginning, the regime deliberately intended to isolate the labour service workers from their families and previous social contexts.[59] In addition, it strategically used the social pressure among the peer groups in the camp and the reciprocal monitoring among the young working women. The focus was placed on the de-individuation of the entire camp workforce: the camp knew "no private sphere" in terms of space or ideology.[60] Everyday life was not designed as a surrogate for *normal* life, but was encoded as *real* life.

Here, visionary postulates coincided with forms of life and lifestyle which were considered as valid and permissible and which already appeared to be 'social reality' in the future-conceived National Socialist social order.[61] The ideological objectives of the regime should materialize here: The camp was considered to be an "ideal space" and, in terms of the NS discourse, as "perfect" and "well-ordered".[62]

From socio-cultural and spatial points of view, the RAD *Reichsführung* attempted to break up previous relations and ties. The camps often remained temporary and were mostly unstable and mutable. Unlike the working men, the young working women were housed exclusively in stable camps (adapted existing buildings, such as castles, former palaces, manors) or wooden barrack hut camps, but not in tent camps. Hegemonic gender norms – which associated

---

every fourth weekend at home. Such permission was granted with increasing rarity after 1939 and the practice was practically suspended in the last years of the war. Cf. Peter Dudek, *Erziehung durch Arbeit. Arbeitslagerbewegung und freiwilliger Arbeitsdienst 1920–1935* (Opladen: Springer Verlag, 1988), 232, quoted after Seifert, *Kulturarbeit*, 170.

58 Cf. Hans-Ulrich Thamer, "Der 'Neue Mensch' als nationalsozialistisches Erziehungsprojekt. Anspruch und Wirklichkeit in den Eliteeinrichtungen des NS-Bildungssystems," in: *"Fackelträger der Nation". Elitebildung in den NS-Ordensburgen*, edited by Vogelsang IP (Wien – Köln – Weimar: Böhlau Verlag, 2010), 81–94.
59 Cf. ibid., 110.
60 Seifert, *Kulturarbeit*, 177–178.
61 Ibid., 179–180.
62 In reference to M. Foucault, Patel defines the RAD camp as "heterotopia", cf. Patel, "Volksgenossen," 323.

women with satedness or domesticity – thus were mirrored in the material configuration of the camps.[63] In addition, the intended non-inclusive nature of the camps played an important role in the given spatial infrastructure. This was especially true for the newly built barrack camps, for which a deliberately solitary location was usually chosen. The RAD(wJ) camps never integrated into existing settlements, social and communicative structures – not even the camps of the female labour service that were housed in formerly existing buildings – nor did they become permanently established there.[64]

The newly built wooden barracks had been standardised since 1935 as had been their arrangement in the landscape and their interior design with the typical, minimalist furniture, the bunk beds, the decorations in the common areas, the garden design on the campgrounds or the outdoor facilities with the camp borders. All these elements functioned as a highly important means of education due to their clear arrangement, transparency and the possibility they offered to control and monitor the camp inmates. As cultural anthropologist Manfred Seifert showed, the effectiveness of many elements within the spatial arrangement are revealed only when considering the intended educational goals of the RAD: in the everyday interplay between educational programs and space, in the potential of the architecture to structurally influence the camp community[65] and in the desire to control and discipline the members. For example, in the newly constructed camps, all the windows and entrance doors of the wooden barracks were visible from one viewpoint in the campsite. This possibility to monitor the young working women was even maintained in facilities built later on, where the barracks were loosely distributed across the available landscape.[66]

Many aspects supported the attempted educational process: the architectural space, the size of the working crews with their subunits, the largely equal age of the staff and the social mix, service rankings, the clothing (uniforms), the rituals and formal aspects of camp life, the accepted rules of behaviour and imparted values, plus the patterns of social conduct based on these or the organisation of the employment. The camp management understood that all these aspects could be used as a means of education, and they used them deliberately. The individual elements of the educational program (work, after-work, local history, state education, folk culture and the nationalist interpretation thereof) were closely intertwined and used consistently in alternating phases of activation and rest. Disciplinary action and comprehensive monitoring became obvious in military morning roll-call or *Ordnungsübungen* [disciplinary exercises] that were used to

---

63 Cf. Backhaus, *Bergkameraden*, 139.
64 Cf. Seifert, *Kulturarbeit*, 238–269.
65 Cf. ibid., 182–184.
66 Cf. Patel, "Volksgenossen," 317.

make the camp inmates tougher, make them practice obedience and obey orders. In turn, the *Innerer Lagerdienst* [internal camp service] was expected to keep the camp running in an orderly manner, encourage order, cleanliness, punctuality and diligence. The sleeping huts and bedrooms were prime examples of this: the military style of bed making [*Bettenbau*] served to a certain extent as proof of a correctly internalised way of living.[67] Ultimately, the entire camp was interpreted as a means of education: barracks, furnishings, badges, duty roster, the formalised interpersonal contact and the communication system – all these aspects created situational contexts by their mere existence and thereby controlled every activity.[68] These aspects substantiate that the educational goal within the RAD was sometimes much more important than employing a labour force efficiently. Last but not least, joint weekend hikes and field courses served the purpose of deepening the social contact among the camp inmates and allowing young urban people to come in contact with nature and rural surroundings. With respect to the young working men, the *Reichsführung* attempted to impart militarily exploitable capabilities while instructing them to spend time in open terrain.

At this point, another aspect of this partial detachment of the socio-cultural camp space from its physical anchor on a certain site should be mentioned, namely, the potential for the regime to use the RAD(wJ) camps as socio-cultural spaces and specifically to transfer the inscribed hierarchies and power relations of an 'organised' camp context to sociocultural spaces beyond the physical confines of the camp. I will address this aspect again in the context of my analysis of autobiographical representations of the camp.

In any case, the 'pressure to become part of the community' meant that the recruited young women had to give up their self-determination, fit in and be subordinate for long periods of time. Many tried to submit to the pressure applied, while a few critically reflected on their time in the RAD, tried to distance themselves, or evade the pressure. Even if they managed to distance themselves internally from the NS ideology, many chose to appear to fit in, in order to complete their labour service period with as few conflicts as possible. In the completely controlled everyday life in the camps, individual freedom could only

---

67 This concept was apparently successful, as is documented by memory texts written by former *Arbeitsmaiden*. In these texts, the RAD education program poses a key element. The former inmates often describe the soldier-like order and accuracy uncritically. Cf. e.g. Friederike Berner, "Wie ich den RAD erlebte," in: Heide Stöckl, *Zeitzeugen erzählen. Reichsarbeitsdienst, Krieg, Gefangenschaft* (Breitenau: Literaris, 2011), 44. In the herein collected texts, the women do not usually critically reflect upon the RAD in their retrospective memories. This is visible even in case of those women who volunteered to extend the period of their recruitment or decided to start a career as an RADwJ leader. A broad analysis concerning gendered cultures of memory regarding the RAD is still lacking. As an exception, cf. Blankosegger, *Im Spannungsfeld*.
68 Cf. Seifert, *Kulturarbeit*, 182–184, 189–195, 203–237, particularly 229.

be gained with difficulty, since the young working women not only were under constant supervision of the camp leaders but were expected – as was mentioned above – to monitor one another. In addition, many military rituals were performed, such as the military double-time cadence, the bellowing of the superiors, subtle penalty systems such as group penalties, initiation ceremonies for new inmates, a rigid pecking order or disparaging individuals in front of the group as well as innumerable inspections to check clothing, shoes, lockers or equipment. All of these measures were carried out to keep order and maintain discipline, but also to intimidate the inmates. Regarding these elements of disciplinary action and control, historian Siglinde Trybek draws a cautious comparison between inclusion camps and exclusion camps – although, of course, the intensity with which the described processes took place was clearly different. Nevertheless, the National Socialist apparatus of power, which operated with "precision" and an "ubiquitous presence", also existed in the integration camps.[69]

But did such camps provide a space for closeness, intimacy or even bodily/sexual relationships to develop?

Self-Narrations in the Context of the Camp Space

Recorded recollections of former *Arbeitsmaiden* show that most people initially found it difficult to adapt to the forced camp community, especially at the beginning of their stay. "In the beginning I suffered a lot", the former *Arbeitsmaid* Lore E. reported, "from the absence of any privacy, among some comrades who spoke obscenely and vulgarly. From the injustice and the primitive pressure applied by some – almost all – leaders, from the senselessness of many orders from the camp management and the resulting dissembling and lying".[70] The dissociation of the young people from familiar social contexts under the guise of a National Socialist "community education" and an "introduction into comradeship" initially evoked uncertainty among many young women. Many were unaware of what to expect in the first place. As Trybek indicates, the camp leaders worked upon the women's desire for affiliation, security and comfort as well as their feelings of insecurity to achieve their own educational goals.[71] The diary of Zaczek, discussed below, shows that the camp leaders even often went one step further and deliberately created and worked on feelings of uncertainty.

In general, Gerta Zaczek primarily described 'the camp' in her diary as a

---

69 Cf. Trybek, *Der Reichsarbeitsdienst*, 92–94.
70 Cf. Written note by the former *Arbeitsmaid* Lore E. to Siglinde Trybek, 30 January 1991, quoted after Trybek, *Der Reichsarbeitsdienst*, 92.
71 Cf. ibid., 98.

socio-cultural space with specific hierarchies and communication patterns. She rarely wrote about equal comrades elders or other young working women who were subordinate, but the crucial point of her entries about different camps concerned the hierarchical positioning that went on within the camp community, the social interactions among members of this community or her relations with particular fe/male functionaries. The thematisation of the camp appears to make it possible for Zaczek, first of all, to reflect on the social contact and exchange with 'her leaders'. In the diary, she meticulously recorded conversations that she remembered she had had with senior leaders (especially in the context of the camp) and described these dialogues using the term "Aussprachen"[72] [discussions or debates], thereby introducing a term that then appears consistently in her diary. In the following analysis, the meaning Zaczek attached to this discursive figure of the *Aussprache*, in terms of a political-cultural and gender-specific knowledge in the sense of Michel Foucault, appears to be of interest.

Aussprachen. Mechanisms of Self-Commitment to the *Volksgemeinschaft*

The term *Aussprache* is used throughout Zaczek's whole diary, but it appears particularly often in the context of the inclusion camps in which she participated. Although she selectively describes dialogues with hierarchically equivalent 'comrades', she usually noted conversations in which her counterpart was a person of hierarchically higher rank: superior leaders, representatives of the leading corps of the Styrian *Untergau* or *Obergau* or individuals to whom Zaczek believed to have political authority on certain issues. The topics of such conversations were mostly existential questions that dealt with her individual integration into the NS (gender) ideology, about religion, "leading qualities", "obedience" and "submission", idealism, honour, visions of the future, love and sexual relations or fundamental, personal decisions she had to make. These dialogues ultimately open up an interface of personal attachment to and integration into the NS *Volksgemeinschaft*. The described social spaces and interactions illuminate comprehensively how the bond to the NS ideology and its representatives could form, how authority was established as a social relationship by higher-level leaders (and vice versa) and how Zaczek herself co-constructed and performatively generated the authority of 'her leaders'. In the

---

72 The etymology of the term *Aussprache* [discussion / debate] points to a spoken dialog, in which something is clarified or present missunderstandings can be cleared up. In the context here, the term can be interpreted as a social space, in which implicitly given cultural aspects are expressed with the aim of self-assurance. https://www.wortbedeutung.info/Aussprache/ (16 October 2018).

Aussprachen recorded by Zaczek, nothing less than her individual process of bonding with the regime is negotiated.

Already in her very first journal entry, which dates back to the end of November 1939, Zaczek refers to a JMB *Landdienstlager* in St. Martin in Graz and describes a personal dialogue that she 'remembers' having with Friedrich Anton Gewolf (called "Tino" for short), who was the head of the press and propaganda department and a high-ranking functionary in the leading corps of the Styrian *Obergau*. At this time, the then 16-year-old Zaczek had a heavy crush on Gewolf (although she seems to have only admired him from afar). In her diary, she describes a (fictional) dialogue that she has initiated about the topics of religion and the church. "Du sagtest mir dann alles ganz klar und jetzt hab ich mich schon durchgearbeitet [...]".[73] Her decision to leave the Roman Catholic Church against the will of her parents can be traced, as she notes, directly back to Gewolf's "clear words". If we refer to Zaczak's diary records, the responsibility for this decision obviously does not (any longer) lie within the realm of parental/fatherly authority; instead, the regime's political representatives are responsible for having guided her through this decisional process – although she writes that Gewolf was a "complete stranger" at that time to her ("Du warst mir ja wildfremd").[74] The power relations that are evident in this (imagined) dialogue appear to be of interest: Even though the hierarchy in the HJ and Gewolf's superior position within it are strongly represented, Zaczek simultaneously claims the *right* to receive advice and discuss such a personally moving topic with an HJ representative. She identifies the training camp for prospective JMB-leaders as the privileged space for such a debate. Her initially indecisive attitude about seceding (or not seceding) from the church is, according to her records, clearly a political question. The secession, therefore, is not to be discussed in a private (family) context, but within the framework of the NS youth organisation to which she belongs. The quoted passage implicitly illustrates the expectations held by the higher-ranked functionaries, who accompanied the state-organised efforts to access young people: Zaczek receives instructions from 'her leaders', which she has "to work through". It is *her* duty to adopt the ideological requirements as her 'personal guidelines' and integrate political rules into the context of her most private life. 'The camp' appears to be the appropriate place to begin this community-building process. In addition, the camp's social and spatially closed context facilitates the elimination of other influencing factors (such as family or

---

73 "You then told me everything very clearly, and now I have already worked through your advice [...]". Cf. [Zaczek], Diary, i.e. entry Jan 1, 1947. Quote: [Zaczek], Diary, Nov 24, 1939, 1.
74 Cf. [Zaczek], Diary, Nov 24, 1939, 1.

school) and enables the regime to gain access to Zaczek as an ideologically 'malleable subject'.

This is vividly evident in a long, retrospectively written diary entry that describes the preceding few months, which Zaczek had spent in a RadwJ camp:

"26.12.41. [...] am 1. Mai (einen Monat verspätet) traf ich im 'Kärntnerhof', meinem nunmehrigen RAD-Lager ein. – Die ersten 14 Tage waren ein Heul – die Lagerführerin war nicht da, auf Tagung in Graz, und Verwalterin H. und Mitschulgehilfin S. konnten mich wirklich nicht begeistern! – Wie dann die Lagerführerin da war, war's bedeutend besser. Sie gefiel mir vom ersten Augenblick an sehr gut [...]. – Zu Pfingsten machten wir dann eine 3-tägige Wanderung auf den Dobratsch, die ich nie vergessen werde! In der ersten Nacht hatte ich eine Aussprache mit Gerl.[inde Hausmann], meiner Lagerführerin. – In aller Früh, es war noch fast dämmrig dunkel, wachte ich schon auf, konnte nicht mehr weiterschlafen (ich lag ja die ganze Nacht balancierend auf der Kante zwischen zwei Betten), und wälzte mich rum (soweit ich das in der Enge überhaupt konnte!) – sie lag rechts neben mir, war scheinbar auch schon wach, – ich kann mich jedenfalls erinnern, daß ich schon sagen wollte: 'Quatsch' ma bissel!', da fing sie von selbst an. – Was wir damals alles sprachen, kann ich nicht mehr sagen – es war wahnsinnig viel! [...]; sie machte den Versuch, dich ganz zu packen, zu erfassen und kennen zu lernen, – und ich wartete direkt auf sowas! Ich war so ganz offene, volle Bereitschaft! – ich erzählte sehr viel von mir – wie ich dann auch davon sprach, daß ich innerlich immer nach dem Spruch gestrebt hätte: 'Rein bleiben und reif werden...'[75], da räumte sie mir alles, aber auch alles runter! – Heute weiß ich, daß ich den Spruch eben nur einseitig, [...] aufgefaßt hatte! – Ich müsse jung sein, lustig, lebensdurstig, froh, aufgeschlossen, frei! Dürfe nicht immer nur Probleme wälzen, philosophieren – durch 'Leben' kommt man weiter, nicht durch 'Theorie'! – ich faßte auf – aber alles, was ich mir so im Jahr derweil zusammengedacht und zusammengebaut hab, stürzte zusammen; das werd' ich nie vergessen, wie sie mir dann so weich über die Haare fuhr und sagte: 'Armes Kind – es tut weh, und ist hart, wenn einem alles so herausgerissen wird und zusammenstürzt – aber da muß man sich durchringen – weiter, durch rauf...' – Ich nickte wohl, hätte aber am liebsten losgeheult! – Wie ich dann meinte, daß ich froh sei, daß ich mich in der Hand gehabt hab, kam's wieder: wozu denn – ist denn das notwendig – u.s.w. – dieser Morgen gab mir viel, wenn er mir auch momentan alles nahm. – [...] – seit damals war's praktisch so, daß ich [mit] Augen [...] und Ohren aufnahm und wieder aufnahm, was sie mir gab. Sie gab bewußt – arbeitete intensiv an mir – und ich war ganz dabei – sie hatte mich vollkommen in der Hand; ich weiß es, wußte es, wehrte mich aber nicht im Geringsten dagegen; ich lernte nur. – [...] und seither arbeitete sie natürlich intensiv dran."[76]

---

75 Zaczek quotes here (as she does often in her diary) a motto from the education literature for JMB leaders: "Rein bleiben und reif werden – das ist die schönste und schwerste Lebenskunst (Walter Flex)." Cf. Mädel-Führerinnendienst des Gebietes Steiermark (30), März 1944, 10.
76 "26.12.41. [...] on May 1 (a month too late) I arrived at the 'Kärntnerhof', my current RAD camp. – The first 14 days were horrific – the camp leader was not there, at a conference in Graz, and the female camp adminstrator H. and her helpmate S. really could not inspire me! – Once the camp leader was there, it was much better. I liked her a lot from the first moment

In this passage, Zaczek records her first closer encounter with 'her camp leader', who hereafter is referred to as Gerlinde Hausmann. Zaczek hauntingly designates the practice of psychological integration into totalitarian groups: affection, creation of insecurity, existential critique and finally indoctrination. The term *Aussprache* is used here as a synonym for opening/openness, something that permits closeness and provides insight into a person's attitude and thoughts. Zaczek presents herself as a recognizably passive subject, implicitly agreeing to undergo the process of indoctrination. In her writing, she transforms manipulation into 'trust', in the figure of the female leader she meets. Diary entries like this one document the profound and sustained self-integration of Zaczek into the NS movement and a – sometimes naïve, sometimes strategically oriented – almost limitless attachment to the regime's representatives. Here, Zaczek first begins to performatively establish her own subordination and subjugation to the given hierarchical figures in her writing. The diary reveals the camp as a specific communication space within which an individual can be connected to the relatively abstract idea of *Volksgemeinschaft*. In Zaczek's entries, the dialogues denoted as *Aussprachen* offer a space in which she can articulate feelings of being part of this imagined national community, her desire for openness, emotional intimacy and closeness. At the same time, however, *Aussprachen* always represent areas of uncertainty; they are places in which power relations are negotiated in hierarchical settings, places where functionaries sometimes express funda-

[…]. – At Pentecost, we then made a 3-day hike on the Dobratsch which I will never forget! On the first night I had a discussion with Gerl.[inde Hausmann], my camp leader. – In the morning, it was still almost dark, I woke up, could not sleep any more (I lay all night balancing on the edge between two beds) and rolled around (as much as I could in the tight space at all!) – she lay right next to me, was apparently already awake, – I can remember at any rate, that I wanted to say: 'Let's chat a little bit', and she already started chatting herself. – I cannot say anymore what we talked about back then – it was so much! […]; she made the effort to grab your attention entirely, understand you and get to know you – and I was waiting for something just like that! I was so completely open, fully ready! – I told her a lot about myself – and I then also spoke about how I would have liked to adhere to the saying: 'Stay pure and mature …', she explained everything to me completely! – Today I know that I had understood […] the motto only from one perspective! – I must be young, funny, eager for life, happy, open-minded, free! I couldn't just always turn problems over in my mind, philosophize – one only gets further by living, not by 'theory'! – I understood – but everything that I had thought and created during the last year has collapsed in the meantime. I'll never forget it, when she caressed my hair so softly and said, 'Poor child – it hurts, and it's hard when everything is so torn out of you and falls apart – but you have to get through it – continue, push on through …' – Yes, I nodded, but wanted to cry! – Then, when I said that I was glad that I had gotten a grip on myself, it came again: why – is that necessary – and so on – This morning gave me a lot, even if it also took away everything at that moment. […] – Since then it was practical, that I opened up my eyes […] and ears and accepted what she gave to me. She gave on purpose – worked on me intensely – and I was fully involved – she had me completely in her hand; I know it, I knew it, but did not in the least revolt against it; I only learned. – […] and since then, of course, she has worked intensively on it." [Zaczek], Diary, Dec 26, 1941, 42–44.

mental critique and often try to modify Zaczek as a person or influence her self-perception. Thus, the 'closeness' that is described always refers simultaneously to distance or hierarchy in the midst of the discursively created community.[77]

It becomes clear how Zaczek is exposed to constant observation in the camp context, depending on whether she does or does not behave in accordance with the expectations of people in her social and spatial environment. One topic present in the diary is the question of 'exposing oneself' or 'playing it close to the vest', of being 'spied on', 'sounded out' or 'deliberately opening up' in different situations and social interactions. This indicates that Zaczek exists in a situation in which she is permanently 'being checked over' – but the dialogues also can contain references to 'checking out' a particular person. 'Observing' thus is not a unidirectional process; Zaczek herself is in the position to observe and to judge, especially in the context of the camp. An inversion can quickly take place concerning who is observing or who is judging whom. In the *Aussprachen* Zaczek describes, she is never merely a subordinate but also the one who must and can concede leadership qualities and competence as a leader. The latter can only play the role of 'good leaders' if she accepts them as her superior.[78] Accordingly, a certain ambivalence about submission and self-empowerment is always present in Zaczek's writing. The dialogues are always about finding a balance between what can be said and what cannot be said, about 'venturing out' or 'having gone too far'. Close social relationships in the closed world of the camp seem always need to be sounded out – with reference to the personal position/ing, but also with reference to those of the opposite counterparts. Sometimes Zaczek regards 'her leaders' critically, judges harshly, acts presumptuously – and not only because she considers herself as one of the rather undefined "leader elite."[79] She claims to "want to have her leaders" in a specific way, and speaks of their ability to serve as a 'role model' or not. These types of paragraphs indicate that it would be inadequate to analyse the process of indoctrination that is described in the labour service camps and consider it as generalised evidence for a one-dimen-

---

77 Cf. [Zaczek], Diary, Nov 24, 1939, 2.
78 [Zaczek], Diary, May 1 and 2, 1940, 21–24. Debates on "good leaders" were very common at that time in public. Since the RADwJ enlarged continually from the mid-1930s and onwards, there was a glaring lack of appropriate leaders who were able to conduct a RADwJ camp and care adequately (in the sense of the regime) for ideological indoctrination and who were capable of organising the specific labour service of the *Arbeitsmaiden*. As Jill Stephenson outlined, since 1936, public media had began to discuss broadly the issue of female leaders in the RAD. On the one hand, these debates were initially aimed at reassuring the parents of volunteers (and respectively those of the young women who had been recruited obligatory since 1939) that the *Arbeitsmaiden* were guided adequately in the camps. On the other hand, those debates served to enlist appropriate leaders and address the chronical lack of trainees. Cf. Stephenson, "Der Arbeitsdienst für die weibliche Jugend," 255–287, here 268.
79 [Zaczek], Diary, June 24, 1940, 28–29. Cf. also Reese, "Einleitung," 9–39, here 11–13, 23–25.

sional process of influence and finally 'successful conformity'. In fact, the *Aussprachen* highlight the way in which Zaczek herself offers to be shaped by those whom she perceives as regime authorities – sometimes painfully exposing herself – and what is at the same time often associated with her specific individual aims: to bring herself and her "symbolic capital" (P. Bourdieu) into a conversation in order to show higher-ranked functionaries 'how far she already is' in her political (self) development or to articulate concrete desires and wishes. This goal is revealed several times in her diary when she discusses, for example, her intended naturalisation in Graz. From the perspective of the NS authorities, Zaczek was a "naturalised German from the occupied territories", who – according to the first implementing provision of the HJ law from 1939 – should not have had to be integrated obligatorily into the BDM. Due to this legal framework, it appears as though Zaczek felt as if her 'German identity' was extremely fragile.[80] This may be analysed as an important motif for her strong over-affirmation of the ideological requirements posed by the NS regime. As far as the personal testimonies show, she always countered criticism of her as a person – mostly issued by authorities whom she had invited to an *Aussprache* – with an increase in self-reflection or an increase in the number of attempts to adapt to the issued directives.[81]

Unwanted Desire. Discursivation of Homosocial/Homoerotic Relations in the Camp Context

In several self-historizing diary entries written between 1941 and 1942, Zaczek intensely worked through the close emotional relationship with 'her camp leader' Gerlinde Hausmann, which obviously irritated her greatly. It was certainly no coincidence that the location in which the quoted conversation occurred, and in which closeness and intimacy in the camp context could take place, was precisely not the regular RADwJ camp at 'Kärtnerhof' in which Zaczek worked at the time. Instead, the location was an alpine hut to which her camp unit had gone for a weekend getaway. In this place, the spatial transparency present in the regular camp – which was assured by the carefully organised 'comrade units', the continuous collective employment or the clearly arranged dormitories – was apparently and generally absent. Nonetheless, even when the outer boundaries of

---

[80] Zaczek refers several times to that point in her diary. After the invasion of Poland in 1939, she was naturalised, but her status as a "German from the occupied territories" represented a kind of 'second-class German identity'. Cf. Erste Durchführungsverordnung zum Gesetz über die Hitler-Jugend (Allgemeine Bestimmungen) March 25, 1939, §2 Abs. (1)–(6), quoted after Gehmacher, "Biografie, Geschlecht und Organisation," 467–493, here 483–484.
[81] Cf. Zettelbauer, *Sich der Nation ver|schreiben*, 292.

the camp changed, the existing sociocultural space and its inscribed power relations remained in place. These undoubtedly led to emotional upheavals and irritation concerning Zaczek's close relationship with Hausmann.

> "26.12.41. [...] Anfang August machten wir unsere große Abschiedsfahrt in's Plöckenpaß-Gebiet, zum Wolayersee. – Als eine der wenigen 'Erfahrenen im Wandern' machte ich 'Schlußlicht' mit [Sauerberg] und [Maurer]. In der Richl-Hütte kamen wir 3 auch ziemlich zum Schluß an und [Hausmann] hatte 2 übereinandergelegene Betten in Beschlag genommen für uns viere. Dann einigte man sich über das Zusammenschlafen und ich lag wieder mit Gerlinde [Hausmann] zusammen unten. – Wir schliefen natürlich nicht viel – sie lag verkehrt, mit dem Kopf gegen das Fenster. (Natürlich nicht zum Aushalten! –) Endlich hatte ich sie doch so weit, sie kroch zu mir rum, es ging gerade. Dann tratschen wir halt wieder. –"[82]

The closeness that is described here would hardly have occurred in the regular camp. In the alpine hut, however, the young women – unlike in the arranged dormitories – sleep together in single beds, creating moments of intimacy. Zaczek describes the narrowness, the small space left for each, the attempts to find something like privacy – her camp leader's head toward the top of the bed, Zaczek's head toward the bottom. A sense of physical closeness is conveyed, which results from the lack of space. But despite all the euphoric feelings that are expressed in Zaczek's diary entry, the situation she describes seems to worry her.

> "Diese Wolayersee-Fahrt war ja so unbeschreiblich schön! [...] – ich war glücklich. Wir kamen am frühen Nachmittag an und bis zum Essen [...] war frei. Zuerst raste alles zur italienischen Grenze rauf, dann beim Zurückgehen meinte [Hausmann] so nebenher: Ich gehe Edelweiß-brocken. – Ohne viel Rede fing ich gleich an, die Halde, die zum Senkopfhaus hinauf führt, auf allen Vieren raufzukraxeln. Nach einiger Zeit kam sie auch nach. Und im Turnzeug, später ohne Turnschuhe, kraxelten wir weiter rauf, und auf einem kleinen Fleckerl fanden wir wirklich die ersten Edelweiß! Ich hatte eine Riesenfreude! – dann kam aber der Abstieg! Nach der selben Seite zurück runter gings garnicht [sic]. Also nach der anderen. Plötzlich schaute aus dem Schutt eine rießengroße Geschoßspitze raus. – Wir buddelten den Blindgänger aus und wollten ihn mit runter zur Hütte nehmen. Zum Tragen war es aber viel zu schwer. Also kollerte wir ihn gemeinsam mit 'Ho-ruck!' immer stückerlweise weiter runter und kletterten nach. – Beim 5. oder 6. Mal ging es dann aber doch plötzlich los. Wir pickten uns direkt an die Wand – aber geschehen ist nichts. Unten glaubte man schon, die Italiener schießen! –

---

82 "26.12.41. [...] At the beginning of August, we made our big farewell trip to the Plöckenpaß area, to the Wolayersee. – As one of the few 'experienced hikers' I took up the last position with [Sauerberg] and [Maurer]. At the end of day we arrived at the Richl-Hütte and [Hausmann] had taken over two beds, one on top of the other, for us four. Then we agreed who would sleep with whom and I lay on the lower bed again with Gerlinde [Hausmann]. Of course, we did not sleep much – she was lying the other way round, with her head against the window. (Of course, this couldn't be endured!) Finally, I got her to turn around and lie next to me, it just worked. Then we gossiped again." [Zaczek], Diary, Dec 26, 1941, 41, 45–46.

> Ich aber hatte selbst 12 Edelweiß gefunden! – Ich hatte [Hausmann] mit der Zeit wahnsinnig gern! Ich kam ihr auch persönlich immer näher."[83]

It appears to be no coincidence that Zaczek associates the feelings she remembers having for Hausmann with the discovery/detonation of the "dud" (unexploded ordnance) she finds. This incident could have been life-threatening – this is the basic message of the paragraph quoted above.[84] Later, in the same diary entry, she recalls a situation that occurred immediately before she was transferred from her former camp 'Kärtnerhof' to the new RADwJ barrack hut camp at Rosegg. Zaczek remembers that Hausmann had taken her to a music concert.

> "Mitte September war nun erste WHW[85] – Sammlung in Villach, wir Kärntnerhofer Maiden sammelten geschlossen mit durchschlagendem Erfolg mit. Gleichzeitig fing auch die 'Paracelsus-Woche' in Villach an. Samstag Abend war ein Konzert der Wiener Symphoniker, ich durfte mit [Hausmann] mit. Wir hatten uns ein Zimmer im Hotel Post genommen. – Nach dem Konzert gingen wir durch die schmalen engen dunklen Gasse mit den vielen Durchlässen zum Hauptplatz zurück – aber da fühlte ich, da waren wir nicht mehr Lagerführerin und Maid, sondern einfach zwei Menschen, einander sehr ähnlich, ganz erfüllt von dem Erlebnis des Konzertes – die so zusammengekommen sind. – dann gingen wir noch ein Stück zum Drau-Kai hinunter. – Da konnte ich nicht [*zwei Blätter herausgerissen*]
> Samstag, den 4. Oktober mit dem Abendzug fuhr ich dann rüber – wurde noch auf die Bahn begleitet – und dann kam aber die große Umstellung und das neue Lager. –"[86]

---

83 "This ride to the Wolayersee was so indescribably beautiful! […] – I was happy. We arrived in the early afternoon and until dinner […] we had leisure time. First, everything raced up to the Italian border, then on the way back [Hausmann] casually said: I'm going to pick up some edelweiss. – Without talking, I immediately began to clamber on all fours up the slope that leads up to the Senkopfhaus. After some time, she followed. And wearing the leotard, later on without gym shoes, we scrambled on up, and on a small place we really found the first edelweiss! I felt tremendous joy! – but then came the descent! We could not go back down the same slope. So, the other one. Suddenly, a huge projectile point peeked out of the scree. – We dug up the dud and wanted to take it down to the hut. But it was too heavy to carry. So, together with a 'heave-ho!', we rolled it down bit by bit and climbed after it. – But on the 5th or 6th heave it suddenly detonated. We pressed ourselves right up against the wall – but nothing happened. Down at the hut they thought the Italians were shooting! – But I had found 12 edelweiss! – As time went on, I really liked [Hausmann]! I also got closer to her personally". Cf. [Zaczek], Diary, Dec 26, 1941, 45–51.
84 It appears to be of interest that this incident was the only situation [Gerta Zaczek] remembered in an oral history interview that took place in spring 2015 when focussing on her activities in the JMB or the RADwJ. Ultimately this emphasizes the importance that [Zaczek] attributed to the relationship with 'her camp leader'. Moreover, she still stored – nearly 75 years after the recalled incident – a dried edelweiss (one of the twelve found?) between the pages of her diary. This object functions as a kind of 'material evidence' for the incident that obviously impressed her deeply.
85 WHW stands for "Winterhilfswerk".
86 "Mid-September was when the first WHW collection in Villach took place, and we maidens

Zaczek retrospectively explains that the hierarchical relationship between her and 'her leader' dissolves, and they reach the same hierarchical level, during an evening walk. At the same time, the readers are cheated of reading the full story, because two pages are missing from the diary. In the few remaining sentences, however, it becomes clear that the feelings she portrays for 'her camp leader' fundamentally irritate Zaczek. The young woman who is so eloquent elsewhere in her writing wrestled with language in the cited paragraph as well as subsequent paragraphs and simultaneously describes herself as being "overflowing" with emotions.[87] The passage above and the torn-out pages indicate that Zaczek perceived the feeling of togetherness with Hausmann to be an existential experience, but interpreted it above all as a threatening feeling. Several subsequent entries support the conjecture that the closeness between the two women also had a physical dimension.

> "27.12.[41] Ich hab mir oft schon Gedanken gemacht drüber, wie Gerlinde [Hausmann] und ich eigentlich zu einander stehen. – Mich zogs direkt hin zu ihr – ich gewann sie mit der Zeit sehr, sehr lieb.– Daß ich stark, ja ganz unter ihrem Einfluß stehe, daß sie mich ganz in der Hand hat, weiß ich. Ich wehre mich aber nicht im Geringsten dagegen – es ist doch gut so – sie gibt mir ja so viel! – Wie ich die erste Nacht bei ihr unten schlief, war's mir so zum Weinen – ich kann garnicht sagen warum – aber sie war so gut und lieb – so weich – das kannte ich nicht – das packte mich so. – Wenn sie mir so ganz leise übers Gesicht, über die Haare fährt, und sagt 'Kleine, was denkst denn schon wieder?' – da bin ich immer so randvoll von – ich kann nicht sagen was mich so ganz erfüllt, beherrscht – ich kann dann nur sagen, ich hab dich so lieb – möchte dir auch gern nur Gutes tun, lieb zu dir sein – dann sagt die Gerlinde mir: bin ja nur froh, daß du da bist – daß ich dich hab! – das ist schon viel, sehr viel! – Du gibst mir ja auch viel   in dir erleb ich mich in meinen Kämpfen direkt wieder – da will ich dir helfen! – Du sollst es nicht so schwer haben wie ich. – Sie zeigt mir direkt Seiten an mir selbst, die ich nie gekannt hab! Ich hätte nie gedacht, daß ich einem Menschen noch so ganz langsam und weich über die Haare fahren könne – bei Gerlinde tu ich's. – Wie das alles kam, kann ich nicht sagen. – Nur, sie kennt mich gut – vielleicht noch besser, als ich glaube; – sie hat so gut erfaßt, wie's bei mir drinnen ausschaut! – Da hat sie einfach mein zweites 'ich', das ich nicht kannte, gepackt. – So kommt's mir direkt vor! – Aber wie steht sie eigentlich zu mir? Hängt sie wirklich auch an mir? Kann ich ihr denn wirklich auch 'geben'? – Wenns wirklich so ist, zeigt sie

---

from the 'Kärntnerhof' collected together with resounding success. At the same time, the 'Paracelsus Week' began in Villach. There was a concert of the Wiener Symphoniker on Saturday evening, I was allowed to go to it together with [Hausmann]. We had taken a room in the Hotel Post. – After the concert, we walked back through the narrow dark alley with its many passages to the main square – but then I felt as though we were no longer a camp leader and a young working woman, but just two people, very similar to each other, completely filled with the experience of the concert – who had come together like this. – then we went a bit down to the Drau quay. – I could not [...] [*two torn out pages*]. Saturday, the 4th of October, I drove over with the evening train – I was accompanied to the train tracks – and then came the big change and the new camp." Cf. [Zaczek], Diary, Dec 26, 1941, 45–51.

87 Cf. [Zaczek], Diary, Dec 26, 1941, 52.

das dann mir deswegen nicht, weil es ihr, (einmal machte sie so eine Andeutung!) sehr schwer fiele – vor ihrem Stolz das eingestehen – u.s.w. Als Lagerführerin hätte sie sich doch schon so viel vergeben vor uns! – [...] wie schauts da eigentlich im Innersten aus?! – Manchmal kommt mir vor, diese Unsicherheit, dieses Ungewisse schaut sie ja! Will sie haben! – Aber wozu? – Aber mich treibt es doch immer wieder dazu, da nachzugrübeln, zu verzweifeln; – warum, kann ich nicht sagen! Ich mißtraue Gerlinde nicht, – aber ich trau ihr zu, daß sie mit mir Theater spielt bis zum Letzten – weil sie weiß, wie ich an ihr häng! – Oder irr ich mich? [...].
Und damals, wie ich die letzte Nacht dort war, wie wir den Zug dann einfach davonfahren ließen – wie der Bub draußen war, haute sie sich plötzlich quer über das Lotterbett auf dem Rücken zu mir hin, daß sie grade so zu mir (ich saß, an die Wand gelehnt!) raufschauen mußte – und meinte – ich weiß nicht, was heute ist – du kommst mir heute so ruhig, so fest, so gesammelt vor, so klar – und ich mir so zerfahren, zerrüttet, so verheerend! – Für mich war's wunderbar dann – ich hab garnicht anders gekonnt, als mit der einen Hand ihr wieder so leise über die Haare fahren und dann bei der Schulter so drüberlegen – aber dann mußte ich immer denken, was denkt sie jetzt? Spielt sie wieder – oder läßt sie sich von ihrer augenblicklichen Regung treiben – und ist froh, daß ich bei ihr bin – lieb zu ihr bin?! –
Für mich ist das arg, wenn ich mich mal so richtig treiben lasse, – nur fühle – und dazwischen kommen mir so bittere Gedanken auf! –"[88]

---

[88] "27.12. [41] I often thought about how Gerlinde [Hausmann] and I actually related to one another. – I was immediately attracted to her – over time I attracted her very, very dearly. – I know that I am strongly, indeed, completely under her influence, that she has me completely in the palm of her hand. But I don't revolt in the least against it – it's just fine – she gives me so much! – Sleeping below with her the first night, it made me cry so much – I cannot say why – but she was so good and sweet – so soft – I had never known that – it affected me in such a way. – When she quietly caresses my face, my hair, and says, 'Little one, what are you thinking of again?' – I'm always so full of – I cannot say what completely fills me, dominates me – I only can say then, I love you so much – I also want to do good things for you, be nice to you – then, Gerlinde tells me: I am only glad that you are here – that I have you! – That's a lot, a great deal! – You also give me so much – in you, I directly experience my struggles with yourself – I want to help you! – You should not have it as hard as I have had it. – She shows me sides of myself that I have never known! I never thought that I could caress a person's hair so slowly and softly – with Gerlinde I can do it. – How did all of this happen? I cannot answer this. – Only, she knows me well – maybe even better than I think; – she understands so well how I feel inside! – There, she simply grabbed hold of my second 'self', which I did not know before. – That's how I feel! – But how does she feel about me? Is she really attached to me? Can I really 'give' something to her? If that's really the case, then she doesn't show her feelings to me, because this would be difficult for her (once she hinted at this!) – with her pride, to acknowledge that. As the camp leader, she already has revealed so much in front of us! – [...] but what does she feel in her heart?! – Sometimes I think that she sees this uncertainty, this doubt! She wants to have it! – But why? – It always makes me ponder, to despair; – why, I cannot say! I do not distrust Gerlinde, – but I believe that she is able to act in a kind of theater with me until the last moment – because she knows how much I'm attached to her! – Or am I wrong? [...]. And back then, when I was there for the last night, when we let the train simply drive away – as the boy was outside, she suddenly threw herself across the bed on her back and towards me, so that she just had to look up to me (I was sitting, leaning against the wall!) – saying – I do not know what it is today – today, you appear to be so calm, so stable, so collected, so clear – and I

Zaczek's description of tenderness, the quite natural, soft touches, emotions that overwhelm her and the notion of 'comradeship' is quite clearly connoted to homoeroticism here: Her language and writing style suggests that she was barely able to categorize her perceptions, even half a year after she had terminated the close relationship with Hausmann. At the same time, doubts and expressions of mistrust appear in her writing or at least a great amount of uncertainty about how she should deal with the feeling of intimacy that has formed between the two of them. Considering the regime's attempts to prevent relations among the camp inmates that were too close, Zaczek's writing also documents her attempts to 'adequately' classify her feelings for Hausmann and to make them fit the political and ideological requirements of National Socialism. Although simplistic, psychologising explanations should not be offered, it appears to be of analytical interest, nevertheless, to investigate the act of splitting that Zaczek herself performed in this section, separating her 'one I' from her "second self". On the one hand, she obviously worked through the ideological prescriptions that had shaped her (the unmentioned 'one I', which could be understood as a referenced superego [Freud's das *Über-Ich*], meaning the political and moral authorities that surrounded her, the ideological ideas, commandments and prohibitions that she also affirmed. On the other hand, with the discursive figure of the "second self", she evidently addressed her emotional, physical (or sexual) desire, which can be identified as "id" [Freuds *das Es*].[89]

The described dissolution of a hierarchical relationship between her and 'her camp leader' obviously did not really work, and the outcome of the indoctrination process that had occurred in the camp context still existed even after she had quit the camp. Zaczek's later personal and emotional relationships were strongly affected by this. This constellation can explain the irritation that arose as a result of the discrepancy: that Gerlinde Hausmann was not only a person for whom Zaczek felt strong emotions but who also embodied a central authority as a camp leader for Zaczek and a personified superego. Thus, it is possible to conclude that Zaczek was extremely uncertain about how Hausmann *really* interpreted the physical closeness between the two young women. Did she approach to her under the aspect of a 'test'; was she 'playing' with her; did

---

feel so muddled, broken, so devastated! – For me it was wonderful then – I could not do anything else, but caress her hair softly again with one hand and rest it on her shoulder – but then I must always think, what is she thinking now? Is she acting again – or does she herself let be carried away by her present feelings – and is glad that I'm here with her – that I care for her?! – For me it's terrible when I let myself get carried away by the moment – just feeling – and then such bitter thoughts surface!" Cf. [Zaczek], Diary, Dec 17, 1942, 51–56.

89 Cf. Sigmund Freud, *Das Ich und das Es* (Leipzig – Wien – Zürich: Internationaler Psychoanalytischer Verlag, 1923). Pages refer to the edition *Gesammelte Werke* (Köln: Anaconda, 2014), 829–872, in particular 847–855.

Hausmann hide her 'true ego' behind her approach or should Zaczek distrust her accordingly? The price that Zaczek might pay for her willingly offered availability as individual becomes visible here as well as the risk she takes of being delivered to a supervising leader. Zaczek could only escape from such a precarious situation by exerting self-control (or by controlling her 'sexual instinct'?). Although she used such strategies elsewhere[90], she obviously did not or could not apply them in the case of her relationship with Hausmann.

Regardless of whether Zaczek describes a desire for a sexual relationship and/or 'real' sexual activities in her diary, she marks the relationship with Hausmann as an act of border crossing in her writing: as an offense against the authority-based relationship between her as a 'comrade elder' and Hausmann as a camp leader, but also as a transgression of what might happen in terms of emotional and/or physical closeness that develops between two young women in the homosocial context of a camp.[91] Her retrospective writing fulfilled the purpose of clarifying and classifying the experiences she had made. By initially describing her emotional and physical attraction and her feelings that oscillated between happiness, uncertainty and exuberance, Zaczek increasingly characterises her connection with Hausmann in terms of devaluation and "dependency", as a precarious relationship. The more time that passed, the more Zaczek specified her feelings – denominating them in terms of "falling in love", and later on qualifying the relationship as "irrational" or "unhealthy".

> "26.9.42. […] Mittwoch/Donnerstag war Gerlinde übrigens hier! Wollte mich eigentlich überraschen, Voß verständigte mich aber vorher. (Die zwei trafen sich auf der Grazer Nervenklinik!) – Typisch für die Verhältnisse im RAD.?! – Man 'uraßt' doch da mit den Führerinnen, wie es höher nimmer geht – und sie selbst, wenn sie in der Arbeit stehen, werden sich dessen kaum bewußt, schinden sich ab, bis sie zusammenklappen, – Idealismus? Arbeitswut? Verantwortungsbewußtsein? – Wohl falsch am Platz? – Wie ich Amd.[Arbeitsmaid], bzw. KÄ [Kameradschaftsälteste] war, sah ich das alles bezeichnenderweise auch ganz anders! (So viele 'Weiberb[r]ut' so lange (besonders die Führerinnen!) zusammen, in Lagern, da übersteigert sich wohl alles? – wird ungesund – Das Verhältnis zwischen Gerlinde und mir war jedenfalls reichlich überspannt!) –"[92]

---

90 A deep difference becomes visible concerning the quoted paragraphs, on the one hand, and some sections, on the other hand, in which [Zaczek] describes how (heterosexual) men approach her in her HJ environment in the Styrian *Untergau*, her physical attitude towards HJ functionaries of the same age or her relations with older men from the NSDAP. In these paragraphs, she stages herself as disciplined, controlled, as renouncing her sexual instincts. Cf. Zettelbauer, *Sich der Nation ver|schreiben*, 338.

91 This uncertainty of [Zaczek's] concerning 'real' or put-on feelings about 'her camp leader' could indicate that she possibly also refers to the fact, that in Austria the criminal law penalised sexual relations between women and her relationship with Hausmann thus would mean a transgression of the contemporary law. Cf. Hauer, "Lesben und Nationalsozialismus," 149.

92 "26.9.42. […] Wednesday / Thursday, Gerlinde was here by the way! She actually wanted to

"Exaggerated" and "overdrawn" are now the terms with which Zaczek categorizes the relationship with 'her camp leader' and demands "from herself" a "new" and a "natural" relation quality concerning Hausmann. Zaczek's self-narration thus evokes the image of a 'progressive' development: her 'one I' (the referenced superego) and the way she acted to conform with the political and ideological guidelines gains the upper hand in the inner conflict described. In the process of writing, she progressively subordinates her desire to comply with the normative political guidelines. From the incisive experience with Hausmann, Zaczek deduces that her future social relations might change fundamentally. The imagined 'return to herself' – as she retrospectively reconfigures the new form of her relationship with Hausmann – is her way of turning away from a homosocial relationship that she interprets as *too* profound. The 'instructive consequence' of this is that Zaczek decides consciously to orientate towards men as potential future love/sexual partners. She now visualizes Hausmann as a 'temptress' who had taken advantage of her adaptability and trustfulness. Indirectly, she even accuses her camp leader of having promoted the closeness between the two of them only to convince her to take a full-time job in the RadwJ. In turn, Zaczek portrays her own decision to withdraw her application to become a full-time RADwJ leader as the first act of resistance against the relationship with her former supervisor and friend, which she now perceives as a 'personal dependency'.

At this point, her self-narration also strongly relies on hegemonic connotations of activity and passivity, which were contemporarily associated with the figure of 'the lesbian'. In fact, the NS judicial system presented arguments in criminal proceedings against homosexuals with ideas of an 'active', 'seductive', lesbian 'disposition', on the one hand, and a 'passive', 'seduced' and sometimes 'naïve' part, on the other hand, in order to describe (sexual) relationships between women. As Insa Eschebach has outlined, this constellation ultimately and clearly illustrates the extent to which hetero-normatively polarised cultures code and negotiate even the ideas about same-sex relations among women against the background of the hegemonic, binary gender concept.[93] Zaczek's self-con-

---

surprise me, but Voß informed me in advance. (The two met at the Graz mental hospital!) – Typical for the situation in the RAD.?! – They wear down the leaders, how it can't get worse, and the leaders themselves, if they are at work, are barely aware of this, toil until they collapse, – idealism? Working frenzy? Responsibility? – Probably in the wrong place? – When I was a young working woman or a comrade elder, I also viewed all of this significantly differently! Such a 'gaggle of hens' staying together for so long in the camps (especially the leaders!), that everything is pushed too far then? – becomes unhealthy – the relationship between Gerlinde and myself was in any case much too exaggerated!)" Cf. [Zaczek], Diary, Sept 26, 1942, 70–76. Cf. the referring to discursive figures analysed in: Eschebach, "Homophobie, Devianz," 67–68.

93 Ibid., 73–74.

struction as a 'seduced woman' paradoxically proves the 'successful' internalisation of such hegemonic knowledge and demonstrates the functionalisation of the implicitly negotiated discursive figure of 'the lesbian'. Actually, this self-construction allows her to externalize her obviously unacceptable feelings. The background for all of this is the concept of the Aryan *Volksgemeinschaft* which represents the unmentioned, absent centre of discourse here. Zaczek herself sets the boundaries between the permitted 'comradeship' and unwanted homo-eroticism/homosexuality in this community. The latter two terms she imagines as a 'transgression of natural limits', as the opposite of heterosexual norms or the antithesis of a 'well-assorted' heterosexuality, which forms the core of NS ideology. She characterizes 'the other', the 'non-Self' as a 'misinterpretation' of what the regime desires in terms of homosociality and, respectively, 'comradeship'. In her version of the story, tender feelings or emotional closeness can be integrated into 'comradeship',[94] but not physical closeness and definitely not erotic or sexual desire. Zaczek's endeavours to redefine the 'natural limits' between Hausmann and herself ultimately indicate the regime's highly 'successful' ideological access to her as an individual person. Zaczek's politically motivated refusal to define her body, erotic feelings or sexuality as a possible place of privacy is also clearly visible here, which directly correlates with the regime's directives. In the context of the 'total institution' of the camp, Zaczek's own desire becomes an entirely political and ideological issue.

Zaczek left the labour service in 1942, and she retrospectively associates this moment with the end of her relationship with Hausmann. This proves ultimately to be a central turning point in her life story. She subsequently left Graz and moved to Heidelberg to study at the Karl Ruprecht University, enrolling in the programme for languages at the Institute for Interpreters. In the following years, she pursued her interests in National Socialist geopolitics and German *Großraumforschung* [research on the 'Greater Germany']. In her diary, Zaczek describes Heidelberg as her "vanishing point", a place where she could "submerge" and where she achieved the necessary distance to 'reorganize' her thoughts about her relationship with Hausmann by writing. Whereas her feelings for 'her camp leader' are often still vague, indefinite and fluent in the contemporary entries made shortly after she had completed her *Pflichtjahr*, her judgement becomes more and more solidified, the further the relationship recedes into the past. One year after her separation from Hausmann, Zaczek first writes of "being in love" and still later she writes about "unreasonable" feelings for Hausmann, which – given a negative connotation – are now categorised as "unhealthy". The act of crossing a border in the relationship with Hausmann now

---

94 Cf. Backhaus, *Bergkameraden*, 143.

leads her to feel "shame"[95]: she feels ashamed of what would happen if someone were to read what she had written about her time in the labour service. These feelings appeared to be so profound that she (?) finally rips the 'shameful' pages out of her diary and – as this act could also be interpreted – 'eradicates' any evidence of her close relationship with Hausmann from an ideologically 're-solidified' life narration.

Several diary sections prove that she hardly succeeded in this attempt. Zaczek is still struggling to classify her relationship with Hausmann two years later – obviously without success. What remains is the result of Zaczek's inability to resolve the boundary between the homosociality that was encouraged, the homoeroticism that was present and the homosexuality that was forbidden by overaffirming the NS ideology. The latter aspect also ultimately indicates that it was a structural impossibility. Although the regime tried to strictly control the borderline between homosocial, homoerotic and homosexual relations, it appears as if such demarcations blurred persistently in the camp context. In any case, the inner conflict that Zaczek describes in her diary actually represents something of a caesura in her life, but only in the sense of trying and not being able to cope with the ambivalent fine lines between the desired homosociality and forbidden homoeroticism in the context of inclusion camps. However, her diary by no means reveals that she politically and ideologically distanced herself from the regime, even though – in the context of her denazification process – she insisted that this act of distancing dated back to 1941. On the contrary and as a matter of fact, Zaczek remained uncritically committed to National Socialism, not only until the end of the war, but even beyond.

As far as can be reconstructed from her diary, Zaczek rarely entered love relationships in the following years (also the first post-war years) and, if then, her partners were men. She kept the physical or sexual aspects of these partnerships at a distance. If she discussed her own sexual desire in her writing, she always did it with an association of "sensual primitiveness", disparaging herself by the attribution of a lack of "breeding", "delicacy of feelings" or as being unable to "restrain herself". In all of her interpretations of closeness, love, body or sexual desire, mainly discursive figures were present which ultimately referred to the National Socialist body of knowledge – even after the end of the war. In this context, the *Reichenberg Rede* held by Adolf Hitler in December 1938 in front of members of the HJ appears to be of interest in that it touched upon the total, deep apprehension of the 'German youth' through National Socialism: "Und sie werden nicht mehr frei, ihr ganzes Leben." As Kiran Klaus Patel outlined, this speech appears to have represented a key moment regarding the efficiency of the

---

95 Cf. Zettelbauer, *Sich der Nation ver|schreiben*, 342.

NS ideology and he stresses that the intended persistent integration of adolescents into National Socialism should be (and was) connected for many with euphoria and feelings of happiness.[96] The camp – which I discussed here as a synonym for a site of indoctrination and disciplinary action, as an attempt to create a 'new human being' in the sense of NS ideology, on the one hand, and a space in which one committed oneself to the regime, on the other – this 'symbolic camp' continued to exist in Zaczek's life story beyond the end of war. Her time in the camp remained a formative moment in her biography during the post-war period, in the sense that she bore the 'camp in the mind'.

---

96 "And they will not be released for their full lives". Adolf Hitler, Reichenberger Rede from December 1938, quoted after Patel, "Volksgenossen," 330.

Annika Wienert

Camp Cartography: On the Ambiguity of Mapping Nazi Extermination Camps

This paper deals with maps of German extermination camps and argues that these maps are ambiguous in several respects. It takes a closer look at a small number of maps from the extermination camp in Sobibór,[1] some of them drawn by survivors. I will present different historical contexts in which maps were produced and/or used and try to shed light on the significance of this less-researched form of Holocaust testimony. As it is disputed among scholars whether the term "camp" is applicable for killing sites such as Sobibór, I will start with a reflection on that matter. Maps constitute a specific form of testimony regarding these sites. In the following section, I comment on their evocative qualities by contrasting a reconstructed plan of Auschwitz-Birkenau with a map drawn by a survivor of the extermination camp in Sobibór shortly after the end of the war. The third and most extensive section deals with the role that maps played in the trials of Nazi perpetrators. While the question of ambiguity is a recurring motif in my analysis of the concrete examples and contexts, I conclude by pondering, on a more abstract level, different aspects of ambiguity that are inherent to maps as media of Holocaust testimony and remembrance. Ambiguity will not be limited to an understanding as a double meaning (which its Latin etymological origin suggests), but as a potentiality for multiple and instable meanings that do not necessarily exclude each other.

---

1 "Sobibór" is the correct spelling of the Polish village next to which the extermination camp was erected by the SS. Some authors use this spelling to distinguish the village from the camp, which is referred to without diacritical mark ("Sobibor"). For reasons of consistency, and to make clear that the crimes were committed not "somewhere in the East," but at concrete places, I will use the Polish spelling throughout my text.

Toward a *Campology* of National Socialism

The camp in Sobibór was one of the three camps of the so-called *Aktion Reinhardt*. This was the code name for the National Socialist plan to murder the Polish Jewry in its entirety.² After mass shootings of Jews in the Baltic and other territories of the occupied Soviet Union by German *Einsatzgruppen*, *Reichsführer SS* Heinrich Himmler sought to implement a procedure for mass murder that would be less exhausting for the perpetrators. To this end he could draw on the expertise of physicians and members of other professions who carried out the murder of patients classified as mentally and/or physically disabled. This so-called euthanasia was halted in August 1941, not least because of public and Catholic protest. In October that year, Himmler ordered Odilo Globocnik to kill all Jews within the district of Lublin in occupied Poland, where he held the position of SS and Police Leader.

This was the beginning of *Aktion Reinhardt*, which would eventually lead to the murder of least 1.8 million Jewish men, women and children.³ They came not only from Poland, but also from the Netherlands, Czechoslovakia, Germany, Austria, France, and the Soviet Union. Under Globocnik's command, three camps were established near the villages of Bełżec, Sobibór and Treblinka with the sole purpose of brutally murdering Jews, in an unprecedented way and at an unprecedented scale. During March 1942 and October 1943, most of the victims died in specially designed gas chambers by means of exhaust fumes. Their bodies were initially thrown in mass graves; later on, they were exhumed and burnt. By the end of 1943 all three camps had been disbanded, the buildings dismantled, the grounds leveled and afforested. An estimated 150 Jews survived the camps. The overwhelming majority of the Nazi perpetrators were Germans and Austrians beforehand involved in the so-called euthanasia, and therefore "experts for extermination"⁴. Additional camp personnel were recruited from among Globocniks paramilitary troops of Soviet POWs trained in a camp at Trawniki, hence usually referred to as "Trawnikis".⁵

The unprecedented nature of the extermination camps raises the question, argued by several scholars, of whether the term "camp" is applicable at all.⁶ The

---

2 For an overview on *Aktion Reinhard* cf. Stephan Lehnstaedt, *Der Kern des Holocaust. Bełżec, Sobibór, Treblinka und die Aktion Reinhardt* (Munich: C.H. Beck, 2017); Yitzhak Arad, *Belzec, Sobibor, Treblinka. The Operation Reinhardt Death Camps* (Bloomington: Indiana Univ. Press, 1987).
3 Numbers are taken from Lehnstaedt, *Der Kern des Holocaust*, 8.
4 Cf. Sara Berger, *Experten der Vernichtung. Das T4-Reinhardt-Netzwerk in den Lagern Belzec, Sobibor und Treblinka* (Hamburg: Hamburger Edition, HIS Verlag, 2013).
5 On this group of perpetrators cf. Angelika Benz, *Handlanger der SS. Die Rolle der Trawniki-Männer im Holocaust* (Berlin: Metropol, 2015).
6 Most prominent: Raul Hilberg in his opus magnum *The Destruction of the European Jews*,

term, however, does help us understand the specific nature of these sites. Firstly, it distinguishes the extermination camps from other sites of mass murders, such as places of mass shootings on German-occupied Soviet territory, often located in the forests.[7]

Nevertheless, a crucial distinction from other forms of camps has to be acknowledged. The overwhelming majority of the victims did not stay in the camp longer than a few hours before their deaths. Hence, scholars have argued that the name "camp" would be a euphemism, indicating a sojourn and not immediate death.[8] It goes without saying that the victims did not camp; nor were they 'encamped'. Nevertheless, they were murdered in a camp, in which some of the deportees were kept as prisoners for a certain period of time, and forced to work. Thus, secondly, using the term "camp" acknowledges what this group experienced.

Thirdly, stating that the crime committed by the Germans was unprecedented does not mean that the way it was carried out had no historical antecedent. The camps of *Aktion Reinhardt* share features with other camps. The term "extermination camp" indicates these features, namely that there was a certain material and personnel infrastructure and logistics. The SS carefully chose a site where a built environment could be put up almost from scratch. The general layout, barracks as the dominant building type, the temporality and reversibility of the facilities, and the formation and implementation of a particular staff to run it, are generic features of modern camps.[9] The stationary gas chambers, newly erected and designed to murder people en masse, and the fact that the camp served no other purpose than this (e.g., economic) fundamentally distinguish extermination camps like Sobibór from other camps.

(first published Chicago: Quadrangle Books, 1961), speaks of "killing centers"; Polish language discourse commonly refers to these sites as "ośrodek zagłady", which is the Polish translation of Hilberg's term. For a discussion of the ambiguous implications of another widely used term, "death factory", cf. Alf Lüdtke, "Der Bann der Wörter: 'Todesfabriken'. Vom Reden über den NS-Völkermord – das auch ein Verschweigen ist," in: *WerkstattGeschichte* 13 (1996): 5–18.

7 For a discussion of the ambiguous role of forests as places of mass murder but also shelter for Jewish refugees cf. Konrad Kwiet, "Forests and the Final Solution," in: *Leerstelle(n)? Der deutsche Vernichtungskrieg 1941–1944 und die Vergegenwärtigung des Geschehens in der BRD nach 1989*, edited by Alexandra Klei and Katrin Stoll (Berlin: Neofelis, 2019), 14–70.

8 Cf. Detlef Hoffmann, "Fotografierte Lager. Überlegungen zu einer Fotogeschichte deutscher Konzentrationslager," in: *Fotogeschichte* 14 (1994), No. 54: 3–20, here 11: "Wir bezeichnen auch die Massenmord-Anlagen von Belzec, Sobibor oder Treblinka als Vernichtungslager. Das Wort Lager suggeriert jedoch einen Aufenthalt für Inhaftierte – dieser Aufenthalt fehlte an den Mordstätten, die Menschen wurden vom Bahnhof in die Gaskammern gebracht."

9 On extermination camps as a building type cf. Annika Wienert, *Das Lager vorstellen. Die Architektur der nationalsozialistischen Vernichtungslager* (Berlin: Neofelis, 2018).

"Camp", however, can mean different things.[10] Filip Friedman, a Polish Jew, historian, survivor of the Holocaust and one of the first people to research it, noted in March 1946 with bitter irony: "Our era owes the 'nation of thinkers and poets' [a common German self-denomination, A.W.] the emergence of a new scientific branch, of which up to now no philosopher could have dreamt."[11] He called this new branch of science "campology". Friedman connects it with yet another new field, the science of the destruction of humans, or genocidal science, which he specifies in parentheses with the German neologism *Vernichtungswissenschaft* (literally: extermination science). Among its most important instruments were camps as an institution.

The respective camps themselves were of different natures, Friedman stresses. In some, he points out, victims were killed immediately upon arrival, but does not consider this to be an argument to dismiss the term. He continues sketching a multifaceted, interdisciplinary research program and elaborates on a classification of German camps according to purpose.[12] In his typology, we find the term extermination camp (*obóz zagłady*), and later references to Treblinka and Sobibór as examples of camps in which the NS administration destroyed material proof and official documents. This, he argues, makes the testimony of witnesses and former prisoners of crucial significance. As early as July 1944, the Central Jewish Historical Commission (CŻKH) in Poland, of which Friedman was the first director, began systematically collecting such testimonies.[13] The members of the commission not only recorded testimonies in writing, but also visual material – photographs, drawings, and maps. Some were sketched by the survivors themselves, others commissioned by the CŻKH. These collected maps are very important and rich sources as to the topography of the camps. While some focus on the gas chambers as the actual site of the mass murder, they also provide information on the larger infrastructure implemented by the SS to carry out the killing.

As images they also possess certain features that distinguish them from

---

10 Kiran Klaus Patel has pointed out the ambiguous (in his terms: janus-faced) role of camps within National Socialist policies, and argued that a comprehensive analysis of Nazi camps would have to include those directed at members of the *Volksgemeinschaft*. Cf. Kiran Klaus Patel, "'Auslese' und 'Ausmerze'. Das Janusgesicht der nationalsozialistischen Lager," in: *Zeitschrift für Geschichtswissenschaft* 54,4 (2006): 339–65.
11 "[…] nasza epoka zawdzięcza 'narodowie myślicieli i poetów' powstanie nowej gałęzi nauki, o której dotąd nie śniło się filozofom. Ta nowa gałąź nauki to – obozologia." Filip Friedman, "Przedmowa," in: *Dokumenty i Materiały. Tom I: Obozy* [=Documents and Materials. Vol. 1: Camps], edited by Natan Blumental (Łódź, 1946), I–V, here I.
12 Ibid., III.
13 The organization was initially named Central Committee of Polish Jews (CKŻP), but changed its name in December 1944. For a short overview cf. Andrzej Żbikowski, "Central Committee of Polish Jews," 12 November 2015 <http://www.jhi.pl/en/blog/2013-11-12-central-committee-of-polish-jews> (5 April 2018).

written sources: Unlike the succession of words in a text, maps provide a synopsis. The beholder is confronted, literally at a glance, with the totality of the camp. Maps, understood as images, simultaneously depict the complexity of structures and relations, with details understood in the context of the whole. In a text, this relationship is inverse: The reader has to recollect the details to construct the whole. This is why images are more capable of depicting spatial relations. Maps also transform time-bound three-dimensional information into a downsized, two-dimensional representation. This transformation is always highly selective, and affected by individual skills and choices, as well as changing cultural norms and conventions. Therefore, the beholder of a map has to engage actively and creatively to make sense of it.

Camp Images – Imagining the Camp

A map is not a mere code to be deciphered. It is an image that both requires and evokes an imagination. A case in point for the evocative capacity is the iconic map of Auschwitz-Birkenau. The term "Auschwitz" has become a metonymy for the Holocaust; maps of Birkenau have to some extent become a cartographical metonymy for the larger complex of different facilities, locations and sub-camps that Auschwitz encompassed.

The SS destroyed most of the documentation produced while the camp was operational, but a "collection of records of the construction management (Bauleitung) of the camp"[14] was preserved. Soviet authorities transferred part of these records out of the country, making it difficult for researchers to access. It was only in the 1990s when the archive of the Museum Auschwitz-Birkenau received microfilms of the documents.[15] The archive possesses several construction plans, the first dating from October 1941.[16] While the literature on Auschwitz is legion, these original plans have been seldom reproduced. Most of the publications draw on a reconstruction of Birkenau's layout (usually without indicating the archival basis). There are two probable reasons for this: Firstly, the historical plans were working drawings, subject to changes and corrections; they show what was planned, not necessarily what was built. Secondly, they were "[p]roduced on poor-quality paper," "[s]tained, folded," and are "in poor con-

---

14 Geoffrey P. Megargee (ed.), *Encyclopedia of Camps and Ghettos, 1933–1945*, (Bloomington: Indiana University Press, 2009), Vol. 1, Pt. A, 213.
15 Cf. Franciszek Piper, "Einleitung," in: *Auschwitz 1940–1945*, edited by Wacław Długoborski and Franciszek Piper (Oświęcim: Auschwitz-Birkenau State Museum, 1999), 14–42, here 20–22.
16 Cf. Irena Strzelecka and Piotr Setkiewicz, "Bau, Ausbau und Entwicklung des KL Auschwitz und seiner Nebenlager," in: ibid., 73–156, here 94.

dition today".¹⁷ Hence, cleared black-and-white redrawings or reconstructions are more accessible and legible, as they provide an unequivocal, stable overview.

The cartographical representation of Birkenau that many scholarly and educational publications make use of reflects a certain understanding of a Nazi camp.¹⁸ The map's monotonous, repetitive and mass character gives an idea of the large scale of the camp even when the reproduction lacks a key or the actual measurement of the camp itself.¹⁹ Evidently, *Schreibtischtäter* (literally: desk-bound perpetrators)²⁰ planned this on the drawing board. Dominated by orthogonality and regularity, the map illustrates a lack of individuality and the inhumanity of the facility.²¹ It corresponds with Wolfgang Sofsky's analysis of the concentration camp as a place of "absolute power".²² Yet, it does not confront the viewer with any individual act of violence. The perpetrators are absent, as are the victims and their suffering. Even geographical information is missing. There is not vegetation indicated and the camp is presented "as built on isotropic surfaces with all traces of topography and geology erased."²³ This idealized order, along with the bird's eye view, and the reduction to black lines on white ground suggest a panoptic grasp, obscuring that the map is, in fact, an abstraction of reality, and in this case: an abstraction in accordance with National Socialist phantasm.

A concept for a memorial in Auschwitz-Birkenau by the Polish architect Oskar Hansen et al.²⁴ rejected such abstraction and its connotations.²⁵ The project was

---

17 Robert Jan van Pelt and Debórah Dwork, *Auschwitz. 1270 to the Present* (New Haven/London: Yale University Press, 1996), introduction to plates' section, without page numbers.
18 Cf. for example the map of Auschwitz-Birkenau in Aleksander Lasik et al., *Auschwitz 1940–1945. Central Issues in the History of the Camp. Vol. 1: The Establishment of the Camp* (Oświęcim. Auschwitz-Birkenau State Museum, 2000), 84–85.
19 140 ha (720 x 2,340 m), cf. *Auschwitz-Prozeß 4 Ks2/63* (exhib. cat. Fritz Bauer Institute Frankfurt am Main, 2004), 583.
20 This is a key term in German-language discourse on Nazi perpetrators that has no standard translation in English or French. It is usually accredited to Hannah Arendt, even though she used the more explicit term "desk murderer". Cf. Christoph Jahr, "Die Täter hinter den Tätern," *NZZ*, 1 January 2017 <https://www.nzz.ch/feuilleton/schreibtischtaeter-die-taeter-hinter-den-taetern-ld.140108> (9 April 2018); Dirk van Laak and Dirk Rose (eds.), *Schreibtischtäter. Begriff – Geschichte – Typologie* (Göttingen: Wallstein, 2018).
21 Which is already indicated by the type of barracks, originally designed as a horse stable.
22 Cf. Wolfgang Sofsky, *The Order of Terror. The Concentration Camp* (Princeton: Princeton University Press, 1997) (first published in German 1993).
23 Andrew Charlesworth, "The Topography of the Holocaust," in: *The Historiography of the Holocaust*, edited by Dan Stone (Basingstroke: Palgrave Macmillan, 2004), 216–52, here 218. In the following, the author elaborates on the significance of the relief ("the contoured landscape") for certain camps.
24 The other team members were Zofia Hansen, Jerzy Jarnuszkiewicz, Edmund Kupiecki, Julian Pałka, Tadeusz Plasota and Lechosław Rosiński.
25 For an overview on the ample literature discussing the project cf. Katarzyna Murawska-Muthesius, "Open Form, Public Sculpture and the Counter-Memorial," in: *Oskar Hansen: Opening Modernism. On Open Form Architecture, Art and Didactics*, edited by Aleksandra

submitted 1958 for an international competition that had been announced one year earlier and that was organized by the International Auschwitz Committee. The authors refrained from established forms of sculptural commemorations, both abstract and figurative.[26] They proposed a road running diagonally through the camp's space, incorporating material remnants of the camp's infrastructure. Instead of a vertical, permanent, immutable monument, the design implied a temporality that is twofold, relating to the spectator and to the site itself. As there is no designated point of view, the spectator cannot remain passive. Walking along the road s/he has to experience the site in time and space. Everything outside this road-monument was to be left untouched and not altered by human interaction, which would lead to continuous change over time through weather conditions, flora and fauna.

The design, suggesting an anti-monument *avant la lettre*,[27] was not realized. The competition entry prepared by Hansen and his team consisted of different materials, among them a partial maquette.[28] Most prominently and widely received was one image altering the map of Birkenau (Fig.1), a pictorial intervention in the two dimensional representation of the camp's space. So, instead of encountering the twofold temporality *in situ* that the artists initially intended, we encounter the project as a single image, be it in publications or within the exhibition space.[29] This image shows a bold black line reaching from the eastern border of the camp to the gas chambers and crematoria south of the camp's internal rail spur. This alteration of the map can be understood as a literal cancellation or crossing out of the Nazi order. In respect to this radical negation, it constitutes an "anti-image", or more specifically, an anti-map.

Whereas the map of Auschwitz-Birkenau is part of the collective, visual memory of the camp, the collective memory of the *Aktion Reinhardt* camps is generally very limited, and contains hardly any images.[30] This, of course, has to

---

Kędziorek and Łukasz Ronduda (Warsaw: Museum of Modern Art, 2014), 199–211, here footnote 4.

26   For a discussion of Rosalind Krauss's reflection on modernist sculpture in the context of the competition cf. Agata Pietrasik, "Abstraction & Figuration in the Auschwitz Memorial. From Consensus to Dissensus," in: *Die Transformation der Lager. Annäherungen an die Orte nationalsozialistischer Verbrechen*, edited by Alexandra Klei et al. (Bielefeld: transcript, 2011), 141–54.

27   On the notion of the anti-monument in the context of public memory in Germany cf. Corinna Tomberger, *Das Gegendenkmal. Avantgardekunst, Geschichtspolitik und Geschlecht in der bundesdeutschen Erinnerungskultur* (Bielefeld: transcript 2007).

28   Photographic documentation online: <https://artmuseum.pl/en/kolekcja/praca/hansen-oskar-jarnuszkiewicz-jerzy-palka-julian-rosinski#> (21 December 2017).

29   Lastly: *documenta 14*, Kassel 2017; *Oskar and Zofia Hansen. Open Form*, Muzeum Sztuki Nowoczesnej, Warsaw 2017.

30   Apart from the station sign "Sobibór", which became known to a wider audience through Claude Lanzman's film *Shoah*.

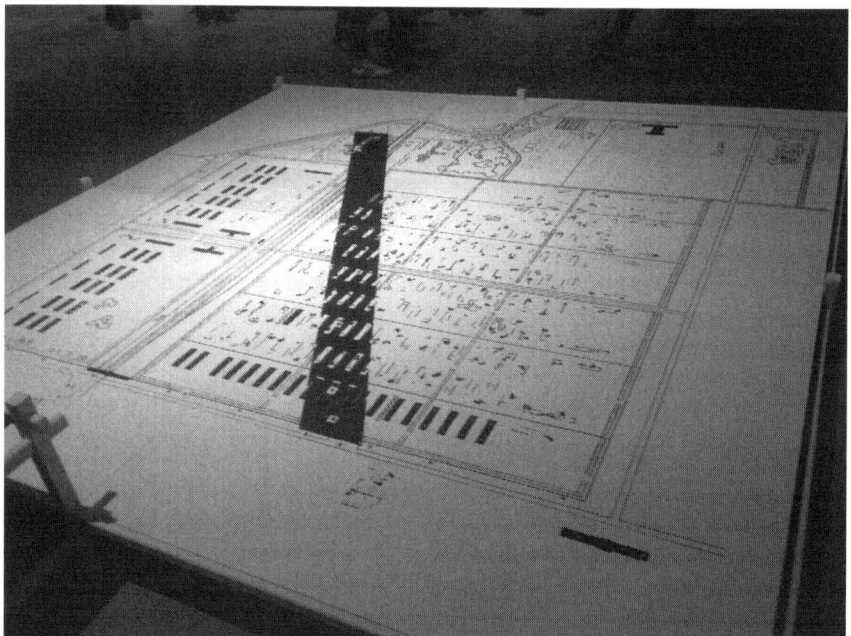

Fig. 1: "The Monument to the Victims of Fascism in Auschwitz-Birkenau Project", 1958. Authors: Oskar Hansen, Sofia Hansen, Jerzy Januszkiewicz, Julian Pałka, Lechosław Rosiński, Edmund Kupiecki, Tadeusz Plasota. Reproduction adapted for the exhibition "Oskar and Zofia Hansen. Open Form", Museum of Modern Art in Warsaw, 2017, installation view. (Photograph: Annika Wienert, with kind permission of the Museum of Modern Art in Warsaw.)

do with the fact that very few historical sources are available. In contrast to most other camps, there are no official Nazi documents with maps or construction plans of the *Aktion Reinhardt* camps. All cartographical representations of their layout and structure were produced from memory *ex post facto*. The Germans succeeded in killing most of the witnesses to their crimes and in destroying almost all evidence and traces. Thus, when visiting the sites today, there seems to be nothing left. *In situ*, the prevailing experience is the absence of the camps and their traces. Thus, visualizations such as maps can function as important means for an imagination of the camps. Some of the maps drawn by survivors create a very different impression than the plan of Auschwitz-Birkenau mentioned above. An example for that is the "sketch of the camp in Sobibór" drawn by Icek Lichtman in December 1945 (Fig. 2).

It is part of his testimony given to the CŻKH in Kraków, recorded by Laura Eichhorn.[31] Born in 1906 Lichtman lived with his family in Żółkiewka, Poland,

---

31 Archiwum ŻIH [=Archive of the Jewish Historical Institute in Warsaw] 301/1204. The account includes two maps; I am focusing on only one of them.

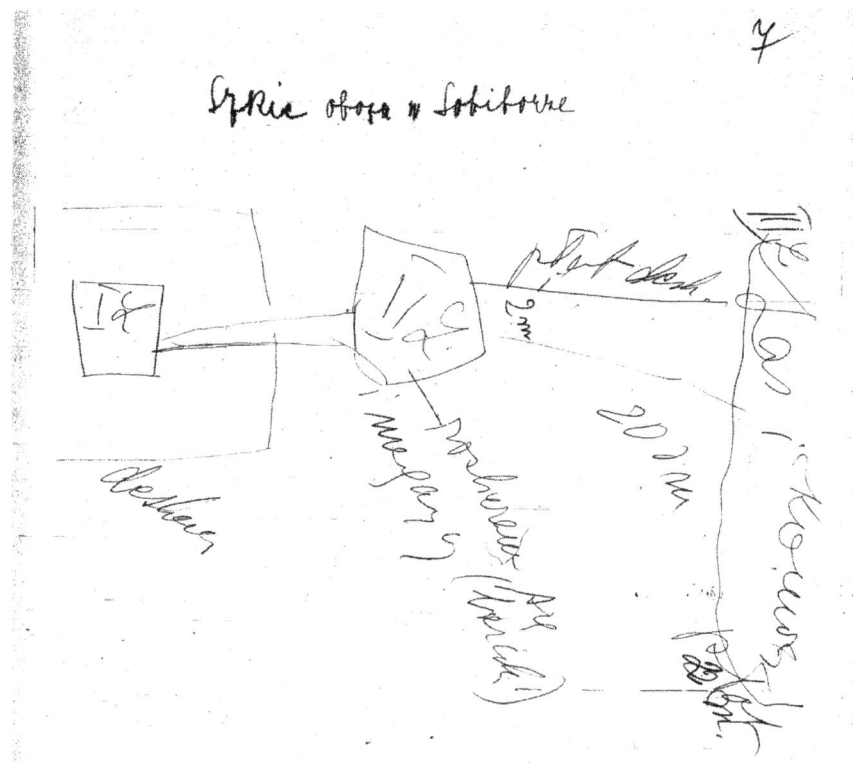

Fig. 2: "Sketch of the Camp in Sobibór", Icek Lichtman, 18 December 1945. (Source: Archive of the Jewish Historical Institute 301/1204)

until being deported to Sobibór in May 1942. During the prisoners' revolt on 14 October, 1943, he was able to escape, and was one of an estimated 70 survivors of the camp, where some 180,000 people were killed.[32]

His drawing on a sheet of paper could hardly serve as a construction plan. However, it qualifies as a map – a graphic representation of the camp's layout from an aerial perspective. As such, it does provide an overview, yet remains enigmatic. We see a few hastily drawn, thin lines, Roman and Arabic numerals, and Polish inscriptions. It is quite literally difficult to decipher, as the writing is barely legible. Inscriptions running horizontally, vertically and diagonally add to the confusion. The author did not use the paper's full format,[33] which might suggest an altogether rather small facility. He does specify certain lengths: 2 m,

---

32 For a discussion of the most recent findings on the accurate number of victims cf. Robert Kuwałek, "Nowe ustalenia dotyczące liczby ofiar niemieckiego obozu zagłady w Sobiborze," in: *Zeszyty Majdanka* 26 (2014): 17–60.
33 Approx. A4 format; exact dimensions: 210 x 295 mm.

200 m, 22 m – but these distances are clearly incongruent with the proportion of the drawing. In fact, everything seems to be out of proportion; it even remains unclear to which distance "200 m" is referring.

Lichtman numbered three parts: I L., II L., III L.,[34] ascending – following the dominant Western reading direction – from left to right. They are connected by (almost) parallel horizontal lines. The first two parts are framed by a quadrangular form, the second being larger than the first. The vertical dimension of the drawing as well as the amount of details also increases from left to right. Thus, upon closer examination, the drawing, enigmatic as it may seem at first, elucidates crucial aspects of the camp by means of composition, scale and inscription. We understand that it consisted of three separate, enclosed parts that were linked by regulated connections. Numbering and composition point out that the third is of the highest significance. With very limited means, the drawing attains a narrative effect.

So while Lichtman's drawing mostly neglects professional cartographical conventions,[35] it does strive for an interpersonal transmission of his experience and knowledge. This experience and knowledge apparently required an additional form of externalization different from the verbal account. How can we characterize this specific form of testimony? In a global sense, Lichtman's drawing is a "value-laden image,"[36] as John Brian Harley has conceptualized maps. Harley emphasizes their contrived character: "Both in the selectivity of their content, and in their signs and styles of representation, maps are a way of conceiving, articulating, and structuring the human world, which is biased towards, promoted by, and exerts influence upon particular sets of social relations."[37] The first part of the sentence is helpful for an understanding of Lichtman's drawing as a map, especially as it recognizes selectivity as a means for making sense rather than a deficit. The last aspect, however, cannot easily be applied to it, as Harley in the article cited conceptualizes the influence that maps exert primarily in political terms. In this sense, Lichtman's map was in no position to cause wider political effects.

Furthermore, one has to take into account that John Brian Harley concentrates on maps produced by professional cartographers. His general considerations

---

34 L. as an abbreviation for "Lager". Lichtman uses this German word (English: camp) referring to the different parts of the camp in Sobibór. Archiwum ŻIH 301/1204.
35 In contrast to the second map that is part of the account.
36 John Brian Harley, "Maps, Knowledge, and Power," in: *The Iconography of Landscape*, edited by Denis Cosgrove and Stephen Daniels (Cambridge: Cambridge Univ. Press, 1988), 277–312, here 278. Harley's writing stimulated an important discussion in the discipline of geography and cartography. Cf. Denis Wood and John Krygier, "Critical Cartography," in: *International Encyclopedia of Human Geography*, edited by Robert Kitchin and Nigel Thrift (Amsterdam etc.: Elsevier, 2009), 340–44.
37 Harley, "Maps, Knowledge, and Power," 278.

nonetheless relate to other forms of maps. The enigmatic, unconventional, and ostentatiously subjective nature of Lichtman's drawing clearly distinguishes it from official maps and building plans produced by professionals. While the former evidently seems to be biased, the latter's impartiality is nothing but a widely shared cultural presumption, Harley argues: "That maps can produce a truly 'scientific' image of the world, in which factual information is represented without favor, is a view well embedded in our cultural mythology."[38] Accordingly, the difference is of degree, and not of kind.

The Ambiguous Role of Maps in the Context of Legal Proceedings

The following discussion will examine the role maps played in the trials of the Sobibór camp's Nazi officers and guards[39] in order to demonstrate their influence in a specific, definite setting. Moreover, I will discuss the effectuality of the understanding of (certain) maps as unbiased, exact representations of reality. In the context of legal proceedings on the crimes committed at Sobibór, the most prominent map was the one drawn by former SS member Erich Bauer, who was stationed there from April 1942 until the end of 1943. It, too, is not a professional map according to official standards of cartography, neither true to scale and nor oriented north.[40] But in principle, it emulates cartographical conventions.

The map originated from the 1950 trial in Frankfurt of two other former members of the SS staff in Sobibór, Hubert Gomerski and Johann Klier. Earlier that year, Bauer had already been sentenced to lifetime in prison in a different trial in Berlin.[41] He was interrogated as a witness for the Frankfurt trial and produced his map in this context in 1950.[42] The main trial of thirteen SS guards of the Sobibór camp took place in Hagen, West Germany from 1965 to 1966. For the purposes of the main hearing, the court issued a large-format reproduction of the Bauer map (Fig. 3).

It was also included in the published judgment.[43] Both, the large-format

---

38 Ibid., 287.
39 On the *Aktion Reinhardt* perpetrators cf. Berger, *Experten der Vernichtung*; on the trials in West Germany cf. Michael S. Bryant, *Eyewitness to the Genocide. The Operation Reinhard Death Camp Trials 1955–1966* (Knoxville: University of Tennessee Press, 2014).
40 An arrow pointing north was added for the publication of the judgment, see footnote 43 below.
41 Initially he was sentenced to death. The sentence was commuted to life imprisonment due to the abolition of capital punishment in West Germany.
42 HHStAW Wiesbaden, Abt. 462, Nr. 36346, Bd. 8.
43 "Urteil des LG Hagen vom 20.12.1966," in: *Justiz und NS-Verbrechen. Sammlung deutscher Strafurteile wegen nationalsozialistischer Tötungsverbrechen*, edited by Dick de Mildt and

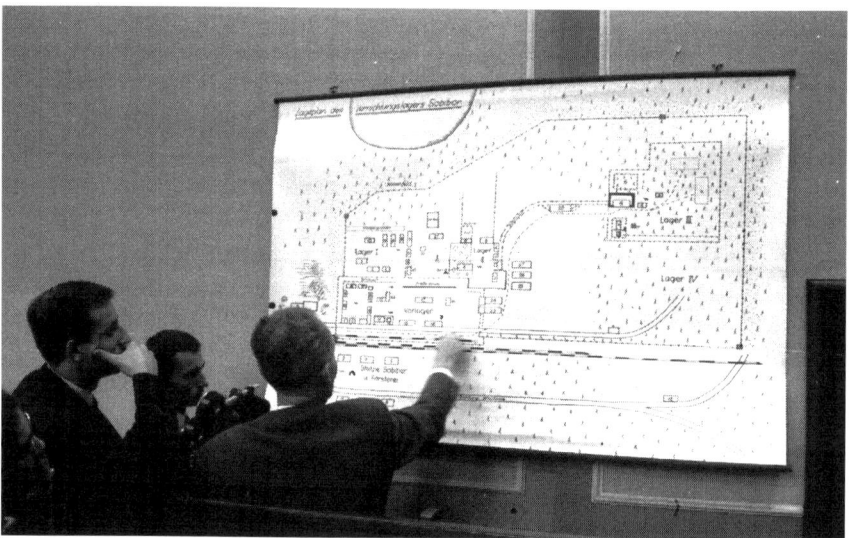

Fig. 3: Picture of the courtroom in Hagen during the trial of former members of the SS in the Sobibór camp, 9 May 1965. (Photographer: Willi Lehmacher. Source: Stadtarchiv Hagen, Bildarchiv)

version used during the hearing and the reproduction in the written judgment have no captions explaining the numerals in the drawing.[44] This suggests an understanding of the map as a self-evident image that needs no further explanation. It was also used as illustrative material in the retrials of Hubert Gomerski in Frankfurt in the 1970s and of Karl Frenzel[45] in Hagen in the 1980s.

The influence of Erich Bauer's map is not confined to the jurisdictional context. Taken as overall correct and objective, it is also referred to in academic studies. A case in point is Barbara Distel's article on Sobibór in the nine-volume German-language encyclopedia on the history of the Nazi concentration camps (2005–2009), co-edited with Wolfgang Benz (Fig. 4).[46]

Apart from its new design, the image Distel uses to illustrate her text is a copy

---

Christiaan F. Rüter (Amsterdam: Amsterdam University Press, 2012), Vol. XXV, 59–252, map 91.

44 Bauer did originally add captions to his map. They were available for the prosecutor and the court.
45 Frenzel had been sentenced to life imprisonment in the first trial in Hagen. The files of the public prosecutor for his retrial contain a copy of the map and its captions. Cf. Wiederaufnahmeverfahren Frenzel. Dokumente. Lagerskizzen., LA NRW, Abteilung Westfalen, Q 234, 4614.
46 Barbara Distel, "Sobibór," in: *Der Ort des Terrors. Geschichte der nationalsozialistischen Konzentrationslager. Vol. 8*, edited by Wolfgang Benz and Barbara Distel (Munich: C.H. Beck, 2009), 375–404, map 377.

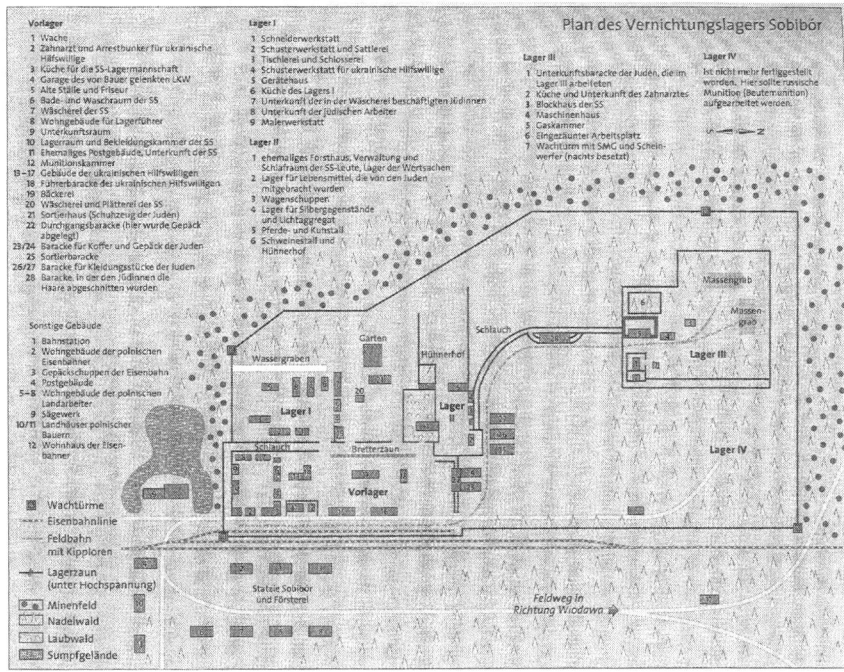

Fig. 4: "Map of the Extermination Camp Sobibór". (Source: Wolfgang Benz, Barbara Distel (eds.), *Der Ort des Terrors. Geschichte der nationalsozialistischen Konzentrationslager*. Vol. 8, Munich 2009, p. 377.)

of the Hagen map, and thus ignores or dismisses research findings from the last forty years. For example, Jules Schelvis, a Sobibór survivor and author of the first academic monograph on the history of the camp, also drew on Bauer's map in his publication, but integrated findings derived from other drawings by SS members and survivors.[47] Although the integration of newer historical and archeological findings[48] on the topography of the camp would not have altered the map drastically, this neglect is somewhat surprising. Even more surprising for an academic publication is lack of attribution.[49] After comparing the two maps,

---

47 Cf. Jules Schelvis, *Vernichtungslager Sobibór* (Berlin: Metropol, 1998) (first published in Dutch 1993), 52–53; map 8–10.
48 At least the results of the first archaeological excavation campaign where already published (Andrzej Kola: "Badania archeologiczne terenu byłego obozu zagłady Żydów w Sobiborze," in: *Przeszłość i Pamięć. Biuletyn Rady Ochroni Pamięci Walk i Męczeństwa* 4 (2001): 115–22); further archeological excavations were being done at the time of the publication, and published the same year: Isaac Gilead et al., "Excavating Nazi Extermination Centres," in: *Present Pasts* 1 (2009): 10–39.
49 Under "Picture Credits" in the appendix, Peter Palm is listed as the creator of this map. Benz and Distel, *Der Ort des Terrors. Vol. 8*, 449.

neglect seems the only explanation, especially since even the incorrect spelling of the Polish word "stacja" as "Statzie" (English: station) is reproduced. Thus, in contrast to Lichtman's drawing, the Bauer map thus clearly exerted influence, as Harley would have it. This influence was not only far-reaching but also shifted context: from criminal prosecution to academia.

While selectivity and bias are inevitable characteristics of maps per se, the effects of these two aspects can be exemplified by a detail: It is striking that the infamous "Lazarett" (English: infirmary), is missing from the map published by Distel and Benz in 2009, which was originally drawn by one of the perpetrators. *Lazarett* was the denomination for a site next to a small wooden chapel, where the SS regularly shot deportees or prisoners considered "unfit for work". The separate execution site plays an important role in many survivors' accounts. During an interrogation in 1962, Bauer confirmed that the *Lazarett* was a place "where people were not healed, but shot."[50] He had included this site in his drawing already in 1950 and marked it with a small cross. He did not assign a caption, though, which might explain why this place is not labeled in the new design from 2009. Barbara Distel speaks of the chapel in her text; in the published map we do find a rectangle on the same spot as in Bauer's map, but without the cross. Therefore, it is impossible to identify this abstract element as the killing site in question.

Before coming back to the issue of the *Lazarett* from the survivor's perspective, it is interesting to look at performative aspects of Bauer's map in its original context. In several trials of Sobibór camp perpetrators in West Germany[51] it shaped both questions and answers of the hearings. Although it was not listed as qualified evidence but only served as illustrative material, it became a key element in the course of the proceedings. In the minutes of these trials, we frequently find such statements as "the witness comments on the map", and witnesses were regularly asked to point out where exactly something happened. Locating their memories on the map, authenticated their testimony. That means that the map provided by the court could help survivors to articulate their stories and to be heard and believed. But, at other times, the map could also call testimony into question when someone was unable to refer to it 'correctly'.

The influence that Erich Bauer's map exerted in court and the power of the

---

50 "Das Wort 'Lazarett' ist hier fehl am Platz, denn dort wurden Menschen nicht geheilt, sondern erschossen." Erich Bauer, Berlin, 10 January 1962. ZStL-251/59-5-990. Quoted in: Schelvis, *Vernichtungslager Sobibór*, 79.
51 Berlin and Frankfurt, 1950; Hagen 1965–66; Frankfurt 1973–77; Hagen 1983–85. Cf. Bryant, *Eyewitness to the Genocide*, chapter 4; Angelika Benz, *Der Henkersknecht. Der Prozess gegen John (Iwan) Demjanjuk in München* (Berlin: Metropol, 2011), 93–100; Sara Berger, "NS-Prozesse gegen Personal der Vernichtungslager der 'Aktion Reinhardt'. Anmerkungen zu Schuld und Sühne eines Massenmords," in: *Einsicht* 1 (2009): 24–31.

cultural assumption of maps depicting factual information without favor reverberates in the memoirs of Andrew Zielinski.[52] His mother, Regina Zielinski, née Feldman, was deported to Sobibór in December 1942 and remained until 14 October 1943, when the prisoners' revolt enabled her to escape. After the war she emigrated to Australia. In 1983, she testified in the trial of Karl Frenzel, who had been convicted in 1966 but succeeded in obtaining a retrial. Andrew Zielinski traveled with his mother to Germany and also accompanied her to court. This is how he describes her initial questioning: Testifying that she had seen through a fence of branches how people were driven naked to the gas chambers, Regina Zielinski was asked to show on Bauer's map where exactly this fence was located. She hesitated to answer. "She then said that there was something wrong with [the map]: it did not correspond with her recollection of the camp at all. We all drew breath, and the accusations made by Frenzel's defense [i.e., her not having been in Sobibór at all, A.W.] hung like a guillotine. [...] Mum walked over to the map, looked at it very carefully, and said it was not a map of Sobibor at all. Judge Kremer came close to the map, examined it, and announced to the court that it had been placed upside down. He apologized to Mum, and turned the map around himself. Then mum was immediately able to point out the location of the brush fence."[53]

This relation highlights the crucial role of the map for the authentication of not only Regina Zielinski's testimony, but also her very identity as a survivor. There is, however, no evidence of this dramatic interaction in the minutes of the trial, and her testimony on the second day of her questioning reads prosaically: "She could hardly show it on the map, because somehow everything was different as it appears on the plan."[54] It is understood that the court's minutes are by no means unbiased, exact representations of the events they record. But the numbers and lettering on the map, as well as the fact that the map was present in court from the very beginning of the trial, make the idea that it was placed upside down highly unlikely. The specific way in which the author relates this event should not be understood as a simple mistake, even less a deliberate distortion, though. We cannot ascertain whether or not this is how he personally remembers it circa 20 years later. The point of the matter is: it reflects the power of the map and fulfills a function in his narrative. Andrew Zielinksi continues to speak about the reaction of the audience present in court: "The students burst into cheers and applause.

---

52 Andrew Zielinski, *Conversations with Regina* (Włodawa: Muzeum Pojezierza Łęcyńsko-Włodawa, 2008) (first published 2003).
53 Ibid., 39.
54 "An der Karte könne sie das schlecht zeigen, weil irgendwie alles anders gewesen sei, als es auf dem Plan erscheine." Protokolle zur Hauptverhandlung vor dem Schwurgericht Hagen, Aussage Regina Cybula-Zielinski am 17.3.1983, LA NRW, Abteilung Westfalen, Q 234, 4406.

[…] The jubilant chorus behind me only stressed this moment as a victory."[55] Thus, the (possible) misremembering allows for portraying his mother as victorious, at last.

His narrative draws on the cultural myth of an unbiased map. Given the implicit understanding of a map's objectiveness, not being able to recognize it would question the survivor's credibility. In this moment, it even seemed plausible to others that she had not been to Sobibór at all. This is instantly obvious to the audience – hence the fact that observers "drew breath". They have to stand the suspense a little longer, as Regina Zielinski stays calm, takes her time and discloses the mistake. The map now no longer serves to delegitimize her, but on the contrary verifies her experience and testimony. She knows more than everybody else in the room; she uncovers a mistake nobody was able to notice before. The judge, a representative of the German state, apologizes; the young audience, composed of members of the post-Nazi generation, applauds her. The word "chorus" brings to the reader's mind the classical Greek theater.

The court transcripts speak an entirely different, ostentatiously nontheatrical language. They still document how witnesses more often than not disagreed with the map on some details, claimed that others were missing, or felt the urge to explain that the camp looked different at the time of the specific incidents that they were talking about. According to the minutes, Regina Zielinski repeatedly told the court that the map did not match her memories of the camp, questioning not only details, but the general proportions and ultimately refusing to point out the site of an execution because of the map's incorrectness.[56]

One argument that can be made in favor of the purported objectiveness of Bauer's map is the fact that he was on duty in the camp from its very beginning to its very end and had access to all parts of the camp. But we have to keep in mind that a map is a static medium, and that the physical reality of the camp dynamically evolved. This, of course, makes the question "What did the camp look like?" even more difficult to answer. Strictly speaking, one has to ask: What did the camp look like at a certain point in time? Accordingly, Regina Zielinski explained her objection regarding the map, emphasizing that "it has to be taken into account that the camp was extended later on."[57]

These general considerations can be exemplified by the testimonies of several

---

55 Andrew Zielinski, *Conversations*, 39.
56 "Die Zeugin erklärt an der Lagerkarte: Irgendwie stimmten die aufgezeichneten Verhältnisse, Proportionen, nicht mit ihrer Vorstellung überein. Sie meine eigentlich auch nicht, daß das Munitionslager da gewesen sei, wo jetzt IV steht. […] Sie könne nicht auf dieser [underlined, A.W.] (falschen) Karte den Platz zeigen, auf dem das Waldkommando erschossen worden sei." Protokolle zur Hauptverhandlung vor dem Schwurgericht Hagen, Aussage Regina Cybula-Zielinski am 17.3.1983, LA NRW, Abteilung Westfalen, Q 234, 4406.
57 "Es sei auch zu berücksichtigen, daß das Lager später auch erweitert worden sei." Ibid.

survivors' during legal proceedings in West Germany. Looking closer at concrete details of some of the interrogations allows for a deeper understanding of the performative power of maps as well as how, on the one hand, they could restrict survivors and, on the other hand, these survivors used them to implement their memories in a context that was fundamentally not set up to include these memories comprehensively.

In court, survivors testify as witnesses in a legal sense.[58] Their testimony is determined by certain rules that govern what can be said, when and how it can be said. These rules are codified under the German Criminal Procedure Code,[59] but of course – as in most situations of social interaction – uncodified rules also come into play. Witnesses have to abide by explicit and implicit rules to be heard and in order for their accounts to be taken into consideration. The map that was present in the courtroom was part of this set of rules. In the retrial of Hubert Gomerski in Frankfurt,[60] the survivor Moshe Bachir was asked to show where the *Lazarett* mentioned earlier was situated. The minutes note: "The witness shows as 'Lazarett' a place to the bottom left of the caption 'Camp IV,' where on the map there is a building without numeration; the building has a cross on it. The witness declares: This site plan does not depict the camp as it was upon my arrival."[61]

In a nutshell, this short section illustrates the ambiguous role the map played in court: Bachir positively referred to a detail while, at the same time, dismissing the map as a whole. He made use of the map to authenticate his testimony and transmit his memories. Nevertheless, he was aware of the map's shortcomings and tried to counteract the restrictions it imposes. Later that same day, he was asked again to show a detail on the map. He then presented a drawing by his own

---

58 There is a rich theoretical reflection on the concepts of testimony and the witness in Holocaust literature; cf. for example *Poetics Today. International Journal for Theory and Analysis of Literature and Communication* 27 (2006), Issue 2: "The Humanity of Testimony," with contributions by Aleida Assmann, Annette Wieviorka, Jan T. Gross, and others. For the purposes of my argument, it is sufficient to note that these concepts crucially belong to three fields: law, (Christian) theology, and atrocity.
59 Cf. Lutz Meyer-Goßner, *Strafprozeßordnung, Gerichtsverfassungsgesetz, Nebengesetze und ergänzende Bestimmungen*, 61st ed. (München: C.H. Beck, 2018); for an English version of the Criminal Procedure Code cf. <https://germanlawarchive.iuscomp.org/?p=754> (26 March 2018). I am thankful to Katrin Stoll for this reference.
60 Gomerski was sentenced to a lifetime imprisonment in 1950; as a result of the retrial, the sentence was reduced to 15 years imprisonment.
61 "Der Zeuge zeigt als 'Lazarett' einen Platz links unten von der Bezeichnung 'Lager IV', wo in der Karte ein Gebäude ohne Nummernbezeichnung eingetragen ist; das Gebäude trägt ein Kreuz. Der Zeuge erklärt: Dieser Lageplan ist nicht so, wie das Lager bei meiner Ankunft war." Zeugenheft Alster / Bachir, Protokoll 26. Verhandlungstag in der Strafsache gegen Gomerski wegen Mord, 12.3.1974, LA NRW, Abteilung Westfalen, Q 234, 4464.

hand (Fig. 5) and answered: "I prepared a plan when I had nothing to do in the hotel, and how I remember it. I can show it to you on that."[62]

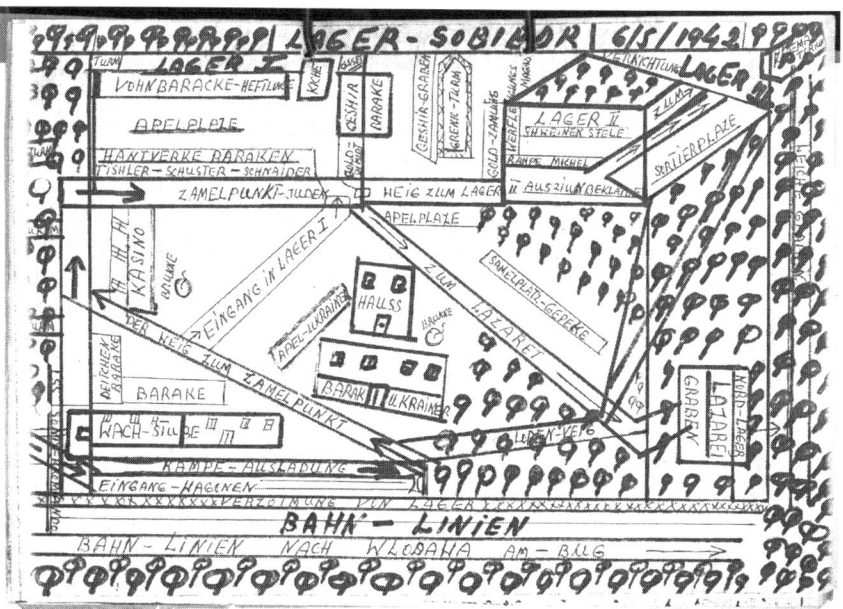

Fig. 5: "Camp – Sobibor | 6/5/1942". Drawing by Moshe Bachir, before March 12 1974 (Archive Copy). (Source: LAV NRW W, Q 234/ Staatsanwaltschaft Dortmund, Zentralstelle für die Bearbeitung von NS-Massenverbrechen No. 4614)

Bachir produced a map in horizontal format, covering an entire A4 sheet of paper, dominated by dense, thick lines, most drawn with the help of a ruler. It shows the camp as surrounded by simple tree symbols (a circle and a vertical line), which on the right half of the paper permeate the camp's space. There is plenty of text in German with spelling errors, and arrows indicating directions of movement. Altogether the graphic elements are disorientating. Following the conventions of architectural floor plans, most of the buildings are indicated as rectangles. In the center, an irregular rhombus frames two buildings: a "hall" for the SS (or: "hauss", misspelled German for house), and underneath a "barracks" for the mostly Ukrainian auxiliary forces, the so-called Trawniki. The two-storey buildings are depicted in schematized front view. This shift in the mode of perspective together with the oversized scale can be interpreted as a use of hierarchical proportion. The author positioned two buildings metonymically in

---

[62] "Ich habe einen Plan angefertigt als ich jetzt hier im Hotel nichts zu tun hatte und wie ich es erinnere. Da kann ich es Ihnen zeigen." Ibid.

the center. Their spatial relation corresponds with the hierarchy among the camp's staff.

From above the buildings and diagonally toward the lower right corner of the sheet, two arrows and the inscription "Zum Lazaret" indicate the way to the so-called infirmary. At the end of this way, there is a rectangle subdivided in three parts labeled "the northern camp," the "lazaret," and a trench. The pictorial downsizing of the *Lazarett* on Bauer's map was among the reasons that Moshe Bachir produced his own map. But that was not the only aspect that he felt required a different visual representation. On the next day of the hearings, he continued to elaborate on his drawing and explained that it depicted the camp during its first months. During the course of his questioning, he repeatedly referred to his own map, and not only when asked. Scholars who study the trials of Nazi perpetrators have stressed how survivor-witnesses – to some extent successfully – tried to act independently from the rules and constraints imposed on them.[63] I suggest that introducing their own graphic representation of the camps' space should be considered agency of this kind.

Indeed, Moshe Bachir was not the only survivor who questioned the official map and eventually confronted the court with a drawing in his own hand. To collect all these maps would require systematic analysis of extensive source material. For the purposes of this study, and due to limited space, we will look at just one more example. The Sobibór survivor Chaim Engel served as a witness in several trials in West Germany.[64] Like Regina Zielinski, he also testified at Frenzel's retrial in Hagen in 1983.[65] During the first two days of his questioning, he repeatedly insisted that a certain courtyard was missing on the map – a square where he and other prisoners had to sort the clothing of the murdered victims. Meanwhile he confirmed other details on the map, making use of the numbering provided. The dissent became pressing when Engel's testimony incriminated Frenzel in the shooting of an inmate. He located this individual act of killing, which could prove crucial for conviction, exactly on the sorting square that was, according to his memory, not adequately represented in the map. The court went back and forth on that matter.[66] The defendant claimed that the map was correct;

---

63 Cf. Katrin Stoll, *Die Herstellung der Wahrheit. Strafverfahren gegen ehemalige Angehörige der Sicherheitspolizei für den Bezirk Bialystok* (Berlin: de Gruyter, 2011), chapter 6.
64 He testified in Frankfurt in 1950 and 1974, and in Hagen in 1965 and 1983.
65 Cf. Protokolle zur Hauptverhandlung vor dem Schwurgericht Hagen, Aussage des Zeugen Chaim Engel, LA NRW, Abteilung Westfalen, Q 234, 4406.
66 "Es war keine geschlossene Baracke, es war ein offener Platz mit einem Zaun darum. Der Platz lag zwischen den Baracken 24 und 25 im Lager II. Der Platz war überdacht. Man konnte alles sehen, was in dieser Baracke vorging, es gab keine Zwischenwände oder so etwas. Ich sehe, wie Frenzel und der Dentist zu einem Tor reinkommt und beide zu dem Tor in dem Zaun zum Lager IV hingehen. [...] Das war nicht unter freiem Himmel. Es war ein offener Platz mit einem Dach darüber. Innerhalb des Platzes war alles offen, das Dach ging über den ganzen

the minutes note further: "The witness insists upon his conception and wants to prepare a sketch in the coming days."[67] On the next day of his questioning, Engel submitted his map (Fig. 6).[68]

Engel confined his drawing to parts of the camp that he had regularly seen, focusing on the area relevant to the specific criminal charge. In contrast to Bauer's map, it does not depict the outer fence of the camp; the parts in question are encircled and surrounded by empty space. Bauer provides an overview of the whole facility and puts it in relation to its surroundings; Engel's perspective is not omniscient, but constricted. The demarcations and fencing within the camp are more significant to him than to Bauer, who partially omitted them in his drawing. Other than one warehouse (German: "Magazin") there are no buildings indicated in Engel's map. Rather than details, his drawing suggests the functional relations of different parts of the camp and indicates utilizations of unbuilt areas that appear solely as empty spaces on the other.[69]

The drawing consists of thin lines and writing in German with minor errors and inconsistent use of upper and lower case. The vertical writing on the left reads "Kremer", the judge's name, and "Koff" (?), and must have been added later on by another hand. At the bottom of the vertical format, and left from the center of the sheet, an approximate square bears the inscription "Lager I". The writing points diagonally towards the upper right corner, where the square opens up and two parallel lines, after a small curve, lead vertically upward. In between the lines, Engel wrote "weg zu arbeit" (English: way to work). This way ends in the center of the sheet where it connects "Lager I" with the "undressing yard / men". This rounded area is separated from the rectangular yard for "sorting clothes" by a horizontal path following "rails for lorries". Left from the two areas the rails and the so-called "Schlauch", the enclosed path on which the victims were driven to the gas chambers, lead upwards to "Lager 3". The sorting yard is the area that Engel claimed to have been misrepresented in the map used by the court. In his testimony, he struggled to explain what it looked like and was contradicted by the defendant. As he was having trouble conveying verbally what was so important to him to explain, he resorted to a visual representation.

    Platz und der Platz war eingezäunt mit einem Zaun, der durchflochten war. […] Wenn in meiner früheren Aussage von einer Barackentür die Rede ist, so mag das auf mein schlechtes Deutsch zurückzuführen sein. Es war ein Tor, keine Tür. […] Der Zeuge versucht noch einmal an der Karte zu erläutern, wie er sich die Sortierbaracken und den von ihm angegebenen Platz vorstellt." Ibid.

67 "Der Zeuge beharrt bei seiner Vorstellung und will in den nächsten Tagen eine Skizze anfertigen." Ibid.
68 Protokolle zur Hauptverhandlung vor dem Schwurgericht Hagen, Bd. 1/2, LA NRW, Abteilung Westfalen, Q 234, 4392, sheet 147.
69 On the function and utilizations of unbuilt areas in extermination camps cf. Wienert, *Das Lager vorstellen*, 160–87.

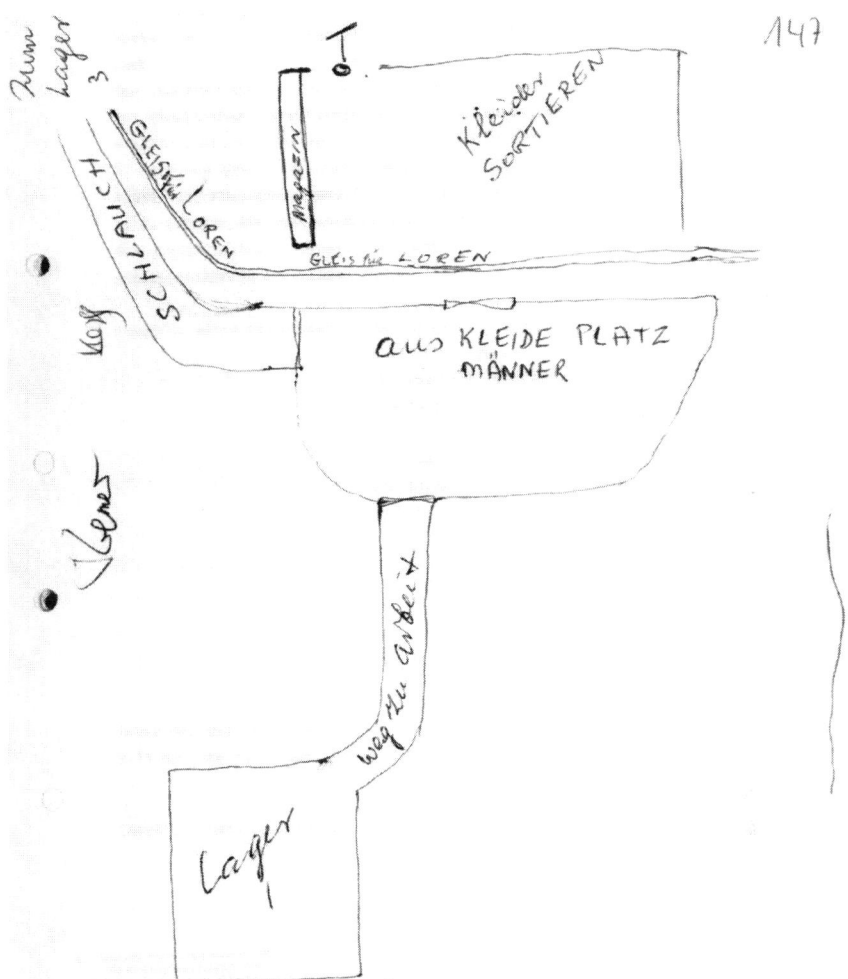

Fig. 6: "Sketch of the Camp in Sobibór", Chaim Engel, before 26 April 1983. (Source: LAV NRW W, Q 234/ Staatsanwaltschaft Dortmund, Zentralstelle für die Bearbeitung von NS-Massenverbrechen No. 4392.)

Chaim Engel and Moshe Bachir's maps definitely had an impact on the course of the legal proceedings, however minimal this impact may have been on the formal outcome of the trial. We find no evidence of any direct influence in the court's final judgment. Nor do the dossiers on the witnesses' credibility that were produced for the Frenzel trial mention that Regina Zielinski and Chaim Engel disputed the official map.[70] Still, maps drawn by survivors were treated as legitimate

---

70 Cf. Glaubwürdigkeit der in der Hauptverhandlung und kommissarisch vernommenen

for further examination; they entered the official documentation of the legal proceedings, and, as part of the written records, continued to exert influence. When Moshe Bachir testified against Frenzel in December 1982, the court introduced his drawing from 1974. On his own map, he specified where a particular cruel punishment of a prisoner was carried out: A father was forced to hang his own son on a tree.[71]

Conclusion

To conclude the analysis of maps produced by survivor-witnesses, I want to elaborate on the question of how theses maps can be conceptualized. The sketch for a memorial in Auschwitz-Birkenau by Oskar Hansen et al. from 1958 (Fig. 1) was characterized as an anti-image, because it fundamentally negates the spatial order introduced by the SS and its cartographical representation. In contrast to this anti-image, the maps drawn by survivors of the Sobibór extermination camp could be characterized as counter-images, or counter-maps. The distinction of the prefixes "anti-" and "counter-" I owe to Mieke Bal. She applied it to her critical engagement with Freudian trauma therapy, that, while altering and amending Freud's thoughts, does not reject it but rather operates within its paradigm.[72] While the prefix "anti-" indicates an exclusionary opposition, "counter-" is more ambivalent, both confirming and contradicting the reference point. The counter-maps were not produced to supersede the map provided by the court, as their authors were very well aware of the fact that they could never succeed at such an endeavor. Survivors who testified as witnesses in German courts were not in a powerful position, and had to acknowledge the rules and constraints. Under this paradigm, they still found ways and space for agency. As a result, they succeeded in broadening the meaning of testimony itself, which in the specific context of the proceeding was meant to be confined to the legal definition of the word.

Zeugen, LA NRW, Abteilung Westfalen, Q 234, 4462.
71 16 December 1982. Other than that the minutes unfortunately read only very general: "The sketch from the main hearing in Frankfurt was discussed with the witness." ("Mit dem Zeugen ist die Skizze aus der Hauptverhandlung in Frankfurt erörtert worden.") Protokolle zur Hauptverhandlung vor dem Schwurgericht Hagen [geordnet nach Zeugen und Beschuldigte, A-B] Aktenzeichen: 45 Js 27/61, LA NRW, Abteilung Westfalen, Q 234, 4404.
72 Cf. Mieke Bal, "Dis-Remembered and MisRemembered: A Confrontation with Failures of Cultural Memory", lecture given at a conference in Warsaw, 6 December 2017, <https://www.youtube.com/watch?v=72atw6dvpHs&list=PL3mposj9_bGskMbGPOLfqYKg0QBS7zb0q&index=2> (26 January 2018). I am here not referring to the predominantly postcolonial practice of countermapping. Cf. Robert Rundstrom, "Counter-Mapping," in: *International Encyclopedia of Human Geography*, 314318.

However, it is not only because of their relative powerlessness that their maps are more usefully seen as corrective addenda than as radical negations. Survivors were aware of the fact that there could never be one single, all-encompassing visual representation of the camp nor of their memories of it, as their insistence on the camp's changing nature shows. Furthermore, the map provided by the court did not unequivocally restrain them. Though maps are, from a critical perspective, usually associated with power and thus understood as oppressive,[73] during the Sobibór trials survivors found ways to make use of the official map for independent, self-determined expression. This may not have happened as triumphantly as Regina Zielinski's son related it retrospectively, but it must also not be underestimated either. What kind of maps survivors produced and how they related to maps produced by others in different contexts are questions that deserve further research.

As this analysis of the maps from Sobibór shows, such research will be confronted with four aspects of ambiguity. First is the need to translate, understand, interpret and sometimes even decipher the maps. That is true for all historical sources, but all the more so for drawings such as the one by Icek Lichtman (Fig. 2) that are simultaneously enigmatic and informative. Traditional historiography provides no established set of tools for an analysis of this kind. It therefore requires an interdisciplinary approach.

Second is the perspective of the author. As noted earlier, all maps were produced *ex post facto* from memory. Memory is always subjective; it is also not fixed, and could fade or change over time. Furthermore, we have to consider, that survivors were deported to Sobibór at different times and kept in different parts, thus experiencing the camp differently. For example, Moshe Bachir never saw the *Lazarett* with his own eyes. Nevertheless, it was a very important part of his experience. The subjectiveness of the testimonies not only applies to the survivors' accounts, but also to the historical source material produced by the perpetrators, and, of course, their postwar statements, most of them given in the context of criminal proceedings. One has to avoid the pitfall of juxtaposing subjective and objective in a way that leads to labeling a perspective incorrect or correct. Maps are more adequately understood as featuring subjective and objective qualities at the same time. Like all forms of individual memory, they are highly subjective, but as external expressions, they aim for an interpersonal

---

73 This assumption lies at the basis on political reflections on mapping and countermapping, cf. ibid. Regarding the Frankfurt Auschwitz trial, Angelika Benz has summarized: "In seiner Dokumentation des Auschwitz-Prozesses hat Hermann Langbein beschrieben, wie die Anwälte und Richter beispielsweise die Architektur des Lagers bis ins Kleinste kannten, während die Überlebenden hilflos vor den detaillierten Lagerkarten standen und Mühe hatten, etwas wiederzuerkennen." Benz, *Handlanger der SS*, 210; Hermann Langbein, *Der Auschwitz-Prozeß. Eine Dokumentation* (Wien: Europa Verlag, 1965), vol. 1.

transmission. Thus, even the most idiosyncratic drawings strive for a certain objectivation.

Third is the context of the testimonies, which produces its own ambiguity. It can be restraining and enabling at the same time. Chaim Engel issued his drawing in a specific way, focusing on a specific part of the camp as context for an event discussed in court, when his memory of an individual act of murder was being questioned (Fig. 6). Although these external factors shaped his drawing, it was also a means of self-determination and agency. It pointed out that Erich Bauer's map, as comprehensive as it may seem, has certain omissions.

Fourth is the dialectical tension between our quest to expand our knowledge and the limits of knowledge. To a certain extent, the maps' richness in details and contradicting data resists the idea of a coherent depiction of the camp. This should not be understood as a deficit. As Ulrich Baer writes: "Even when archives, sources, memoirs, and testimonies have been consulted, there remains something confounding and inexplicable about the existence of a place like Sobibór."[74] This assertion reflects a conceptualization of the Holocaust as an event that demands "representational modes, explanatory models, and ethical attitudes which conventional professional historiography, with its fetishism of facts and nothing but the facts could not provide,"[75] as the late Hayden White wrote. Maps of extermination camps drawn by survivors defy such a mere factual approach. Their representational modes point to that which cannot be represented. Analyzing them helps to increase our awareness of the contrived character of all maps and allows for a deeper understanding of maps as acts of memories. It reminds us not to identify the camp with the cartographical representation but to understand the map as a means of encountering the memory of a survivor.

---

74 Ulrich Baer, "To Give Memory a Place: Holocaust Photography and the Landscape Tradition," in: *Representations* 69 (2000): 38–62, here 46.
75 Hayden White, "Historical Truth, Estrangement, and Disbelief," in: *Confronting the Burden of History. Literary Representations of the Past*, edited by Izabela Curyłło-Klag and Bożena Kucała (Kraków: universitas, 2012), 15–43, here 16.

Abstracts

Reflections on Camps – Space, Agency, Materiality

Ulrike Krause
Protection | Victimisation | Agency? Gender-sensitive Perspectives on Present-day Refugee Camps

All over the world, refugee camps serve as humanitarian spaces for the protection and assistance of refugees in host countries. But how do these camps function, which effects do camp structures have on refugees, and how do they cope with these effects? These questions form the core of this article. By drawing on the growing multidisciplinary body of literature and, in part, original research conducted with refugees in Uganda, practices of humanitarian agencies as well as refugees in camps are explored from a gender-sensitive perspective. The article shows how camps are shaped by various forms of ambivalence, including provisional setups vs. protracted situations, protection measures vs. insecurity, female victims vs. male perpetrators or actors, and territorial inclusion vs. social exclusion. Based on that, it is argued that refugee camps are neither 'neutral' spaces of humanitarianism nor 'safe harbours' for refugees but purposefully established enterprises in which women, men, girls, boys, and other people determined as refugees (try to) create meaningful lives, despite the adversities they face.
Keywords: Refugee camps, humanitarianism, agency, Global South

Robert Jan van Pelt
Labour Service Barrack-Huts in Germany and the United States, 1933–45

Since the mid 19th century, the prefabricated barrack-hut that can be easily dismantled has become a standard element of soldiers' camps, prisoner of war camps, emergency hospitals created to combat epidemics, internment camps, refugee camps, and labour service camps. This case study compares and contrasts the different design philosophy, construction practice and social use of barrack-huts created in the 1930s for the German Reichsarbeitsdienst (RAD; Reich Labour Service), and the American Civilian Conservation Corps (CCC). The RAD barrack-hut was a developed as part of a nation-wide system of modular, standardised, and cost-effectively produced parts. The barrack-huts that could be assembled from these parts by the RAD men without the involvement of locally available trades, were meant to reflect the organisational structure of the RAD in a direct and constant manner, creating a universal matrix of representation and social control. The CCC barrack-huts were more pragmatic in conception and execution: their development allowed for regional variations, demanded on both ideological and economic grounds the involvement of local labour, and did not more than very loosely fit the organisational chart of the camp.
Keywords: barrack-hut, Reichsarbeitsdienst, Civilian Conservation Corps

Antje Senarclens de Grancy
Different Housing Spaces – Space, Function, and Use of Barrack-Huts in World War I Refugee Camps

This paper argues that the modern standardised camp barrack-hut is far more than a simple temporary dormitory for specific inhabitants. It is a complex spatial structure that is not solely generated by factors such as design, construction or equipment, but also by its use and its symbolic functions. The huge housing barracks in the refugee camps of the Habsburg monarchy in World War I serve as a case study for investigating the relationships between space, function and use of this building type. The paper focuses on the interwined factors of the (bio)political aims of the government, the design decisions of the planners in the construction offices who translated these ideas into a material form, the regulations of everyday life by the camp management, the appropriations of the refugees to whom these rooms had been allocated, and finally, the external visitors' reception of the camps.
Keywords: refugee camps, barrack-hut, space, use

Annika Wienert
Camp Cartography: On the Ambivalence of Mapping Nazi Extermination Camps

The paper deals with maps of German extermination camps and argues that these maps constitute a specific form of testimony. It takes a closer look at a small number of maps produced in different contexts, some of them drawn by survivors. In order to exemplify the ambivalence inherent to maps as media of Holocaust testimony and remembrance, the paper analyzes the role that maps played in the trials of Nazi perpetrators in Western Germany. Depending on the context, they could function as both restraining and enabling the agency of the survivor-witnesses. The paper concludes by suggesting that maps can be understood as a means of encountering the memory of a survivor.
Keywords: Holocaust Drawings, Maps, Prosecution of Nazi Crimes, Sobibór

Heidrun Zettelbauer
Unwanted Desire and Processes of Self-Discipline. Autobiographical Representations of the Reichsarbeitsdienst *Camps in the Diary of a Young Female National Socialist*

She fell "right in love" with her camp leader – this is how a young female National Socialist, retrospectively described the relationship with her superior in a camp for the *Reichsarbeitsdienst für die weibliche Jugend* (RADwJ) in her diary. Considering the absolute compliance with heterosexual gender norms which characterised her self-narrations elsewhere, this choice of words is astonishing. It is generally known that the National Socialist regime established living environments for youth as gender specific and homosocial spaces, and the extent to which they did so was unprecedented. At the same time, homosexuality was considered a criminal offense and grounds for persecution in the so-called *Ostmark*, which allowed people to be brought to court, jail, or concentration camps during the *Third Reich* period. In the present article, diary records serve as a starting point and objects of analysis, which raise the question of how narrow the gap was between the desired homosociality and the unwanted/forbidden homoerotic/homosexual desire in camps for *Volksgenossinnen*. The article places a particular focus on forms of agency and the ways in which the addressed young female adults could assume the roles of protagonists with specific scopes of action. Autobiographical representations are discussed not only with respect to the norms that structured the "space of the camp", but also regarding the processes of attachment between the self and the ideological guidelines that took place in the camp context.
Keywords: Reichsarbeitsdienst für die weibliche Jugend, RADwJ camps, gender, autobiographical representation, homosociality, homoeroticism/homosexuality

Rezensionen

Henning Fischer, Überlebende als Akteurinnen. Die Frauen der Lagergemeinschaften Ravensbrück: Biografische Erfahrung und politisches Handeln, 1945 bis 1989, Konstanz/München: UVK 2018, 542 Seiten.

In der beeindruckend recherchierten Arbeit rekonstruiert Henning Fischer die Geschichte von deutschen Kommunistinnen des Frauenkonzentrationslagers Ravensbrück im norddeutschen Brandenburg. Dabei leistet er in zwei Bereichen Pionierarbeit: Mit dem über 500 Seiten umfassenden Buch liegt die erste Geschichte der Lagergemeinschaften in der DDR und BRD vor: eine chronologische und thematische Überblicksdarstellung der Organisation in Ost- und Westdeutschland bis in die 1990er-Jahre. Zugleich ist diese Rekonstruktion mit einer Kollektivbiographie in Collageform verwoben, in der Fischer exemplarisch die Lebensgeschichten von fünf Protagonistinnen der Lagergemeinschaft (Emmy Handke, Rita Sprengel, Erika Buchmann in der DDR, Doris Maase und Gertrud Müller in der BRD) nachzeichnet. Zusätzlich sind Informationen aus 20 weiteren Biographien in die Arbeit eingeflossen (S. 29). Dies ist umso wichtiger, als über die Nachgeschichte der Überlebenden nach wie vor wenig Wissen existiert.

Ein zentrales Anliegen Fischers ist es, die Lebensgeschichten der Frauen als politische Biographien zu erzählen. Die Überlebenden sollen weder als Opfer noch unreflektiert als Heldinnen, sondern als Handelnde, als Akteurinnen ihrer eigenen Geschichte dargestellt werden. Den methodischen Fokus legt Fischer insbesondere auf die Erfahrungen, die die Biographien und das Handeln der porträtierten Frauen prägten. Der bestimmende Rahmen für deren Selbstverständnis war ihre kommunistische Identität sowie die Hafterfahrung in den Konzentrationslagern.

Der Autor verfolgt die Lebensgeschichten der Protagonistinnen von ihrer politischen Sozialisation in der Weimarer Republik und ihrem Engagement für die KPD über die Zeit der Verfolgung, des Widerstands und der Haft im Nationalsozialismus bis in die nachfolgenden beiden deutschen Staaten. Dieser Blick auf biografische Kontinuitäten und Brüche über verschiedene politische Regime und Systeme hinweg ermöglicht Fischer, längerfristige gesellschaftspolitische Entwicklungen zu analysieren: so beispielsweise, wie die individuelle und kollektive Verarbeitung der Vergangenheit mit gesellschaftspolitischen Entwicklungen verbunden ist.

Formal ist der Beginn der Lagergemeinschaft mit der Gründung des ersten Komitees ehemaliger Ravensbrücker Häftlinge in Berlin 1947 datiert. Insbesondere die Involvierung in die Beweissammlung für die Ravensbrück-Prozesse (1946–1950, 1966) hat dem Organisationsprozess Dynamik verliehen. Akteurinnen wie Erika Buchmann dokumentierten die Verbrechen im Lager und organisierten frühe Formen des Gedenkens sowie Zusammenkünfte der (v. a.

kommunistischen) Überlebenden. Lange Zeit kaum oder keinen Platz im allgemeinen Gedenken hatten Juden und Jüdinnen, Sinti und Roma sowie die von der SS als „kriminell" und „asozial" kategorisierten Häftlinge.

Viele der Kommunistinnen waren im Konzentrationslager Funktionshäftlinge und als solche in der Grauzone zwischen der SS und den Mitgefangenen tätig. Durch diese Stellung verfügten sie oft über ein größeres Wissen über die Verbrechen im Lager, das sie auch in die Prozesse einbrachten. Zugleich bargen diese Positionen die Gefahr in sich, selbst der Zusammenarbeit mit der SS beschuldigt zu werden und nach 1945 vor Gericht oder zumindest im Fokus von Nachforschungen zu stehen.

Dass die Frauen die politische Arbeit sofort nach der Befreiung wiederaufnahmen, interpretiert Fischer als Möglichkeit zur Trauma-Bewältigung, die dem Alltag Sinn und Struktur verlieh. Der Kommunismus spielte dabei als ideologisches Sinngerüst eine wichtige Rolle für das Weiterleben der Frauen, die in der Regel mit chronischen psychischen und physischen Leiden zu kämpfen hatten. Als Idee stiftete der Kommunismus Kontinuität und Sinn, als Milieu und Organisation gab er sozialen Halt.

Mit der Konsolidierung der BRD und der DDR trennten sich die Wege der kommunistischen Überlebenden von Ravensbrück in Deutschland. Während die Staatsgründung der DDR für die politische Identität der porträtierten Frauen den Sieg über den Nationalsozialismus bedeutete, erlebten die kommunistischen ehemaligen Häftlinge in der BRD eine politische und gesellschaftliche Marginalisierung und juristische Verfolgung.

In der DDR etablierten sich die Ehrung der Überlebenden und eine Institutionalisierung des Gedenkens an Ravensbrück, die zugleich eine Instrumentalisierung war: Die Erinnerung fand im Rahmen der offiziellen Doktrin vom antifaschistischen Staat Platz, den viele der Frauen unterstützen. Beispielsweise fungierten die Widerstandskämpferinnen und Überlebenden Charlotte Müller (S. 221) und Maria Wiedmaier (S. 224, 239) als überzeugte Mitarbeiterinnen des Ministeriums für Staatssicherheit. Die Protagonistinnen in der DDR waren staatlich anerkannt und privilegiert – solange sie auf Parteilinie blieben. Konflikte und Aushandlungsprozesse um die Erinnerung zeigen allerdings, dass in den ersten Jahren nach der Befreiung und dann in der DDR die Diskussionen offener waren und erst später eine Zentralisierung der Erinnerung im Einklang mit der offiziellen Staatspolitik stattfand.

Die Geschichte der Kommunistinnen in der BRD ist vom Niedergang des eigenen politischen Milieus, dem Verbot der KPD (sowie dem partiellen Verbot der Vereinigung der Verfolgten des Nazi-Regimes), von Strafverfolgung sowie vom Kampf um Anerkennung und Entschädigung geprägt. Der Staat verwehrte Überlebenden den Anspruch auf Entschädigung mit dem Vorwurf, dass sie die „freiheitliche demokratische Grundordnung" bekämpften (S. 261, 276). Der omnipräsente Antikommunismus als Teil der Identität der jungen BRD delegitimierte die Anliegen der kommunistischen Überlebenden. Beispielhaft dafür steht die Biographie der Ärztin Doris Maase, die wegen ihrer politischen Tätigkeiten mit Strafverfolgung und Haft konfrontiert war und Entschädigungsleistungen sogar rückwirkend an den Staat zurückzahlen sollte. Bis in die 1970er-Jahre bemühte sie sich um Wiedergutmachung. Die formelle Gründung der Lagergemeinschaft in der BRD fand erst im Jahr 1966 in Frankfurt am Main statt.

Mit der geschichtspolitischen Wende der 1970er-Jahre – als längerfristige Folge der Aufbruchsstimmung der späten 1960er-Jahre – wurden die Überlebenden in Westdeutschland schließlich vermehrt als Zeitzeuginnen des Nationalsozialismus wahrgenommen. Die BRD öffnete sich schrittweise gegenüber der NS-Vergangenheit und ein neues Publikum für die Erzählungen der Überlebenden formierte sich. Fischer argumentiert, dass in diesem Prozess eine Transformation der Akteurinnen und ihres Auftretens stattfand: Von der Marginalisierung als Kommunistinnen zur Anerkennung als Überlebende, von politisch Handelnden der Gegenwart zu Erzählerinnen der Vergangenheit, von der revolutionären Rhetorik zu einem Bewahrungsdiskurs über Demokratie und Frieden (S. 403).

Im Jahr 1991 vereinigten sich die ost- und westdeutschen Lagergemeinschaften schließlich. Die Lagergemeinschaf Ravensbrück/Freundeskreis e.V ist bis heute eine wichtige Akteurin der Erinnerungspolitik, aber auch in Bezug auf die Thematisierung aktueller Formen des Rechtsextremismus.

Die vielschichtige Arbeit Fischers basiert auf einer eindrucksvoll großen Fülle an Quellenmaterialien, die der Autor in zahlreichen öffentlichen und privaten Archiven, in verschiedenen deutschen Städten und Gedenkstätten recherchiert hat. Zudem finden sich mehrere Seiten mit Fotografien von Protagonistinnen der Lagergemeinschaften sowie von Demonstrationen und Gedenkfeiern in dem Buch, das als Standardwerk in der Forschung zur Geschichte der Lagergemeinschaften bezeichnet werden kann.

Veronika Duma

Christian Merlin, Die Wiener Philharmoniker. Band 1: Das Orchester und seine Geschichte von 1842 bis heute. Band 2: Die Musiker und Musikerinnen von 1842 bis heute. Aus dem Französischen von Uta Szyszkowitz und Michaela Spath, Wien: Amalthea 2017, Band 1: 368 Seiten, Band 2: 272 Seiten.

Die beiden Bücher des Musikwissenschafters und Musikkritikers Christian Merlin basieren auf seiner an der Sorbonne Université erfolgreich verteidigten Habilitationsschrift mit dem Titel „Prosopographie de L'Orchestre Philharmonique de Vienne. Histoire d'un orchestre à travers ses membres, de 1842 à nos jours". Es ist die erste musikwissenschaftliche, aber auch sozial- und kulturhistorische Kollektivbiographie dieses großen, europäischen Orchesters, wobei insgesamt 854 Biographien aus dem Untersuchungszeitraum mit unterschiedlichsten Quellen recherchiert wurden und bis auf 137 auch entsprechendes Datenmaterial verwendet wurde.

Der Autor hat sich direkt auf den Spuren des berühmten französischen Soziologen Maurice Halbwachs bewegt, der seinerseits bei seinen Versuchen, das kollektive Gedächtnis soziologisch zu analysieren und zu begründen, immer wieder auf die Erfahrungen und das Beispiel von Orchestern zurückgegriffen hat. Im Falle dieses österreichischen Orchesters kommt natürlich eine multiple Identität hinzu, die sich in den quantitativen Studien von Christian Merlin deutlich zeigt: Beispielsweise sind im Jahr 1869 14 Prozent der Musiker jüdischer Herkunft, 1903 18 Prozent. Interessant ist natürlich auch der damit verbundene Identitätskonflikt im Rahmen des Orchesters. Natürlich gab es auch zahlreiche Musiker aus Böhmen und Mähren, wie der prominenteste Fall, der Soloklarinettist Franz Bartolomey, der – schlecht Deutsch sprechend – 1892 nach Wien geholt wurde und eine Philharmoniker-Dynastie begründete.

Zusammenfassend kann festgehalten werden, dass es Merlin gelungen ist, eine umfassende, sehr stark an musikwissenschaftlichen, aber auch kulturwissenschaftlichen Fragestellungen orientierte Arbeit zusammenzustellen, mit einer Reihe innovativer Schwerpunkte, die weit über die engere Orchestergeschichte der Wiener Philharmoniker hinausgehen und die österreichische und deutsche Musikgeschichte direkt betreffen.

Wichtig ist, wie gesagt, Merlins Analyse der Identitäten der Orchestermitglieder, da es bis 1914 aufgrund des starken Anteils an Mitgliedern aus Böhmen, Mähren und anderen Teilen der Monarchie verschiedene Bindestrich-Identitäten im Orchester gegeben hat und es zunehmend bereits vor 1918 zu einer „stärkeren Assimilierung im Orchester kommt". Auch die Orchestermitglieder jüdischer Herkunft passen sich meist dem katholischen deutschen Mainstream an.

Bezüglich der Frage, welche Dirigenten der Wiener Philharmoniker am wichtigsten für die Innovation des Repertoires waren, zeigt sich, dass aufgrund seiner quantitativen Studien hinsichtlich der Erweiterung der Orchesterstellen, aber auch im Hinblick auf die Aufführungen, sicherlich die Phase von Gustav Mahler die wohl prägendste Phase des Orchesters war. Wie übrigens jene Dirigenten, die – wie beispielsweise Clemens Krauss – auch Operndirektoren waren, den wichtigsten Einfluss auf das Orchester gehabt haben. In weiterer Folge verweist Merlin bezüglich des spezifischen Impacts auf Clemens Krauss, Wilhelm Furtwängler, der nicht Operndirektor war, und Herbert von Karajan.

Ein immer wiederkehrendes Thema betrifft den spezifisch österreichischen und Wiener Klangstil der Wiener Philharmoniker. Merlin kennzeichnet die Phase der NS-Zeit als stilprägend, wie auch entsprechende Stellungnahmen von Otto Strasser dokumentieren. Wesentlich ist dabei die direkte Konkurrenz zu den Berliner Philharmonikern, auf deren Präzision, die in dieser Form bei den Wiener Philharmonikern nicht anzutreffen sei, Wiener Kollegen hingewiesen haben. Es hat hier durchaus einen Vorbildcharakter gegeben.

Die Studien von Christian Merlin leisten einen wichtigen Beitrag zu einer intensiveren Auseinandersetzung mit der österreichischen Kulturgeschichte im späten 19. und in der ersten Hälfte des 20. Jahrhunderts. Besonders wichtig ist die von Merlin in der Studie erwähnte Internationalisierung des Orchesters, die nach 1945 langsam begann, ab den 1960er-Jahren stärker und besonders ab den 1970er- und 1980er-Jahren intensiver wurde, wie auch die Zunahme an Tourneen außerhalb Österreichs anschaulich verdeutlicht.

Oliver Rathkolb

Matthias Marschik/Rolf Sachsse, Rauchende Sportler. Ein obszönes Sujet, Wien: Verlagshaus Hernals 2017, 174 Seiten.

Die größte Sensation im US-Sport des Jahres 1925 war, als der Football Star der University of Illinois, Harold „Red" Grange, erklärte, er werde noch vor seinem Abschluss die Universität verlassen, um zukünftig als Profi für die Chicago Bears zu spielen. Im Anschluss wurde er einerseits von traditionalistischen Sportjournalisten und Verbandsvertretern des Verrats am Amateurideal bezichtigt, während er andererseits zum Zuschauermagneten der noch jungen Profiliga aufstieg. Grange machte nie einen Hehl daraus, dass sein Seitenwechsel mit der Aussicht auf finanzielle Absicherung für sich und seine Familie begründet war: Schon in den ersten Wochen bei den Bears unterschrieb er hochdotierte Werbeverträge u. a. für Schokolade, Ginger Ale und Sportbekleidung. Ein Angebot einer Zigarettenmarke lehnte er indes ab, weil die Firma verlangt hatte, Grange solle sich als Raucher bekennen und mit Zigarette ablichten lassen. Trotzdem konnte man schon kurze Zeit danach großformatige Anzeigen für Old Gold Cigarettes sehen, auf denen Grange abgebildet war – doch dieser Marke genügte sein Porträt, ohne dass der Sportler beim Rauchen selbst zu sehen sein musste.

Diese Geschichte steht beinahe prototypisch für das Verhältnis des Sports zum Rauchen: Für lange Zeit während des 20. Jahrhunderts gehörten die Zigarette und die Tabakwerbung wie selbstverständlich zur Welt des Sports, doch war diese Beziehung stets zugleich auch problematisch und von zahlreichen Widersprüchen wie Ambivalenzen gekennzeichnet. Diesem spannungsreichen Verhältnis gehen Matthias Marschik und Rolf Sachsse in ihrer Kulturgeschichte des Rauchens im Sport nach. Als Ausgangspunkt ihrer Argumentation dient ihnen genau die paradoxe Beobachtung, dass obwohl „Zigarette und Sport in besonderer Weise verwoben sind, […] Abbildungen rauchender Spieler_innen oder Sportler_innen etwas Anrüchiges, ja Obszönes an sich" haben; „Sportler_innen rauchen heimlich beim Hintertürchen oder nur im privaten Kreis. Manchmal kann man darüber lesen, sehen kann man es kaum" (S. 11–12). Vor dem Hintergrund der Tatsache, dass Tabakindustrie und Tabakkonsum in den vergangenen zwei Dekaden besonders nachdrücklich und erfolgreich aus der Öffentlichkeit und somit auch aus dem Sport verdrängt worden sind, beleuchtet „Rauchende Sportler" auf knapp 160 Seiten Text und mit Hilfe von mehr als 120 Abbildungen facettenreich die Geschichte des Rauchens im Sport vor allem als eine Geschichte seiner (Un-)Sichtbarmachung. Dabei ist es nicht das Anliegen der Autoren, die offensichtliche Gesundheitsgefährdung durch das Rauchen zu leugnen, vielmehr geht es ihnen darum, „die diskursiven Formationen des Rauchens und seiner heutigen gesellschaftspolitischen Ächtung nachzuzeichnen und nach der dahinter liegenden Biomacht zu fragen" (S. 27).

Das Buch ist ungleichgewichtig in zwei Abschnitte gegliedert. Im ersten und weit längeren Teil offeriert der Kulturwissenschafter und Historiker Matthias Marschik einen in erster Linie chronologisch, bisweilen aber auch von thematischen Exkursen geleiteten Überblick über die Rollen von Tabak und Rauchen im internationalen Sport seit dem späten 19. Jahrhundert. Werbung und Sportsponsoring werden breit diskutiert, darüber hinaus thematisiert Marschik aber auch komplexe soziale und kulturelle Zusammenhänge wie Geschlecht (v. a. ans Rauchen gekoppelte Entwürfe von Männlichkeit), Urbanität, Modernität, Gesundheit und Leistungsfähigkeit. Auch die politische Ebene, etwa die Spaltung zwischen bürgerlichem Sport und Arbeitersport oder die Vereinnahmung des Sports durch den Nationalsozialismus, wird breit angesprochen. Die Spurensuche führt von Österreich und Deutschland aus nach Europa, Nordamerika und bisweilen auch darüber hinaus. Bei den behandelten Sportarten dominieren Fußball und Motorsport, in beiden Fällen erweisen sich die wechselseitigen Referenzen zwischen Sport und Tabak als besonders zahlreich und besonders anschlussfähig an umlaufende Diskurse. Doch auch in anderen Disziplinen kann der Autor den vielfältigen Spuren des Tabaks sowie den Versuchen, diese vor der Öffentlichkeit zu verbergen, nachspüren; auch im Tennis wie beim Skilaufen und Radfahren wurde geraucht, und das Verhältnis zwischen Genuss einerseits und dem Gefühl von Unangemessenheit andererseits war gleichfalls evident. Der angekündigte Rückgriff auf visuelle Quellen (Presse- und Privatfotos, Werbung) gelingt konsequent und wird auch zumeist von dichtem zeitgenössischen Textmaterial unterfüttert. Insgesamt entsteht so im ersten Teil des Buchs ein breiter, kenntnisreicher und stringent argumentierter Überblick, dem man freilich an manchen Stellen etwas weniger Tempo und stattdessen eine kleine Zigarettenpause wünschen würde: Während die übergeordnete These klar zum Ausdruck kommt, fehlt es diesem Teil bisweilen an Tiefenschärfe, an einem Innehalten, das sich einzelnen Zusammenhängen oder auch einzelnen Bildern detailreicher widmen könnte.

Dieses Manko wird im zweiten Teil von „Rauchende Sportler" in gewisser Hinsicht kompensiert. Weit kürzer konzipiert, auf nur knapp 13 Seiten, widmet sich Rolf Sachsse darin „einer kleinen Typologie sportlicher Raucherbilder" (S. 152). Der emeritierte Professor für Design entwickelt dabei zunächst eine Reihe von medientheoretischen Gedanken zur Sportfotografie im Allgemeinen, bevor er sich ausführlich der Ikonographie des Sujets vom rauchenden Sportlers zuwendet, hier vor allem im Automobilrennsport. Marschiks Tour de Force im ersten Teil wird also auf den letzten Seiten des Buchs durch eine eingehendere Studie des Zusammenspiels von Sportfotografie und Visualisierungen des Rauchens sinnvoll ergänzt und erweitert. Sachsse gelingen diese Ausführungen gut, und so wünscht man sich am Ende der Lektüre, die beiden Autoren hätten sich zu Beginn ihrer Zusammenarbeit auf eine andere Struktur ihres Buchs und eine engere Verzahnung ihrer jeweiligen Analysen geeinigt. „Rauchende Sportler" bietet einen klugen, thesengeleiteten Einstieg und Überblick in das Themenfeld Sport und Tabakkonsum sowie seinen komplexen Formen der Visualisierung, doch hätte das Buch insgesamt davon profitiert, wenn die Interventionen Sachsses an mehreren Punkten des Texts erfolgt wären und dabei die dichte Diskursgeschichte Marschiks um je eigene kunst- wie medientheoretische Bemerkungen erweitert hätten. Trotzdem wird der Band sowohl Expertinnen und Experten als auch einer breiteren, interessierten Öffentlichkeit wichtige Impulse dabei geben, den kultur- und konsumhistorischen Dimensionen des Sports und der für seine Wirkung so wichtigen Welt der visuellen Medien in angemessener Weise nachzugehen.

Olaf Stieglitz

Autor/innen

Veronika Duma, Dr.
Historikerin, wissenschaftliche Mitarbeiterin am Ludwig-Boltzmann-Institute for Digital History, Wien, veronika.duma@univie.ac.at

Ulrike Krause, Dr.
Politikwissenschaftlerin, Juniorprofessorin für Flucht- und Flüchtlingsforschung am Institut für Migrationsforschung und Interkulturelle Studien (IMIS), Universität Osnabrück, ulrike.krause@uni-osnabrück.de

Robert Jan van Pelt, Dr.
Architekturhistoriker, University Professor an der School of Architecture, University of Waterloo, rjvanpel@uwaterloo.ca

Oliver Rathkolb, Univ.-Prof. DDr.
Zeithistoriker, Institutsvorstand am Institut für Zeitgeschichte der Universität Wien, oliver.rathkolb@univie.ac.at

Antje Senarclens de Grancy, Dr.
Architekturhistorikerin, Assistenzprofessorin am Institut für Architekturtheorie, Kunst- und Kulturwissenschaften, Technische Universität Graz, antje.grancy@tugraz.at

Olaf Stieglitz, PD Dr.
Historiker, Privatdozent am Historischen Institut der Universität Köln, olaf.stieglitz1@uni-koeln.de

Annika Wienert, Dr.
Kunsthistorikerin, Wissenschaftliche Mitarbeiterin am Deutschen Historischen Institut Warschau, wienert@dhi.waw.pl

Heidrun Zettelbauer, PD Dr.
Historikerin, Assoziierte Professorin am Institut für Geschichte, Karl-Franzens-Universität Graz, heidrun.zettelbauer@uni-graz.at

Zitierregeln

Bei der Einreichung von Manuskripten, über deren Veröffentlichung im Laufe eines doppelt anonymisierten Peer Review Verfahrens entschieden wird, sind unbedingt die Zitierregeln einzuhalten. Unverbindliche Zusendungen von Manuskripten als word-Datei an: agnes.meisinger@univie.ac.at

I. Allgemeines

Abgabe: elektronisch in Microsoft Word DOC oder DOCX.

Textlänge: 60.000 Zeichen (inklusive Leerzeichen und Fußnoten), Times New Roman, 12 pt, 1 $\frac{1}{2}$-zeilig. Zeichenzahl für Rezensionen 6.000–8.200 Zeichen (inklusive Leerzeichen).

Rechtschreibung: Grundsätzlich gilt die Verwendung der neuen Rechtschreibung mit Ausnahme von Zitaten.

II. Format und Gliederung

Kapitelüberschriften und – falls gewünscht – Unterkapiteltitel deutlich hervorheben mittels Nummerierung. Kapitel mit römischen Ziffern [I. Literatur], Unterkapitel mit arabischen Ziffern [1.1 Dissertationen] nummerieren, maximal bis in die dritte Ebene untergliedern [1.1.1 Philologische Dissertationen]. Keine Interpunktion am Ende der Gliederungstitel.

Keine Silbentrennung, linksbündig, Flattersatz, keine Leerzeilen zwischen Absätzen, keine Einrückungen; direkte Zitate, die länger als vier Zeilen sind, in einem eigenen Absatz (ohne Einrückung, mit Gänsefüßchen am Beginn und Ende).

Zahlen von null bis zwölf ausschreiben, ab 13 in Ziffern. Tausender mit Interpunktion: 1.000. Wenn runde Zahlen wie zwanzig, hundert oder dreitausend nicht in unmittelbarer Nähe zu anderen Zahlenangaben in einer Textpassage aufscheinen, können diese ausgeschrieben werden.

Daten ausschreiben: „1930er" oder „1960er-Jahre" statt „30er" oder „60er Jahre".

Datumsangaben: In den Fußnoten: 4. 3. 2011 [Leerzeichen nach dem Punkt, nicht 04. 03. 2011 oder 4. März 2011]; im Text den Monat ausschreiben [4. März 2011].

Personennamen im Fließtext bei der Erstnennung immer mit Vor- und Nachnamen.

Namen von Organisationen im Fließtext: Wenn eindeutig erkennbar ist, dass eine Organisation, Vereinigung o. Ä. vorliegt, können die Anführungszeichen weggelassen werden: „Die Gründung des Oesterreichischen Alpenvereins erfolgte 1862." „Als Mitglied im Womens Alpine Club war ihr die Teilnahme gestattet." **Namen von Zeitungen/Zeitschriften** etc. siehe unter „Anführungszeichen".

Anführungszeichen im Fall von Zitaten, Hervorhebungen und bei Erwähnung von Zeitungen/Zeitschriften, Werken und Veranstaltungstiteln im Fließtext immer doppelt: „"

Einfache Anführungszeichen nur im Fall eines Zitats im Zitat: „Er sagte zu mir: ‚….'"

Klammern: Gebrauchen Sie bitte generell runde Klammern, außer in Zitaten für Auslassungen: […] und Anmerkungen: [Anm. d. A.].

Formulieren Sie **bitte geschlechtsneutral bzw. geschlechtergerecht.** Verwenden Sie im ersteren Fall bei Substantiven das Binnen-I („ZeitzeugInnen"), nicht jedoch in Komposita („Bürgerversammlung" statt „BürgerInnenversammlung").

Darstellungen und Fotos als eigene Datei im jpg-Format (mind. 300 dpi) einsenden. Bilder werden schwarz-weiß abgedruckt; die Rechte an den abgedruckten Bildern sind vom Autor/von der Autorin einzuholen. Bildunterschriften bitte kenntlich machen: Bild: Spanische Reiter auf der Ringstraße (Quelle: Bildarchiv, ÖNB).

Abkürzungen: Bitte Leerzeichen einfügen: vor % oder €/zum Beispiel z. B./unter anderem u. a. Im Text sind möglichst wenige allgemeine Abkürzungen zu verwenden.

III. Zitation

Generell keine Zitation im Fließtext, auch keine Kurzverweise. Fußnoten immer mit einem Punkt abschließen.

Die nachfolgenden Hinweise beziehen sich auf das Erstzitat von Publikationen. Bei weiteren Erwähnungen Kurzzitat. Wird hintereinander aus demselben Werk zitiert bitte den Verweis „Ebd." bzw. mit anderer Seitenangabe „Ebd., 12." gebrauchen. Kein „Ders./Dies." Zwei Belege in einer Fußnote mit „;" trennen: Gehmacher, Jugend, 311; Dreidemy, Kanzlerschaft, 29. Bei Übernahme von direkten Zitaten aus der Fachliteratur „Zit. n." verwenden.

Monografien: Vorname und Nachname, Titel, Ort und Jahr, Seitenangabe [ohne „S."].
Beispiel Erstzitat: Johanna Gehmacher, Jugend ohne Zukunft. Hitler-Jugend und Bund Deutscher Mädel in Österreich vor 1938, Wien 1994, 311.
Beispiel Kurzzitat: Gehmacher, Jugend, 311.
Bei mehreren AutorInnen/HerausgeberInnen: Dachs/Gerlich/Müller (Hg.), Politiker, 14.

Reihentitel: Claudia Hoerschelmann, Exilland Schweiz. Lebensbedingungen und Schicksale österreichischer Flüchtlinge 1938 bis 1945 (Veröffentlichungen des Ludwig-Boltzmann-Institutes für Geschichte und Gesellschaft 27), Innsbruck/Wien [bei mehreren Ortsangaben Schrägstrich ohne Leerzeichen] 1997, 45.

Dissertation: Thomas Angerer, Frankreich und die Österreichfrage. Historische Grundlagen und Leitlinien 1945–1955, phil. Diss., Universität Wien 1996, 18–21 [keine ff. und f. für Seitenangaben, von–bis mit Gedankenstrich ohne Leerzeichen].

Diplomarbeit: Lucile Dreidemy, Die Kanzlerschaft Engelbert Dollfuß' 1932–1934, Dipl. Arb., Université de Strasbourg 2007, 29.

Ohne AutorIn, nur HerausgeberIn: Beiträge zur Geschichte und Vorgeschichte der Julirevolte, hg. im Selbstverlag des Bundeskommissariates für Heimatdienst, Wien 1934, 13.

Unveröffentlichtes Manuskript: Günter Bischof, Lost Momentum. The Militarization of the Cold War and the Demise of Austrian Treaty Negotiations, 1950–1952 (unveröffentlichtes Manuskript), 54–55. Kopie im Besitz des Verfassers.

Quellenbände: Foreign Relations of the United States, 1941, vol. II, hg. v. United States Department of States, Washington 1958.
[nach Erstzitation mit der gängigen Abkürzung: FRUS fortfahren].

Sammelwerke: Herbert Dachs/Peter Gerlich/Wolfgang C. Müller (Hg.), Die Politiker. Karrieren und Wirken bedeutender Repräsentanten der Zweiten Republik, Wien 1995.

Beitrag in Sammelwerken: Michael Gehler, Die österreichische Außenpolitik unter der Alleinregierung Josef Klaus 1966–1970, in: Robert Kriechbaumer/Franz Schausberger/Hubert Weinberger (Hg.), Die Transformation der österreichischen Gesellschaft und die Alleinregierung Klaus (Veröffentlichung der Dr.-Wilfried Haslauer-Bibliothek, Forschungsinstitut für politisch-historische Studien 1), Salzburg 1995, 251–271, 255–257.
[bei Beiträgen grundsätzlich immer die Gesamtseitenangabe zuerst, dann die spezifisch zitierten Seiten].

Beiträge in Zeitschriften: Florian Weiß, Die schwierige Balance. Österreich und die Anfänge der westeuropäischen Integration 1947–1957, in: Vierteljahrshefte für Zeitgeschichte 42 (1994) 1, 71–94.
[Zeitschrift Jahrgang/Bandangabe ohne Beistrichtrennung und die Angabe der Heftnummer oder der Folge hinter die Klammer ohne Komma].

Presseartikel: Titel des Artikels, Zeitung, Datum, Seite.
Der Standestaat in Diskussion, Wiener Zeitung, 5. 9. 1946, 2.

Archivalien: Bericht der Österr. Delegation bei der Hohen Behörde der EGKS, Zl. 2/pol/57, Fritz Kolb an Leopold Figl, 19. 2. 1957. Österreichisches Staatsarchiv (ÖStA), Archiv der Republik (AdR), Bundeskanzleramt (BKA)/AA, II-pol, International 2 c, Zl. 217.301-pol/57 (GZl. 215.155-pol/57); Major General Coleman an Kirkpatrick, 27. 6. 1953. The National Archives (TNA), Public Record Office (PRO), Foreign Office (FO) 371/103845, CS 1016/205
[prinzipiell zuerst das Dokument mit möglichst genauer Bezeichnung, dann das Archiv, mit Unterarchiven, -verzeichnissen und Beständen; bei weiterer Nennung der Archive bzw. Unterarchive können die Abkürzungen verwendet werden].

Internetquellen: Autor so vorhanden, Titel des Beitrags, Institution, URL: (abgerufen Datum). Bitte mit rechter Maustaste den Hyperlink entfernen, so dass der Link nicht mehr blau unterstrichen ist.
Yehuda Bauer, How vast was the crime, Yad Vashem, URL: http://www1.yadvashem.org/yv/en/holocaust/about/index.asp (abgerufen 28. 2. 2011).

Film: Vorname und Nachname des Regisseurs, Vollständiger Titel, Format [z. B. 8 mm, VHS, DVD], Spieldauer [Film ohne Extras in Minuten], Produktionsort/-land Jahr, Zeit [Minutenangabe der zitierten Passage].
Luis Buñuel, Belle de jour, DVD, 96 min., Barcelona 2001, 26:00–26:10 min.

Interview: InterviewpartnerIn, IntervieweriIn, Datum des Interviews, Provenienz der Aufzeichnung.
Interview mit Paul Broda, geführt von Maria Wirth, 26.10.2014, Aufnahme bei der Autorin.

Die englischsprachigen Zitierregeln sind online verfügbar unter: https://www.verein-zeitgeschichte.univie.ac.at/fileadmin/user_upload/p_verein_zeitgeschichte/zg_Zitierregeln_engl_2018.pdf

Es können nur jene eingesandten Aufsätze Berücksichtigung finden, die sich an die Zitierregeln halten!